# The High Price of Socialized Medicine

# The High Price of Socialized Medicine

A HISTORY OF GOVERNMENT
MEDDLING IN AMERICAN HEALTH
CARE, AND HOW A FREE MARKET
WOULD SOLVE OUR PROBLEMS

———

*Dr. James W. Brook*

**Published By James Brook, D.O.**

**Credits:**

**Cover Art – R.J. Wright**

**Electronic Formatting – Jim Sevy**

ISBN: 1507803281
ISBN 13: 9781507803288

# Table of Contents

# Introduction

———

Now that Obamacare has gotten off to such an ignominious start, people are looking at tax increases. The economy is being hit hard. Companies are laying off workers or cutting back their hours to avoid the penalties for not providing a government-sanctioned insurance policy. Many people think these are small problems in comparison to all the good that the new legislation will bring about. After all, it is named the "Affordable Care Act." Who could be against affordable care? Actually, a look into the history of health care in America shows that we can expect nothing but a worsening of our current problems as a result of this legislation.

If we want to fix the problems of high cost, long waiting times, and lack of customer-friendly service such as thorough care and house calls, then we have to identify what caused those problems to occur in the first place. If we just apply more of the same kind of pressures that have led to our current problems, then we will find our problems getting worse, not better. That is exactly what Obamacare is doing.

This book is not so much a dissection of Obamacare as it is an examination of the historical forces that have led us to this situation over many decades. It does discuss Obamacare, but that is actually a small part of the book. I will not be recommending a restructuring of government programs controlling healthcare. I will not be advocating some sort of "Obamacare-lite" alternative. I suggest removing the root causes of our problems, by reinstituting freedom in this country.

Freedom works. It has brought prosperity everywhere it has been tried. This has been proven time and time again. Freedom works in health care - this has also been proven. There are many examples of free market medical practices, including my own. These practices bring affordable health care to people of modest means, while providing thorough, personal service. Freedom means non-interference by outside forces in our transactions and pursuits. When it comes to bringing goods and services to ordinary people, freedom works.

I was board certified in family practice in 2003, after completing a Duke University family practice residency, following medical school. I have turned away from the typical modern medical practice model in which somebody besides the patient pays the majority of the bill. I practice as closely to free market principles as is possible in America today. My patients pay me in full at the time of service. This results in cutting fees and improving service drastically. I even offer housecalls.

I fully understand the way supporters of "universal coverage" think. I used to be one of them. I will now outline their views before I proceed to thoroughly debunk them.

Many people say we have to institute universal health care, or socialized medicine, in America, because it is the only way to help the less fortunate get the health care they need. Our technological advancement has outpaced our ability to pay for such care. We all need to contribute, for the greater good of society. These advocates of socialized medicine say that with government running things, our administrative costs will be much less, resulting in more of the money going to actual care. This is proven, they say, in countries like Canada, where a smaller percentage of their national income is spent on health care. Canadians spend less while they get more.

Here in America, as the story goes, the insured subsidize the care of the uninsured. People without insurance go to emergency departments for care. This ends up costing more than if they went to an outpatient clinic. They do not pay their bills, and the insured end up paying for these higher costs.

Everybody is said to have health care in the government-run systems, as opposed to the 40 to 50 million Americans without access to care. Longevity is better in the socialized systems. Infant mortality is better. The United States is the only country in the developed world that has not progressed to a government-run health care system. Enlightened people throughout the world have moved forward to these systems, while Americans are still trying to hold onto free markets. This is an obsolete way of thinking Americans have.

According to this philosophy, free market capitalism has been given its chance, right here in America, and it has been shown to be a failure. We have no system. We just have a patchwork of different government programs and capitalist players, leaving many holes in the pattern for people to slip through. We are spending way too much and getting too little for our money.

It is widely proclaimed that everybody has a right to health care. It is one of the fundamental rights of human existence. As a society, we have an ethical responsibility to ensure that right to all members of society, no matter what their material situation. With government-run medicine, access will be guaranteed to all Americans. There will be no haves and have-nots, like there are now.

I used to think that way too, when I began medical school. I even argued for socialized medicine while I was applying to medical school, during an interview with the school president, who was a staunch supporter of free markets. I wanted to finish my training and go to work for a state-subsidized indigent care clinic.

Most of the academic leaders teach these same philosophies. In medical school, we even had a one-hour lecture given by a member of some socialized medicine advocacy group, entirely devoted to pushing the cause. I was completely in agreement. We never had even a portion of a lecture devoted to the merits of free market principles in health care.

I soon came to realize the arguments for socialized medicine simply do not hold up to reality. I saw the results of our government programs, and what they did to the people whom they were supposed to be helping. This experience caused a profound change in my viewpoint. By the time I finished my training, I had evolved from a big-government socialist into a pro-constitution supporter of freedom.

There are points on which agreement can be reached between a supporter of government control and a supporter of free markets. Our goals are often the same, but we would use entirely different methods to achieve these goals. We often see the problems as being the same, for example, unaffordability and poor service.

We need to examine the causes of these problems, however, if we are to find solutions that will work. We need to figure out what incentives apply to different people. Doctors, patients, hospital administrators, insurance company executives, medical equipment producers, and pharmaceutical manufacturers all respond to *incentives* much more than they respond to the *intentions* of policy makers, no matter how good the stated intentions might be.

This book will bring these incentives into the light of day, in a way that is easy for anybody to understand. It is thoroughly documented, from reliable sources, most of which can be easily verified by anybody with Internet access. As we will see, we do not have a free market in American medicine. We have not had one for many decades. We have government interventions into every aspect of health care. These interventions completely distort the free market, with incentives that directly cause the problems we see today.

While increasing technology drives cost down and satisfaction up in other sectors of the economy, in health care, technology drives prices up, because somebody besides the patient is paying the bill. Cost is disconnected from the consumer, more than it is in most developed countries, even in the ones that are usually considered to have socialized medicine.

In free markets, business leaders bend over backwards to please the customer. They constantly work to achieve low prices, high quality, and good service. They do this to keep the customers coming. They know if they do not, their customers will go elsewhere. In health care, the patient is not the customer. The customer of the doctor is usually the insurance company. The customer of the insurance company is usually the employer. There is little reason for anybody involved to bend over backwards to please the patient.

What we have in America is not a free market economy in health care, but a semi-socialized system. It is a system of third party payment, caused by tax incentives. It is a heavily regulated, centrally controlled economy. It is controlled through the Medicare and Medicaid programs, and the regulations that they have initiated which have then spread throughout the insurance industry.

It is a system wherein government permission is needed to buy medications, to sell medications, or to practice a trade in health care. Physician supply is controlled. The types of insurance policies that can be sold are heavily regulated by the state. A doctor needs government permission to perform simple laboratory tests. There are many more types of regulations that strangle the efficiency of health care delivery.

Litigation has become a plague on every doctor, and indeed on everybody who produces and contributes to American society. This is the result of a deliberate effort on the part of legal theorists for the past several decades. Our system of civil law has changed from one in which blameworthy conduct was punished, into one in which losses are redistributed as a matter of social justice. Practicing a trade with extreme diligence and care, to avoid mistakes, does not protect one from lawsuits. This pushes costs up and drives doctors away from the practice of medicine.

Privacy of medical records has been abolished by recent legislation from Washington. Fraud has become a problem when a distant third party is paying the bill, and the effort to detect fraud is perhaps even more costly than the fraud itself.

The economic impact of these problems extends far beyond just health care. Its contribution to our national debt is enormous. Our long-term national debt has reached staggering proportions. It has already gotten beyond our ability to pay, and Medicare comprises the majority of that debt. It is mathematically certain that if we continue on our current course, health care will bankrupt our country.

High fees, difficulty finding thorough care when and where we need it, and high cost of medications are all problems that have resulted from a lack of free markets in American medical care. Many people simply cannot afford the health care they need.

Other, more heavily socialized nations, face an even more dire economic future. Shortages that would shock the sensibilities of ordinary Americans are just a part of life in those countries. Government-run medicine is causing drastic hardship in Canada, Great Britain, and every other nation where it has been tried. People in the lower economic classes are harmed the most, because they do not have the resources to flee their countries to find care.

The solutions to our problems have to be based on correcting the causes that led to those problems. If we just apply more of the same incentives that led to the problems, we can only expect the problems to get worse. Removing the incentives will correct the problems. We can have the same kind of prosperity in health care that we have in other areas of our economy. We just need to see why those areas are prosperous, and apply the same principles to health care.

Obamacare is an attempt to fix the problems that have been directly caused by government interference in free markets, by increasing government interference even more. It is like trying to treat a patient in congestive heart failure with fluid overload by giving a large bolus of IV fluid. This can only make our situation worse. The only possible results are worsening waiting times, higher costs, and loss of personal control over our health decisions.

I offer a perspective that is not often heard in this critical debate. After changing my philosophy during my training, I decided to put these principles to work. I now run a solo family practice that operates as closely to free market concepts as possible. I do not work with Medicare or Medicaid, and do not have contracts with insurance companies. People pay me directly. Most of my patients are uninsured. Some are on Medicare, paying me out of pocket without reimbursement. Some have traditional insurance, but see me even though I am not on their networks. My fees are typically just a fraction of what most doctors charge, with the kind of service that was expected in the days of Marcus Welby, including house calls.

My practice is one example of what can be done in health care when free market principles are applied. There are many others that will be discussed, some in the United States, some in other parts of the world. There are examples in family practice, and also in complex surgical care, with surprisingly reasonable fees.

America has led the world in freedom. We can stand apart from the more socialized nations in health care, as we have stood apart in so many other ways, if we remove government controls and establish free markets. Specific ways of doing this will be discussed later in this book. If we generate the political will to make these changes, we can have affordable health care with high levels of service once again. Our economy can be saved from the disaster that now threatens us. We can become the envy of the world, and show other countries the way to fixing their broken systems.

If you are opposed to a government-run system of health care, then read this book. It will confirm your suspicions about socialized medicine, and give you intellectual ammunition to argue your case in a logical and thorough way. If you are undecided, then read this book. It will explain the workings of our health care economy in a way that you probably have not heard before. If you are dedicated to socialized medicine, then read this book. If you want to elevate the condition of the lower classes, which socialists say they want to do, then you need to use capitalism to accomplish that goal.

# Why Free Markets Lead to Prosperity
# and Socialism Leads to Misery

# Crisis? What Crisis? Conditions Before Government Interference

———

*"I predict future happiness for Americans if they can prevent the government from wasting the labors of the people under the pretense of taking care of them."*

- THOMAS JEFFERSON

IN AN EFFORT TO UNDERSTAND the current health care problems in America, it is important to realize that there was no major crisis prior to the institution of socialism. People were generally satisfied with their doctors, and widely regarded them with great respect. Marcus Welby was a symbol of purity and goodness. The family doctor was readily available, did housecalls, and was affordable.

The state of American medicine was the finest in the world. People often came to the United States from many other countries for the most expert medical care that could be found. Indeed, they still do, even though many Americans are starting to go elsewhere. Personal, committed service was expected among American doctors. They spent the time needed with a patient.

Doctors still want to be able to provide quality service, and to do their best for their patients. Most would probably love to be able to do house calls, and to spend the time a patient needs. Most would want to see patients quickly when they have a need.

Unfortunately, these doctors are handicapped by systems that do not allow for this type of service. In medical school and beyond, almost all of the doctors and student doctors I met were dedicated to doing their best for their patients. They got into medicine because they wanted to do something useful.

While there was inflation in health care, it was not until the past several decades that we started to experience runaway inflation. Between 1929 and 1940, annual health care expenditures per person inflated only slightly, from $383 to $472, in 2010 dollars (adjusted for inflation).[1,2,3]

This amounted to just 1.9% per year above the general inflation rate. Around the time of World War II, health expenditures started to inflate more, and then in the late 1960s health spending started to take off like a sprinter coming out of the blocks.

While Americans have been increasing their spending on health care by leaps and bounds in recent decades, there has not been a corresponding increase in longevity. Longevity increased quite steadily and rapidly in the first half of the twentieth century, when there was very little increase in health care spending. Longevity continued to increase in the latter half of the twentieth century, but at a much slower rate. Average lifespan for Americans increased 44% in the first half of the twentieth century, but it only increased 13% in the second half.[4,5]

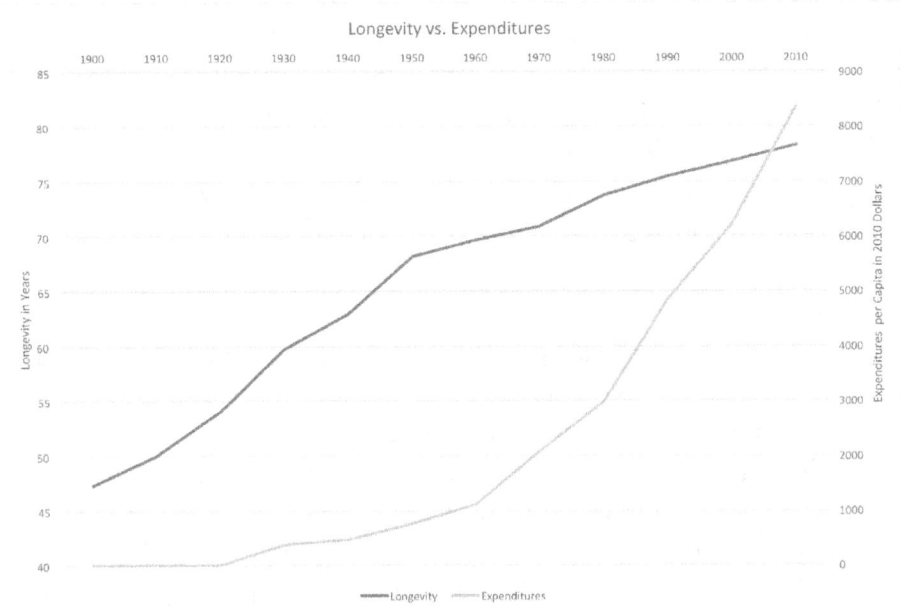

American longevity vs. average annual health care expenditures per capita, adjusted to 2010 dollars.[1,2,4,5] No data on expenditures available before 1930.

Does the lack of a large increase in longevity mean that our health care is not much better now than it was in 1950? No, of course not. In fact, it is so much better, that it is able to overcome our increase in obesity and generally lazy, unhealthy lifestyles. If not for improvements in health care, we might even expect longevity to be decreasing in America.

The tremendous increases in the first half of the century do, however, indicate that it does not take a huge portion of our economic resources in order to advance our health. There were tremendous breakthroughs in the first part of the century, which simply did not cost an arm and a leg. Advances such as X-ray technology, pharmaceutical discoveries, new surgical techniques, and many others gave us tremendous benefits without being unduly expensive.

Sulfonamide antibiotics became widely used in the 1930's.[6] Penicillin reached clinical use in the early 1940's.[7] Tetracycline was developed in 1953.[8] Streptomycin was another antibiotic that was discovered in 1943,[9] and chloramphenicol in 1947.[10] The dawning of the antibiotic era in the 1930's and 40's was an enormous benefit to the health of mankind.

Some advances were improved upon in later years, but the main technological breakthrough was made before 1950. For example, plain X-rays, which were invented in 1895, were a tremendous boon at the time, and are still very useful. Then researchers figured out how to apply that technology using moving emitters and receivers, putting the images together with a computer. Thus, computed tomography (CT) scans were born. Essentially, they are complicated X-rays.

Anesthetics and improved infection control made surgeries possible beginning in the nineteenth century.[11] It became possible to perform increasingly complex procedures. According to a modern textbook of surgery, by 1945, "essentially all organs and areas of the body had been fully explored," and "the domain of surgery had become so well established that the profession's foundation of basic operative procedures was already completed."[12] Surgeons had been successfully operating in every part of the body, including the brain and the heart. A mitral valve (one of the valves of the heart) was even repaired surgically in 1923.[13] The electrocardiogram was developed in 1902.[14] Blood banking began in 1932.[15] These advances occurred well before health costs started increasing rapidly.

There were tremendous leaps in our understanding of physiology (how the body works) in the first part of the twentieth century. Some of this understanding led to clinical treatments then, and some of it formed the groundwork for future cures.

One example of these increases in knowledge, and our ability to use that knowledge, is that of the adrenal medulla. That is a gland near the kidneys where some important hormones are made. A medical text I read recently lists the history of important discoveries relating to the adrenal medulla, and a tumor in it, which is called a pheochromocytoma. Fourteen discoveries with their dates are listed in the book. All but one of the discoveries was made before 1951. This includes the first successful surgery to remove a pheochromocytoma, in 1926, at the Mayo Clinic in Minnesota.[16]

Improvements in general hygiene also played a large role in increasing longevity, but medical advancements were probably at least as important in improving our lifespans. This happened without accelerations in cost.

Of course, life expectancy is just an educated guess anyway, until a life-time has passed. Nobody really knows how long somebody is going to live if that person was born five years ago. It is a prediction of the future. With that in mind, we do not really know how well our life expectancy has improved in the past few decades. We do know there was a tremendous improvement in longevity in the first half of the twentieth century, however. The main point is that health care costs do not have to inflate dramatically while medical technology advances and life expectancy improves.

What happened in the 1940s that started health care costs inflating, and then why did costs start accelerating so dramatically in the late 1960s? During World War II, health insurance started to become something that was frequently offered by employers, as a result of government interference in the labor market. Then in 1965, Medicare and Medicaid were enacted. These two events have done more than anything else to drive health care costs through the roof, and decrease the quality of service, in American health care. I will discuss each of these subjects in detail in subsequent chapters.

So total spending on health care has climbed enormously. This means that we are doing more for our health, doesn't it? No, that is only a part of the increase. Take a couple of specific health procedures, and look at what they cost in 1950 and 1960, compared to today.

People suffered from appendicitis decades ago just as they do now. The treatment is the same, with slight modification. The appendix needs to be taken out surgically. The slight change is that it is usually done laparoscopi-cally now (via small instruments introduced through small cuts), rather than opening up the abdomen. It is often still done in an open procedure, however. The cost does not differ by all that much between these techniques, when the hospital stay is included. A CT scan or ultrasound is often done now for diagnosis, but often the surgeon does not need these tests.

The delivery of a baby has not changed all that much either, unless there are complications. The only real changes in most cases are fetal heart moni-toring, and epidural pain control, which are small parts of the overall cost. Yet, even though these procedures were not greatly different in past decades, their costs were quite affordable to the typical manual laborer, without any insurance.

"In the days of direct payment, a bill for a 4-day maternity and 4-day nursery stay, including $10 for the delivery room, was $52.50 in 1950 at Memorial General Hospital in Las Cruces, NM. The statement was handwritten on a half-sheet of paper. The hospital bill for an uncomplicated appendectomy at St. Mary's Hospital in Tucson, AZ, was $150 in 1960, about 10 days' wages for a common construction laborer."[17] A patient of mine told me of a bill she had seen for the delivery of a baby. The bill was framed and hanging in the office of her doctor who has since retired. That bill was for $50. Adjusting for inflation, $52.50 for the delivery in 1950 equals $475 in 2010, and $150 for the appendectomy in 1960 equals $1105 in 2010.

I have queried my older patients and others on the subject of service from doctors. Invariably, they have told me that service was much better in the 1950's and 60's. Back then, it was not too difficult to get a doctor to come to the home. They spent sufficient time with the patient. There were not the waiting times that are so commonplace today.

It is difficult to find data on patient satisfaction from those days. If anybody did patient satisfaction surveys, I have not been able to find any. They probably simply did not need them. There was only one satisfaction survey that mattered, and that was whether patients patronized a doctor or not. If they were unsatisfied, they just went elsewhere. Doctors knew this, and provided the service that was needed to keep the patients coming.

To summarize, there was no major problem with health care costs until recent decades. Technology was racing forward. People were starting to live substantially longer, without spending all that much for the benefit. House calls and prompt service were commonplace. People were generally happy with the service that was provided. Things were really going quite well. Then the situation started to change. I will discuss the problems that started to occur, describe the causes, and then propose some solutions.

The treatment will be based on the diagnosis. It does no good to propose a solution to a problem if the cause of the problem is ignored. A careful analysis of the causes of our health care problems gives a great deal of hope to a reasonable person. Health care can be saved in the United States, but not using the methods that Congress and the President have recently foisted upon us. We can have excellent care that is affordable, with the kind of service we have come to expect in other areas of our economy. The solutions are not complex. All that is needed is an understanding of the causes, and the willingness to make the changes.

# America Is the World
# Leader in Innovations

———

*"Politics is the conspiracy of the unproductive but organized
against the productive but unorganized."*

*- Joseph Sobran*

AMERICA HAS NOT ONLY HAD affordable health care in previous decades, but
it has been at the forefront of medical advancement. For centuries, America
has been the place where more innovations have been developed than any
other place, both in the medical field and outside of medicine. It is the place
where modern medicine has been nurtured and grown.

Fifty percent of the Nobel Laureates in Physiology or Medicine, from the
first prize in 1901 through 2008, have been from American institutions. The
count is 96 of 192. Of those who left their native lands to do their work, 29
came to the United States, and none left the United States to do their work
elsewhere. The vast majority of the non-American Nobel Laureates are from
Europe. Aside from those who emigrated from Russia, there was only one
Russian winner, Ivan Pavlov, but his work was before the Bolshevik takeover.
There were no Nobel Laureates affiliated with institutions in communist nations.[1] There was one major advancement in the practice of medicine that I
can think of that came from the Soviet bloc, and that was blood banking.

This really says something about the value of freedom to society. Countries that have freedom at the core of their political institutions lead the world in technological advancement, while countries that bind their people with the shackles of intrusive government lag far behind.

Other nations benefit tremendously from the work that is done in America, because they end up with the technology. An economist observed, "If all countries squeezed profits in the health sector the way Europe and Canada do, there would be much less global innovation in medical technology. Today, the whole world benefits freely from advances in health technology that are driven largely by the allure of the profitable U.S. market. If the United States joins other nations in having more socialized medicine, the current pace of technology improvements might well grind to a halt."[2]

Of course, we could just become completely socialist, and be happy with what we have now. Most people would prefer to continue with medical research, however.

If we look at all fields of interest, not just medicine, we find the following. Of all the inventions that were found worthy enough to be listed in the 2006 World Almanac and Book of Facts, from 1790 until 2006, there were 213 American and 125 non-American inventors.[3] Considering that the United States has roughly 5% of the population of the world, it is pretty impressive that 63% of inventions came from here. Of the 125 non-American inventions, a mere 8 were from outside of Western Europe (west of the iron curtain). From communist nations, there was only one invention.[4]

Concerning medical advancements, "U.S. innovators hold 80% of patents issued in the U.S., but also 50% of the patents issued in Canada, 40% of patents issued in Japan, and two-thirds of patents issued in Mexico."[5] Americans lead the world in innovation, hands down.

I would add that I believe it is the example of freedom in America, which led to greater freedom in Europe, which then led to an improvement in their output of technology.

It has been said that our greatest export has been our constitution. Our example of freedom has been emulated by many other nations. Too bad we have left the idea behind. There has been an enormous acceleration in world-wide technological advancements since the founding of freedom in America.

Does all this mean Americans are just plain smarter than other people? Hardly. Other people do not have the same incentives to fully develop their ideas. We are not held back by caste. Government power is not as much of a drag on advancement as it is in other nations, although it is becoming more of a drag with each passing year. Given the same system of freedom, I believe people anywhere would be just as productive as Americans are.

# The Reason for Our Prosperity Is Freedom

———

*"Government's view of the economy could be summed up in a few short phrases: If it moves, tax it. If it keeps moving, regulate it. And if it stops moving, subsidize it."*

*- RONALD REAGAN*

AMERICAN FREEDOM HAS BEEN A driving force behind medical innovations for the past couple of centuries. It has also been the cause of prosperity in general, medical and otherwise.

There has never been anything in all of history to compare with that amazing engine of prosperity we call the United States of America. We have produced more wealth than any other nation on earth. We achieved prosperity in a very short time. Our wealth has benefited everybody, from the highest to the lowest strata of society. Even the so-called poor have more than most people in other nations.

Does this sound overly simplistic and naive? Could it just be the rantings of a radical pro-America simpleton? Let us look at some specifics, and see if it is naiveté, or if being pro-America is the logical conclusion of an honest student of history.

A careful historical analysis performed by some economists compared the American economy in the nineteenth century to the economy of Great Britain, the greatest economic power in the rest of the world. They determined that the U.S. led the United Kingdom in terms of income per capita and output per worker between 1830 and 1870.[1] Real GDP per capita of the US was 20% higher than that of Great Britain, the second mightiest industrial nation on earth, as early as 1831.[2] British GDP was at about the same level just prior to World War I, about 82% of US GDP, after which it declined relative to the United States, to a low of 47% of ours following World War II.[3]

Apparently, it was indeed a very short time for the United States to surpass the economic production of Great Britain, in spite of our catastrophic financial condition shortly after our War of Independence, wherein we seceded from Great Britain. We suffered horrendous debt and terrible conditions under the Articles of Confederation, but during the 42 years following the ratification of the Constitution, we surpassed the mightiest economic power on earth, and maintained our lead to the present day.

Professors Ward and Devereux conclude, "American leadership in living standards and productivity is long standing. It dates at least to the early part of the nineteenth century. These results raise questions about the source of American prosperity."[4]

I maintain that the source of American prosperity is in large part our Constitution, which recognizes and guarantees our God-given freedoms.

Germany was another economic powerhouse of Europe. Its economy also paled in comparison to that of America. "Germany's powerful industrial revolution did not get fully started until 1870. By that time America's industrial revolution had been well under way. Starting from a much lower base, therefore, Germany's rate of growth would have been expected to exceed America's, at least for a while. Yet despite Germany's takeoff (the fastest of a major European nation over these years), the American economy continued to grow faster ... All this time, America was providing jobs for tens of millions of immigrants."[5] The conclusion from this study was, "it cannot be said strongly enough that the economy we have come to take for granted has been remarkable."[6]

While the American economy has produced enormous wealth, it has benefited all who care to contribute, and even those who do not. With few exceptions, the so-called "poor" in this country are really quite well off by the standards of anyone, except another American. "More than 92 percent of Americans below the poverty line said they had enough food, as of 1998. Some 86 percent said they had no unmet need for a doctor, 89 percent had no roof leaks, and 87 percent said they had no unpaid rent or mortgage."[7]

What? Mortgages being held by the "poor?" How can that be? As it turns out, America is such an unusual phenomenon in world history that ownership of substantial homes among those called "poor" is actually quite common. In fact, our standards are so high that most people in the rest of the world would probably be astonished.

Robert Rector, Senior Research Fellow at The Heritage Foundation analyzed Census Bureau data on "poor" Americans. He found the following about those below the official poverty line in the U.S.: 43% own homes, with an average of three bedrooms, one and a half baths, a porch or patio, and a garage. Eighty percent have air conditioning. Only 6% of "poor" households are reported as overcrowded. Over two-thirds have more than two rooms per person. On average, they have more living space than the average person in Athens, Vienna, Paris, London, and other European cities. This is comparing "poor" Americans to average, not poor, Europeans. Almost three-quarters of "poor" households own a car, 31% own at least two. Ninety seven percent have a color TV, over half have at least two color TVs. Sixty two percent have cable or satellite TV. Seventy eight percent have a VCR or DVD player. Over half have a stereo. Eighty nine percent have at least one microwave oven. Over a third have an automatic dishwasher.[8]

How many poor Banglades his have air conditioners? How can we say that someone is "in poverty" if he owns an air conditioner, a home, a microwave, two cars, and most of the other luxuries on this list? We really should avoid using the words "rich" and "poor" when talking about Americans. More accurate would be the terms "wealthy" and "less wealthy."

It is rather obvious that our economy lifts those of all classes of society to greater material well-being. "But the rich are getting richer, and the poor are getting poorer! The gap between rich and poor is widening!" Even if that was true, so what? How is a wealth gap wrong anyway? How is it wrong for industrious people to be rewarded for their industriousness? Should laziness or inability be rewarded just as much as hard work and ability? But let us think about that gap a little more.

When I was younger, and did not have many of the above luxuries, I certainly did not consider myself poor. I figured I was just starting in life, and that my material situation would improve as I developed more skills and experience. This is actually what happens in the vast majority of cases. Of those in the lowest fifth of income in 1996, 29% moved to the second quintile by 2005, and another 29% moved up to the middle fifth or higher of income.[9] So while there are inequalities in wealth, the "poor" among us are for the most part not really poor, and with some effort they elevate their material situation in time. The "widening gap between the rich and the poor" is not even making valid comparisons. People move from the "poor" class into the middle and even higher classes. So a study comparing the rich and the poor in 1985, compared to the rich and the poor in 1990, will have some of the people in the poor class in 1985 included in the rich class in 1990. Any analysis of the width of the gap between rich and poor is, therefore, somewhat meaningless.

In summary, America has become wealthy in a very short time. It has outproduced the other industrial powers, hands down. Its economy raises all levels of society. Why, then, has this happened? What makes America so incredibly prosperous?

Some people attribute our wealth to our natural resources and/or our isolation from the wars of Europe. While these factors undoubtedly help, they cannot be the only, or even the primary, reasons for our success. If so, Mexico would be a wealthy nation. It has the same conditions of isolation from Europe, and it has a bounty of natural resources. Mexico was a colony of Spain, much like the United States was a colony of Great Britain. Mexico won its independence a little later than we did, and has had plenty of time to begin to prosper. We are still waiting for that prosperity to occur.

Mexico has resources of petroleum, silver, copper, gold, lead, zinc, natural gas, and timber. While the GDP per capita in the United States is $45,800,[10] the Mexican GDP per capita is only $12,400.[11] Wealth is very unevenly distributed, with corrupt government officials raking it in; but with the peasants truly being poor, not like the official poverty class in America. The blight throughout Mexico is obvious to anyone who travels there, outside of the resort areas.

As to the natural resources of some other nations, Nigeria has natural gas, petroleum, tin, iron ore, coal, limestone, niobium, lead, zinc, and arable land, and only has a GDP per capita of $2,100.[12] Zimbabwe has coal, chromium ore, asbestos, gold, nickel, copper, iron ore, vanadium, lithium, tin, and platinum group metals, and has a GDP per capita of an incredibly low $200.[13] The "Democratic Republic" of the Congo has cobalt, copper, niobium, tantalum, petroleum, industrial and gem diamonds, gold, silver, zinc, manganese, tin, uranium, coal, hydropower, and timber, and their GDP per capita is $300.[14] Even Saudi Arabia only has a per capita GDP of $19,800,[16] or 43% that of the United States, in spite of having over 20% of the known petroleum reserves on the planet.[17]

So obviously, natural resources do not make a country wealthy. Some of these nations are abounding in natural wealth, and yet are cesspools of poverty, rife with disease and starvation. Imagine a person on an official government poverty list in Zimbabwe. Would that person have two color televisions, a car, his own three bedroom house with a garage and patio, a microwave, air conditioner, cable TV, etc., as the average "poor" person has in the U.S? He would be lucky to find clean water.

What differentiates these countries from the United States? They do not have the freedom we do. The Heritage Foundation compiles an Index of Economic Freedom every year, based on many objectively measured variables from sources such as the World Bank. There is a direct correlation between freedom and prosperity, as illustrated in the following graph.

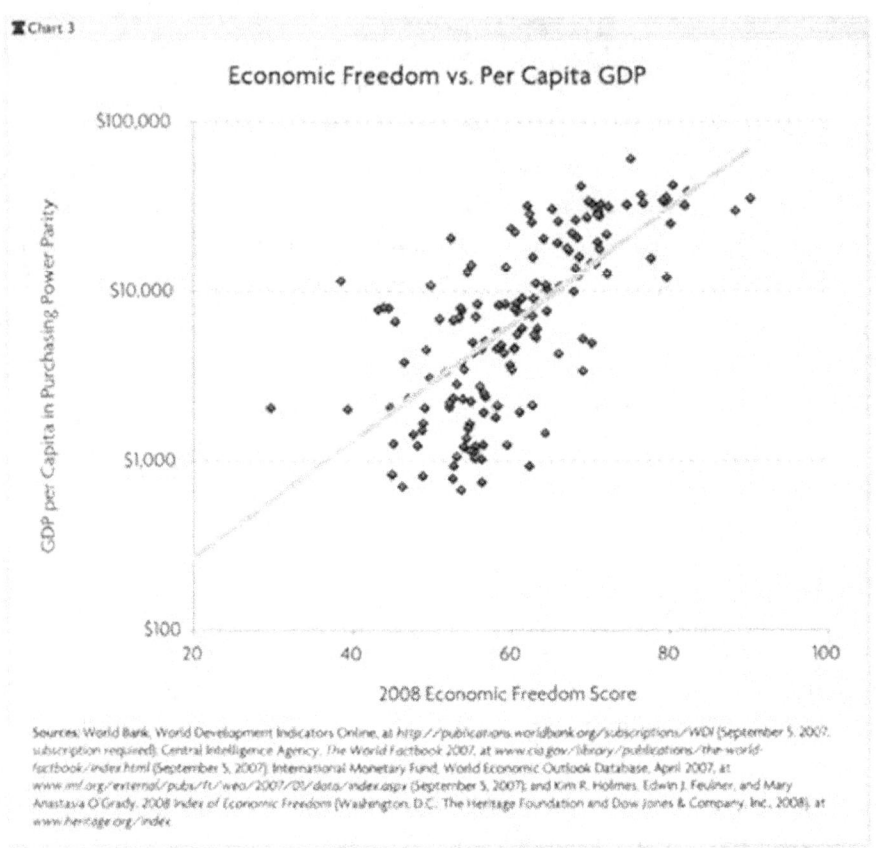

Per Capita Income of Nations vs. Economic Freedom in those Nations[18]
Reproduced with permission.

Without economic freedom, a society simply does not prosper. Some of the tin pot dictators in these countries are quite wealthy, but the average prosperity is much less than we enjoy in the United States, and the lower classes barely cling to life in many of these countries. It is not natural resources, or geographic position, that prospers a nation and its people. They may help, but they are not sufficient.

Then there is the completely ludicrous idea that we are wealthy and powerful because we exploit other nations. How does a weak and poor country exploit other nations in order to become wealthy and powerful in the first place? Until that is answered, it is absurd to suggest that is how America became prosperous.

Some people claim that a lack of population density is the cause of our wealth. With room to work and grow, they say, we have the conditions that enable success. If that is true, why do small, densely populated nations like Singapore and Luxembourg prosper? Why did small, dense Japan, which also has few natural resources, become such an economic power? The Index of Economic Freedom ranks these countries highly in their levels of freedom. They are much more dense with people than the United States, and much more dense than many impoverished nations of the world. Lack of population density cannot be the cause of success for these nations, or for the United States.

Freedom has been vital to the prosperity of America, since it's founding. Without freedom, we would have nowhere near the level of wealth and comfort we do. America was revolutionary, in that the powers of its government were limited by a written constitution, which specified the areas in which the federal[19] government has jurisdiction. It says that the federal government may exercise power over this, and this, and this, and that is all. Hands off everything else.

The constitution was also unique in that it recognized and guaranteed the inherent, God-given freedoms of individuals. It did not give us these freedoms; God did. If you do not believe in God, you can still recognize that our freedoms are inherent to us by virtue of our humanity. They predate the institution of governments, and their protection was the reason that people combined to form governments in the first place. The constitution was a contract that formally recognized these freedoms. That recognition was based upon the section of the Declaration of Independence which stated: "We hold these truths to be self-evident, that all men were created equal, that they are endowed by their Creator with certain unalienable rights, that among these are life, liberty, and the pursuit of happiness; that in order to secure these rights, governments were instituted among men."[20]

It is, therefore, the purpose of government to secure the rights of individuals, which they were endowed with by their creator (God). It is not the purpose of government to provide for people, but to secure them in their rights. This means that people band together to form governments, to provide for their mutual protection, against criminal attack, foreign armies, etc. Anything that threatens the lives or property of the people is an enemy from which protection is sought through the combined strength of government.

People are then secure, and able to pursue happiness. Whether any individual will find that happiness is up to himself, but his liberty to do so, unmolested by others, is secured by government. Whether someone succeeds financially or not, and what someone is able to buy, is up to that individual. Government establishes the conditions under which success is possible, by securing our rights, but does not guarantee success for any individual.

Under these conditions of freedom, secured by the constitution, people are able to profit from their hard work, resourcefulness, and risk taking. Because they can enjoy the fruits of their labors, they work hard to succeed. By doing so, they raise their own standard of living, and the standard of living of others around them. Because Thomas Edison found 2,000 ways not to make an electric light, and still persisted until he found a way to make it, we all benefit from having electric lights. Why did he keep at it? He continued because he profited from his inventions. The amount of innovation, medical and non-medical, that has come out of America has been breathtaking, as I have already discussed.

Because of the freedom of people to pursue their happiness, the ingenuity and creativity of individuals was unleashed. There was no more aristocracy of birth; this was replaced by an aristocracy of talent. Work, risk, and intelligence were rewarded as nowhere else in the world. Government did not stand in the way of progress.

In other nations, governments determined what a person may aspire to, based on birthright. This is not the case in America. Anybody can pursue whatever vocation he sets his mind to, and enjoy the fruits of his labors. The profit motive is the driving force of progress.

Early in our nation's history, race and gender did play a defining role in the potential of a person. We suffered from the blight of slavery, and women were also denied opportunity. This kept some of the brightest minds from contributing to societal progress. However, the Judeo-Christian culture was not unique in practicing slavery; rather, it was unique in eliminating it. Most other cultures on every continent had practiced slavery, and some still do. The United States was part of the movement by Jews and Christians, both American and European, which put a halt to slavery. Men and women of all races now have opportunity to reach their full potential, and by doing so, to advance the state of our technology.

The United States Constitution is a contract that was formed by the separate states, which at the time were affiliated but separate nations. They had their own forms of currency, their own import duties and customs, and their own armies. The economy was in chaos. Congress owed back pay to soldiers, and debts were owed to other nations, but they could not collect taxes to pay those debts. The financial situation was bleak for the people, and it was not improving.

In order to form a cohesive nation, the Constitution was written. Its purpose was to define a federal government, with its framework, powers, and limitations. Some specific limitations on federal jurisdiction and power were laid out in the Bill of Rights, the first ten amendments. These were specific restrictions, but they were not the only limitations on federal power. The tenth amendment made this clear; it said that any powers not given to the federal government by the Constitution were to be reserved to the states or to the people. Four of the biggest states of the original thirteen would not ratify the Constitution until they were promised that tenth amendment.[21] The Constitution was then ratified by the states, making it official.

It became a binding contract between the states, the "supreme law of the land; and the judges in every state shall be bound thereby, anything in the constitution or laws of any state to the contrary notwithstanding."[22] This means that any law contrary to the constitution is not legitimate. Judges are bound by the Constitution as the supreme law of the land. If a state passes a law that is contrary to the Constitution it is null and void. If the federal government passes a law contrary to the constitution it is also "void and is as no law. An offence created by it is not a crime."[23]

During the ratification process, the states agreed to form a national government on the terms that were specified in the Constitution. It thus became a binding contract. It is no more of a "living, breathing document" than any other contract is. It is changeable, but only by the amendment process, which was very clearly delineated. It does not discuss situations in their specifics, but declares principles, which are then to be applied to specific situations as appropriate. In that sense, it may be called "living and breathing," but its principles do not change without amendment.

The power of the federal government was restricted from meddling in the affairs of the citizens. It was limited to securing the rights of people, through the protection of armies, navies, copyright protection for intellectual property, etc. Standards of weights and measures, postal roads, and currency were established to provide for a cohesive nation, under a rule of law, which would be able to work together.

From the start, there was no power recognized in the federal government to take wealth from one person and transfer it to another person, in any form, for any purpose, no matter how worthy the cause may be. It was observed that the power to tax is the power to destroy. If there is a cause that is worthy of charity, then that is the province of individuals acting on a voluntary basis. It is not an act of charity to confiscate money from someone to give to another, and such acts were not permissible under the Constitution. There was never any amendment that altered the Constitution so fundamentally to make such acts legal. Legislatures and courts simply began to ignore the supreme law of the land, and rob from Peter to pay Paul, thereby winning the approval of Paul. Such theft also wins the approval of those who feel guilty about their wealth, even though their prosperity was made possible by the freedoms that were recognized in the Constitution. There are also a great many people who have no comprehension of the Constitution, and approve wholeheartedly of socialist redistribution of wealth, because they think it is for the good of mankind. I will describe at length in a subsequent chapter how socialist redistribution of wealth actually diminishes the well being of everybody, except those in power.

There are many people who say our constitution is outdated, archaic, and no longer valid. They say that we should not limit ourselves by its constraints in this technologically advanced society. Yet, we would not live in this type of society if not for the prosperity that our constitution brought to us. As we abandon the principles of freedom that have been embodied in the constitution, we also begin to lose our prosperity.

We started our national existence heavily indebted to the major powers and financiers of Europe, without much realistic hope of overcoming that debt. Within a very short time, against all odds, we overcame those bleak beginnings, and became a power on the world stage, economically and militarily. Not too much later, we had become the industrial and military leader of the world, without peer. In all of recorded history, there had not been such a stunning rise to power as that of America. The reason was limited constitutional government, and the freedom of the individual to prosper, that such a government established. This held true in all fields of endeavor, including medicine. Let us learn from our history, stay with what works, and shun that which does not.

# What is Money?

———

*"Property rights is a radical Republican idea!"*

THIS CHAPTER WAS INSPIRED BY my brother-in-law, who blurted out the above quotation, while standing on his property. I suspect that if I started chopping up his kayak into kindling he might have remembered that it was his property. It did not occur to me that some people do not understand the concept of property, but there may be many others like him. I do not think he was referring to republicanism; i.e., government by elected representatives. I believe he was talking about Republicans, as in the Republican Party.

In reality, property did not come about as a result of any political ideology. Governments came about because of the need for protection of people's lives and property from the assault of others who were stronger than them. People banded together to form a collective strength that would defend the individual members from predations. Along with property came the need for money, a medium of exchange, to trade that property.

In order to understand health care economics, it is first necessary to understand economics in general. The idea of a discussion of economics may sound rather dreary, but it is one of the most important subjects a person can know. Bad economic theory led to abject poverty for a huge portion of the world's population. To understand economics, a person needs to know what money is. Let us go back in time several millennia and study the origins of money.

Og, Kanook, Neewob, and Gar each made spears to hunt mastodons for the meat and fur. Soon they came to realize that Og was really good at shaping and sharpening the heads of the spears, and Kanook excelled at making nice straight smooth shafts, but Gar's methods of attaching the heads to the shafts were best. Neewob was far and away the best hunter of mastodons. He could really throw that spear into the X ring on a mastodon. Therefore they decided to specialize.

Og's spearheads were not lost or broken at the same rate as Kanook's shafts. The attachments did not last the same as either. And those mastodons sure took a long time to eat. They could not just keep trading one thing for another. Gar could attach the heads and shafts, in exchange for a mastodon from Neewob, but he still had plenty of meat from the last one. So they developed money to help the barter system along. They found some rare seashells that they exchanged and the various items were assigned different values.

We have become even more specialized in our day than they were in Og's day. Simple barter would not work. Imagine that you want an iPod. Your specialty is painting houses. You find out who succeeded Steve Jobs, and offer to paint a small bit of his house. Too late, he already exchanged iPods to three thousand other house painters, and there are no little bits of his house left needing painting. You need some means of currency to facilitate the exchange.

You paint somebody's entire house, and they give you those certificates of service[1] that we call dollars. You then use those certificates of service to exchange for an iPod, and whatever else you want to buy with the remainder. The owner of Apple can then pay his employees, and they can buy food or clothes or whatever they need.

Money is therefore nothing more or less than certificates of service. It came into being through the need for a separate currency to simplify barter of goods and services.

Following Og's time, better forms of currency were developed than the shells they used. That was because Kanook found a large deposit of those supposedly rare shells. He now had thirty times the amount of shells as were previously in circulation. He did not have to do anything to obtain the services of others; he simply gave up some of his shells of which he had a lot more.

Now the group had nobody that was good at making really straight, smooth shafts for their spears. Their money had decreased to 1/30 of its original value. It used to take 3 shells to buy a good spearhead, and now it took 90, because of Kanook's inflating of their money supply. They had to find another form of currency.

Advancing societies eventually settled on gold as currency, for several reasons. It was scarce. It was easily divisible. It could be easily transported and exchanged. Gold, and other rare metals such as silver, became the currency that people used to exchange goods and services. The situation remained stable for millennia. The value of gold has remained approximately the same for centuries; in terms of what it can buy.[2]

While the value of gold has been fairly constant, our paper "dollars" have dropped precipitously in value for the past century. That is because of what governments have done to money.

After people had been trading gold for centuries, banks started offering gold certificates - paper notes that could be carried instead of gold, but which could be exchanged at the bank for the gold that they certified. People could then carry those notes, which were much lighter, and then exchange them later.

Then along came governments, including the United States government, which also issued gold or silver certificates like the banks did. The difference is that they passed laws that said people had to take their certificates as money, or they would be imprisoned. Resisters, of course, would be shot. People decided to take the government gold certificates, rather than being shot. After all, they could always exchange them for gold.

After enough time passed for people to get used to the government-issued gold certificates, the United States government said the certificates could no longer be exchanged for gold or silver. People would still be required to take them, however, or they would be imprisoned. Once again, resisters would be shot. They also forced everybody to give any gold they had to the government. People complied rather than being shot.

Now, "dollars" were no longer backed by anything more than the confidence of people that other people would still honor them. They could still be useful as certificates of service, so long as Kanook Jr. was not put in a position of authority in the banking cartel called the Federal Reserve. Unfortunately, he was.

Those paper certificates that we now call dollars have been printed in massive quantities. At the time that the Federal Reserve was instituted, 1913, a dollar was worth 1.64 grams of gold.[3] Now a dollar is worth only 0.023 grams of gold,[4] or 1.4% of the value in 1913. Remember, gold has remained roughly steady in value. "Sound as a dollar" is a phrase that we no longer hear except in classic movies.

Kanook Jr., Alan Greenspan, Janet Yellen, et. al. have been printing our modern certificates of service so that they can use them to pay for things the American people would never willingly pay for if they knew the cost. It is usually done now by the Federal Reserve digitally creating money with which they buy the Treasury notes that the U.S. Treasury prints. It amounts to the same thing as printing new dollars.

Certificates of service are being printed to give to people who provide no service to others, through our many forms of welfare. These certificates have been used to pay for a century of war, the like of which would astonish the founders of our country. We now have soldiers in 135 countries around the world.[5]

Our welfare-warfare state would never have been willingly paid for by productive members of society, if they knew the full cost. Therefore Kanook Jr. came along and inflated our money supply with relatively worthless paper dollars to pay for these things.

Now people are being taxed without knowing it. If Kanook Jr. and company at the Federal Reserve double our money supply, each dollar is worth 50% less, with the government keeping the remainder. The typical poor sap in America does not know he has been taxed 50%. He might recognize that goods cost twice as much as they used to, and blame the people that sell. He might rant and rail against evil capitalists for charging high prices. He does not figure out that the government stole half his money.

Your ability to make a good living reflects the value of your service to others. Some, like me, choose to charge less than they are worth (proven by tips), but your ability to do so means that you are valuable to others. If you learn a more valuable skill, then people will voluntarily pay you more. This does not apply to government workers or criminals, as their living is made by confiscated money. This does not mean that there are no government workers who do useful work, but that is not reflected in what they make for a living. If it was being voluntarily given in exchange for their work, then this would also apply to government workers, but the mechanism by which government works is force.

Now that money has been explained, property needs to receive its due respects. Property is the result of people's effort. If somebody takes something that is commonly available to all, and puts effort into its improvement, it becomes his property. It cannot then rightly be taken by another. Somebody can find a stick that is just laying on common ground where anybody can take it. When it is laying there, it is not his property. Anybody can take it. If he picks it up, and then whittles it into a beautiful artistic form of a horse, then it is no longer in the common domain. He can sell it, or keep it, or give it to somebody else. Nobody else can lay claim to it once he has put his effort into it.[6]

In the days of staking claims for mining, if a person declared a patch of ground to be his claim, and put some work into development of a mine, then that made it his property. A simple declaration of ownership without any development work was not sufficient.

The right to hold and control property is vital to the well being of society. Without it, nobody could be confident that the work they do would end up benefiting themselves. Why would anybody develop something into a useful enterprise if others could just take it from them? We would have none of the comforts of modern society, because nobody would be able to develop their means of production.

If I wanted to run something as simple as a lemonade stand, I would need to have a property right to all the materials that went into it. Otherwise, as soon as I started to put it together, and brought some lemons and sugar and water, somebody else could just take it, leaving me in the lurch. Whatever is given to me in exchange for the lemonade then becomes my property also. Nobody has a right to take it from me by force to give it to another.

Once something becomes the property of a person, then that person can rightfully do whatever he wants with it, so long as it does not interfere with the rights of another. He can give it to his children upon his death. He can sell it. He can develop it further.

What about taking my money to give to other people? If I have forty percent of my money taken to give to other people, then that means that forty percent of my work is being taken by force to be spent for the benefit of others. Forcing somebody to work for you is a reasonable definition of slavery. This means I would be forty percent enslaved. Personally, this author is opposed to slavery. How about the reader? Is making somebody a forty percent slave okay with you? Twenty percent? To what extent can a person rightfully be enslaved?[7] This author believes that voluntary exchange, or free markets, are a much more moral approach. Free markets also lead to much greater practical benefits, by increasing the standards of living of the people who live in those systems.

# Socialism – The Equal Sharing of Misery

———

*"Socialism is simply Communism for people without
the testosterone to man the barricades."*

*- GARY NORTH[1]*

A COMPREHENSION OF SOCIALIZED MEDICINE, or in other words, universal coverage, or single-payer health care, requires an understanding of the underlying principles of socialism. In order to compare socialist systems of health care to free market systems, we need to study the methods and results of socialist economies in general. In the next chapter, a study specifically of state-controlled health care systems will be undertaken.

Socialism has always led to economic problems, in every place it has been tried. The Union of Soviet Socialist Republics is just one example of this. Their failed experiment in utopian ideals has been replicated to varying degrees throughout Europe, in Canada, Cuba, Cambodia, and many other areas. It has never brought improvements in living conditions to any group of people, except for the rulers who feed off of the people. Winston Churchill correctly observed, "The inherent vice of capitalism is the unequal sharing of blessings; the inherent virtue of socialism is the equal sharing of miseries."[2]

Socialism and communism are very closely related. I define socialism as government control over the resources and means of production, whereas communism is government ownership of the resources and means of production.

There is very little difference between the two, with the chief difference being the level of violence needed to be employed by the government in order to enforce compliance and maintain the system. What government controls, they may as well own. The effects are very similar. There are varying degrees of socialism seen throughout the nations that are recognized as such. Pure socialism would involve complete government control over all aspects of business, rendering the business owner a mere employee of the state, in effect becoming communism. Socialism has been seen as a necessary intermediate step toward communism in those states that could not be directly communized by violent revolution or conquest.

Both socialism and communism deny to the individual the fruits of his labor. This must, of course, be done by force. While most people are very willing to give to causes they believe in, they are generally unwilling to give to the state, and so must be forced to do so. With the profit motive gone, productivity declines. Efficiency of resource use declines. Administrative costs increase. Shortages develop. Quality declines. When the producers and achievers are able to escape a socialist economy for a more free one, they often do, leaving a shortage of bright and capable people behind. In an effort to provide everything equally to all, the economic decline that results from the government interventions reduces everybody's conditions down to that of the lowest.

By contrast, in capitalism, the conditions of everybody are raised, as a result of their own efforts and abilities, and being rewarded for their work. Some are raised more than others, resulting in a gap of wealth, but everybody is more wealthy than they would be without freedom. There is nothing wrong with a gap between the wealthy and the less wealthy. It is to be expected when the conditions of some people improve dramatically, and the conditions of others are only somewhat improved. The results of freeing an economy from government shackles approximate the following graph:

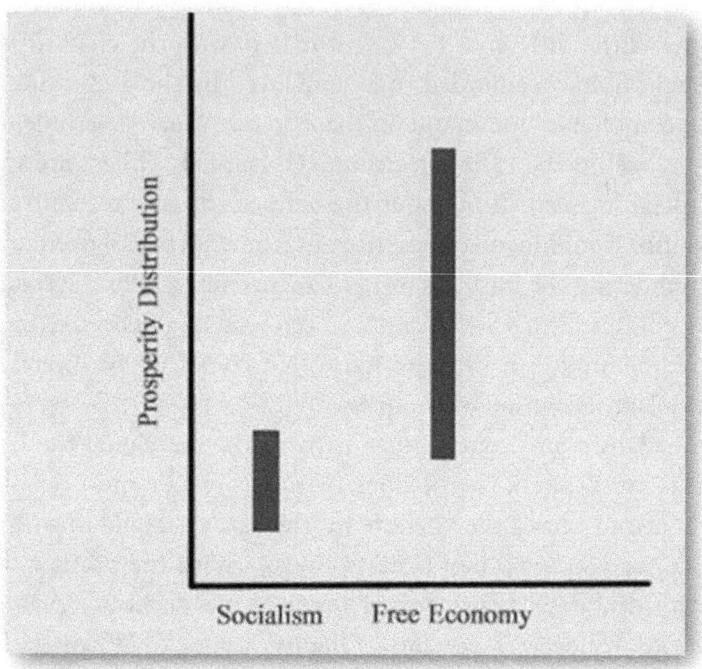

Some European nations have been experimenting with socialism recently. This change has been very hard on their economic well-being. Compared to the United States, unemployment rates are high, and the standard of living is low. The situation in health care is even worse, as we will see in the next chapter.

"America is close to full employment, whereas in Europe millions of poorly educated people can't find an employer willing to pay them the artificially high minimum wage or willing to take a chance on such hires because they may be impossible to fire in the future. In other words, Europe seems to be so productive only because a large portion of its people are simply left out of the productivity statistics (and working life). If labor productivity in Germany and in the U.S. continues on the same path as from 1996 to 2003, per capita income in Germany will grow by only 44 percent by the time American incomes double in 2026. Put differently, within a generation, Americans will enjoy twice the economic status that Germans do. [There has been] persistent mass unemployment in many European countries— with jobless rates hovering near double-digit levels in Germany, France, and other parts of the continent for most of a decade now."[3]

Unfortunately, the above quote from 2005 is no longer true, as Americans have followed the example of the Europeans economically. We are no longer close to full employment, chiefly because of the damage that interventionist government policies have caused in the American economy. The crash in the housing market in 2008, which caused the nationwide economic downturn, was primarily driven by government pressure on banks to lend money to high-risk borrowers.[4] Our drive for "fairness" and "social justice" has driven everybody down. As America becomes more socialist, we become less affluent, just like Europe.

To compare how Europeans fare to Americans, the average European does not even do as well in material well-being as someone below the official poverty line in America. The average "poor" American has more square footage of living space than does the average person living in London, Paris, Vienna, and Munich.[5] "Poor Americans eat far more meat, are more likely to own cars and dishwashers, and are more likely to have basic modern amenities such as indoor toilets than is the general West European population."[6] Just like Churchill said, "The chief vice of capitalism is the unequal distribution of wealth, but the chief virtue of socialism is the equal distribution of misery."

Then we get to outright communism. The people suffered even more under that. The early days of the Soviet Union were described thus: "Without any personal incentive among the workers, production on the farm and in the factory dwindled to a trickle. The factories were soon down to 13 percent of what they had been producing before the war started, and the farmers cut their production in half. Black markets began to flourish. Workers stole goods from the factories to exchange for food, which the peasants secretly withheld from the government. Before long, the peasants were holding back more than one-third of their crops."[7] The poverty under communism was legendary. Even Lenin had to re-institute elements of capitalism, such as the farmers getting to keep a portion of their crops, and the hiring of workers, in his New Economic Program. Otherwise, mass starvation would have resulted.

I had a Russian athlete stay with me in my house once, shortly after the collapse of the Soviet Union. There was not enough time yet for any significant change in their economy, and they were still reeling from the effects of communism. When we took him to the local supermarket, he was almost catatonic with shock at our abundance. It seemed as if he had never seen fresh food before. Indeed, we had some peaches hanging around that should have been thrown away a week before, when they started to go bad. This poor deprived soul downed those peaches like they were the best thing he had in his whole life. Keep in mind; this was an elite athlete, one who enjoyed far more luxury than the average Russian.

One of the many reasons for economic problems under socialism is the lack of any incentive to excel. "The same problems with incentives that plagued the Soviets also effect (sic) the workers under socialized medicine. In India, with a two-tier system, it was found that the less wealthy were better off paying doctors who did not have as much training, than going to the government doctors for free. This was because the private sector doctors did more of what they were supposed to do. The gap between what doctors do and what they know responds to incentives: Doctors in the fee-for-service private sector are closer in practice to their knowledge frontier than those in the fixed-salary public sector.... What doctors do in practice is very different from what they know they should do... Households in poorer neighborhoods are better off visiting less-qualified private practitioners than more-qualified public doctors."[8]

People always respond to incentives. It is no different in medicine than in other areas. The difference between intentions and results is due mostly to incentives. It does not matter so much what the goals are, if the results are exactly opposite. The advocates of socialism may espouse lofty, flowery sounding goals, but the results of socialism are precisely the opposite of those goals.

The goal of socialists, at least the goal they publicize, is helping the little guy. They say they want to help the unfortunate lower classes of society. Yet, it is precisely this group that is harmed the most by socialism. People who have more money are able to work around the system. They can still get what they want by hiring servants to wait in lines for them. They can take advantage of black markets. They can travel to other countries for health care.

Free market capitalism, on the other hand, has benefited the lower classes immensely. The lowest socioeconomic classes in a wealthy country like America now have an abundance of food; indeed, the "poor" are very often obese. They have gizmos and gadgets galore. They have large-screen televisions, automobiles, microwave ovens, and computers. If you want to pursue the espoused goal of socialism, the lifting of the masses, then you need to use capitalism to do it.

Great Britain has a "two-tier" health care system, like that of India. This means that there is a government system and a market-based, fee-for-service system. We do not have to hop the pond, however, to see what happens in a two-tier system. We have a perfect example of that here in the land of the free and the home of the brave. It is found in education.

There is a government side, the "public" schools, and a free market side, the "private" schools. In my town of Idaho Falls, Idaho, there is a private school called King's Academy. They charge $200 per month for tuition. This is enough to cover most of their operating costs, with 7% of their budget coming from donations.[9] They also have teachers who have experience in their fields of instruction. For example, the math and science teacher actually has a background in math and science, which she used while working in the pharmaceutical industry.

Contrast this with the government schools, which spend an average of $7,959 per pupil in Idaho.[10] It is not typical in the government schools to have a teacher with expertise in his or her subject. They generally graduate with degrees in education, rather than in chemistry, physics, or mathematics.

The annual expenditures, per pupil in government schools, varied by state from a low of $6,387 to a high of $16,665 for the school year 2002-2003. The percentage of eighth-grade students with grade-level proficiency in reading, varied by state from 12% to a high of 44%. The percentage of eighth-graders who were up to grade-level performance in math was from 7% to 43%.[11] These kinds of results would never be accepted from private organizations.

People generally expect much better schooling for their children in the private schools than in the government schools. This is why those who know best - the teachers - so often send their own children to private schools. Forty-four percent of the children of government school teachers in Philadelphia are enrolled in private schools. The figure for Chicago is 39%, and for Washington D.C. it is 27%. Nationwide, 21.5% of the children of government school teachers in urban areas attend private schools. This is compared to 17% of all urban children in general (not just the children of teachers) being in private schools.[12] Why are government school teachers in our cities sending their own children elsewhere? Presumably, it is because the teachers know that the quality of education is poor in the government schools.

Again, only in government can we find such terrible quality for such enormous prices. Even though the schools in Washington D.C. cost over $16,000 annually per pupil, they only achieve eighth grade proficiency for math in 7% and for reading in 12% of their eighth-grade students,[13] and over one fourth of their teachers turn elsewhere for education for their own kids. They do this even though they are being taxed heavily to pay for the government schools, and have to pay a second time to enroll their children in the private schools.

Jay P. Greene of the Manhattan Institute, using U.S. Department of Education data, pegs the average annual expenditure per pupil nationwide to be $8,032 in government schools, and $4,689 for private schools.[14] This means that only 58% as much is spent per pupil in private schools as is spent in government schools, on average.

Critics of this argument about schools most often say that private schools get better results while spending less money because they do not have the burden of special-education children. However, as studies of the Milwaukee and Florida voucher programs reveal, private schools do accept many disabled students, and even provide them with a better education, at a much lower cost than the government schools. They often do it without labeling the students as having disabilities.[15]

This is the difference between a government service and a free market service. Much less money is spent, and much better results are achieved, in free markets. We should not expect it to be any different in health care. In the following chapter, we find that government health care is exactly as we should expect, as a result of the incentives that socialism creates.

Socialism destroys sociality. People associate together, form communities, and bond together in families, for mutual support. Socialism leads people to depend on government instead of family, church, and community. It is therefore destructive of family, church, and community association. It becomes very difficult for family to support their own when massive amounts of money are being extracted from them to pay for socialist programs. People have less to give to church charities and community charitable drives. People usually think of government first as a means of support now when they run into hard times.

Socialism has great appeal to the innate sense of justice and morality that humans fortunately have. Unfortunately, as we have seen, those nations that fall victim to its charms have suffered economic stagnation. They have endured falling standards of living for everybody except the rulers. Research efforts have been sluggish and relatively unproductive. As we shall see next, health care in particular has suffered tremendously in those countries that have become more fully socialized.

# The Disasters of Fully
# Socialized Medicine

———

*"Democracy is the theory that the common people know what they want,
and deserve to get it good and hard."*

*- H.L. Mencken*

Everywhere socialism has been tried, it has failed to bring about the results most people hope to achieve. If the goal is increased power and control, then it is fabulously successful. However, the goal for most people is to increase the well-being of all the population. In this, it has been a dismal failure, time and time again. It actually achieves the directly opposite result, the "equal sharing of miseries." The health care arena is no exception.

It is said that the United States is the only developed nation that does not have socialized medicine. I will go on in subsequent chapters to refute this idea. I contend that our health care is mostly socialized, through various government controls. It is in the more completely socialized medical systems that we can see the real problems that result, even more directly than we do in the United States.

Take Great Britain, for example. They have a "two-tier" system, meaning that the private practice of medicine has not been criminalized, and there is also a government system.  These are the two tiers, the free market and the government system.

The British, because of the private tier, have more freedom than Canadians do.  If two mutually consenting adults, one a doctor and the other a patient, engage in the act of health care in exchange for monetary compensation, then the government will not punish them in England as it might in Canada.

In Great Britain, the government tier, or National Health Service (NHS), has become plagued with shortages, lengthy waits, and rationing way beyond anything we would consider reasonable here in America.  Whenever the people come to feel entitled to services for which somebody else is compelled to pay, government must resort to drastic measures to limit the extent of spending.  "When the people find they can vote themselves money, that will herald the end of the republic."[1]

One example of the extent to which the British overseers have had to resort in order to limit spending is the following:  "Overweight patients have been denied hip and knee replacement surgery on the NHS as some health authorities try to cut costs.  Those with a body mass index (BMI) of 30 or above are classed as obese and will not be allowed surgery to replace worn out joints."[2] This was proposed in some regions of the NHS, to limit costs.

To get the full picture of this kind of rationing, consider that Mike Tyson, when he fought Razor Riddock, was 5' 11 1/2" tall, and weighed 218 lbs, for a BMI of 30.  He was considerably heavier for other fights.  Picture Iron Mike weighing in for his hip surgery, and not making weight.  He might have to sweat off some weight to make the proper weight class before surgery.  It is good that people need to fast for surgery - it will help them make the weight cutoff.

Elderly patients have often been left to die, by withholding food and fluids, under the "Liverpool Care Pathway" in Britain.  This was often done without even informing family.  85 year old Olive Goom was put on this protocol, and just hours before her death, well after doctors removed food and fluid, her family was told there was no urgent need to visit.  Families had been forbidden by staff to even provide a sip of water to their dying loved ones, even though they were seeming desperate for it.  130,000 patients per year have been put on this pathway, often without consent, and many times these patients would likely be able to recover with proper medical care. Sometimes they did recover when family found out about what was happening and intervened.[3]

The retirement speech of the former chairman of the British Medical Association was very enlightening. He referred to the "creeping, morale-sapping erosion of doctors' clinical autonomy brought about by micro-man-agement from Whitehall, … stifling of innovation by excessive, intrusive audit, … shackling of doctors by prescribing guidelines, referral guidelines and protocols, … suffocation of professional responsibility by target-setting and production-line values that leave little room for the professional judg-ment of individual doctors or the needs of individual patients," and the "ex-traordinary lengths to which some hospitals will go to pull the wool over the auditors' eyes."[4]

Sarah Lyall of the New York Times described the situation at St. George's Hospital in London. "At times as many as 30 patients have been sprawled on gurneys outside his emergency room, waiting for treatment for things like pneumonia, heart attacks, stabbings and injuries from car accidents." Patients often have to wait for over two days as their conditions become worse. She quotes Dr. Don Wijetunge as saying that the situation is now "almost rou-tine." The same despair is found all throughout Great Britain.[5]

There is only one place in the United States where I have seen anything approaching the scenario described above, in all the years of my training and medical practice. That was in our government system, the Veterans Affairs (VA) hospital where I spent some time in medical school. There, patients were left in the emergency department for a day while awaiting admission. They were admitted into recliner chairs in the outpatient surgery department. It takes government to produce such shortages in a land of plenty.

The waiting times for specialists in the United States will be described in more detail in a subsequent chapter. Orthopedic surgeons in the worst city of the U.S. had an average wait of about 6 weeks.[6] What of Britain? Surely they must do better with their wonderful, free care. "A [2008] study has shown that waiting times after referral by a GP are up to four years - or 208 weeks - for one orthopedic surgeon. The research by the charity, the College of Health, also shows patients are waiting 147 weeks and 145 weeks to see foot specialists in two separate hospitals. The worst waiting time for an out-patient appointment in neurology was 126 weeks, with one example of a 95-week wait to see an eye specialist, the study showed."[7]

The leadership in England is proud of the progress they have made. Only 155,439 people have been awaiting hospital admission for over four months after referral from their general practitioner as of May 2012. Only 3,500 have been waiting for over a year.[8] Imagine the pain and anguish patients endure through these waits. Do you really think this situation would be acceptable in the United States, where we can get just about anything delivered to our doors within a few days? Is four months waiting for hospital admission an admirable goal in the first place? NHS officials are doing their level best to achieve mediocrity, and are failing in that quest.

How many people are taken off the lists because they have decided to have their surgery privately is anybody's guess. Nic Fleming of The London Daily Telegraph reports that the number of Britons travelling for their surger-ies has been increasing. He reports on a poll of general practitioners, 74% of which find an increasing number of their patients fleeing England for sur-gery.[9] Another way the four month target is often met is by contracting out for medical services outside of the government system. The administrators of the NHS are coming to realize that the government system cannot provide for people, and they need to rely increasingly on the private sector.

These British numbers sound pretty bad, but what is the human cost? Just how does a sluggish socialist system affect an individual? A patient of mine answered this question. I had diagnosed a hernia and recommended he be evaluated by a general surgeon. I got a call from him the next day, after he had his surgery. Yes, he got in immediately, happened to be fasting at the time, and even though his hernia was not incarcerated and was not an urgent condition, the surgeon had an opening and operated that day. I told him about my research toward this book, regarding the waits for surgery in Britain, and his response was very striking. He used to live in England. Concerning surgery there, he said, "Unless it's extremely critical, you may as well go to the Home Depot and get the do-it-yourself kit, because it's just not going to happen." This may not be an exaggeration. The New York Times reports people pulling their own teeth in Britain because they cannot get into a dentist.[10]

What a wonderful, benevolent system has been created by those loving, utopian socialists. Do we really want that here? As much as I enjoy the Home Depot for my lumber and tool needs, I would really rather avoid them for surgery. By the way, the reason the Home Depot can do such a great job of supplying lumber, tools, etc., with great prices, and no shortages or waiting lines, is because it is a free market business. If they do not have what I want, when I want it, for a good price, I can go to their competitor just down the street. They do not struggle under as much bureaucratic government control as doctors do.

How about Canada? The situation is about the same there. Like the British, they have a horrible system of waiting, waiting, and more waiting. For this system, they pay through the nose in taxes. Like the British, they also have an escape to free markets, but they have had to leave their country to find it. They often head south.

MD Anderson, an American cancer center, has opened an office in Toronto to help meet the demand from Canadians for more prompt cancer treatment. "When Dawn Reimer of West Vancouver was diagnosed with breast cancer, she was told it would take two weeks to get a consultation with a surgeon. Surgery would take place some time after that. Instead, she headed to Houston-based MD Anderson because 'I wanted the best care possible. I wanted to be part of the decision-making. The doctors there, they have more time, they'll spend however long with you that you want to talk.' Within a week of contacting MD Anderson in May, the 48-year-old mother of three had a treatment plan and breast-conserving surgery, and she was home, recuperating. When she returned, they called to follow up on her care."[11]

MD Anderson is by no means the only American health care institution that has been experiencing an influx of frustrated Canadians. The Cleveland Clinic has an office in Mississauga, Ontario, to facilitate care of Canadians that come to their state-of-the-art facilities in Ohio. Also, "the Mayo Clinic, based in Rochester, Minn., has seen its Canadian clientele grow over the past few years, with an estimated 1,500 to 2,000 of them travelling to its three clinics for care each year, said Misty Hathaway, the clinic's international relations administrator."[12] Over 45,000 Canadians are estimated to have left Canada to find health care in 2011.[13]

Why do tens of thousands of Canadians flee their country, as medical refugees, every year? It is because they otherwise would have to wait for ages, to get mediocre care. People die on waiting lists in Canada and England. "Health expenditures in nationalized systems are kept lower chiefly by price controls and the frank rationing of services. In Canada waiting lines for many medical procedures are legendary. [In 2004], lawyers in Quebec filed a class action suit on behalf of 10,000 breast cancer patients who contend they had to wait too long for radiotherapy."[14]

Dr. Brian Day was medical director of the Cambie Surgery Centre, a "rogue" private facility that is "technically prohibited" in Canada. "Public hospitals are sending him growing numbers of patients they are too busy to treat," yet "no one is about to arrest [him], or any of the 120 doctors who work there."[15] He since became President of the Canadian Medical Association.[16]

Marsh Canada Limited, an insurer, has started to offer private health policies to Canadians. This is not typical insurance, however - it pays for care in *United States* medical facilities.[17]

For all the problems that the Canadian system has caused, they are being soaked. "Canadians pay an average of 48% of their income in taxes, and in Ontario, 40% of every tax dollar goes to medicare."[18] Their health care may be free, but it sure does cost a lot of money.

Of course, we do hear the statistics of how much less of a percentage of GDP is spent on health care in Canada than in America. We could also reduce our spending with a government system. We could outlaw private doctors. Send everybody to jail who commits health care outside of the government system. Then we decrease services. Government can decide how much to spend on health care resources. If more is demanded, which it will be, then just let people suffer. That is the socialist way. If we wanted to, we could spend only 1% of our GDP on health care. It costs nothing to just let sick people die. The amount spent is determined not by demand, but by the withholding of care by government officials.

Just as the British and Canadians are coming to realize they need to turn toward capitalism, the Swedes have seen that light years ago. As their health costs began consuming ever higher portions of their resources, in 1985 the Swedish national government introduced capitation. They gave each county only so much money per person in order to meet their health care needs. That led to a worsening of waiting lists, and a very upset population. The waiting time for an angiogram of the heart was up to eleven months, then up to eight months further to wait for coronary bypass surgery.

The Swedish answer was found in competition. Instead of government-run facilities, in the 1990s they shifted to private ownership with government reimbursement. These private health care facilities then competed with one another within the counties and even between counties. This brought costs down and shortened the waiting lists, as private owners were able to innovate and improve efficiency. These private owners were often the doctors themselves.[19]

The Swedish government set a goal in 2012 to have no more than 20% of patients waiting for over three months for surgery. The counties that achieved that were rewarded extra money from the national government. Only 16 of 21 Swedish counties were able to accomplish that very low standard. These waiting times are considered to have been "cut substantially."[20] Partial market-based reforms have resulted in partial improvement in waits, but leave a lot to be desired.

The waiting times are long enough that roughly a half million Swedes, or 5% of their population, now have private health insurance. It is usually offered by their employers. As one Swedish insuree said, "It's quicker to get a colleague back to work if you have an operation in two weeks' time rather than having to wait for a year."[21]

What happens to someone who has cancer if he is unfortunate enough to live in a nation that has socialized medicine? A rough idea of likelihood of survival is obtained by dividing the number of people diagnosed with it in a given year by the number of deaths due to that disease in that year. This is not perfect, because these are not the same people. Someone can succumb to cancer in a later year. This method, however, does provide a good basis for comparison between countries, for health care.

Using the above method to obtain the likelihood of dying from breast cancer if she develops it, a woman will find she is indeed blessed to live in the United States. In the United Kingdom, 37% of women who are diagnosed with breast cancer will die from it, in New Zealand 36%, Japan 33%, France 31%, Australia 27%, Canada 26%, and Germany 24%. America outshines them all, at 17%.[22]

For colon cancer, the corresponding data are: United Kingdom 74%, New Zealand 62%, France 58%, Germany 57%, Australia 53%, and Canada 36%. The United States beats all these socialized medical systems once again at 33%.[23]

Proponents of a government takeover of health care often point to infant mortality data as their proof that our health care is inferior to the Marxist way. Data on lifespan, infant mortality, and such things do not provide very meaningful comparisons of health care however, because they are so dependent on factors other than health care. For example, infant mortality is higher in the United States than in most developed nations, but a further analysis shows our outcomes are actually superior, from the health care standpoint. How can this be?

The Congressional Budget Office (CBO) analyzed infant mortality data by birth weight, comparing results in the United States to Japan and Norway. A mortality of 7 per 1,000 means that 7 babies die in their first year of life for every thousand born. The study found that for each weight category of low birth weight babies, American babies were more likely to survive than Japanese or Norwegian babies. This was in spite of the fact that Japan and Norway were ranked much better in overall infant mortality. Japan was number 4 and Norway was number 5, while the United States was number 20.

Birthweight-specific Perinatal Mortality Rates per 1,000 Single-Delivery Births[24]

| Birthweight (grams) | Japan | Norway | U.S. (Black) | U.S. (White) |
|---|---|---|---|---|
| All weights | 10.8 | 10.5 | 19.8 | 11.1 |
| <500 | 990.3 | 1,000.0 | 886.7 | 916.7 |
| 500-999 | 735.2 | 680.3 | 525.6 | 601.0 |
| 1000-1499 | 485.4 | 352.9 | 160.4 | 237.9 |
| 1500-1999 | 215.6 | 158.9 | 60.6 | 106.6 |
| 2000-2499 | 40.2 | 54.9 | 20.7 | 30.4 |
| 2500-2999 | 6.3 | 13.9 | 5.3 | 7.7 |
| 3000-3499 | 3.0 | 4.1 | 3.1 | 2.9 |
| 3500-3999 | 2.8 | 2.0 | 3.2 | 2.2 |
| 4000-4499 | 6.5* | 2.9 | 5.1 | 2.3 |
| >=4500 | --- | 3.1 | 14.4 | 5.8 |

* Perinatal mortality rate for all births 4,000 or more grams
- Japan did not separate this group further

Several things are worth noting from these data. Low birth weight babies are much more likely to die than heavier ones. Low birth weight babies born in the United States are more likely to survive to one year of age than those born in Norway or Japan. These perinatal figures do not differentiate cause of death. Any death up to one year of age is included. Anything in the home environment, such as drug abuse or violence that could lead to death would be reflected in these numbers.

If infant mortality in most weight classes is better in America, then why is the overall mortality worse? The most obvious pattern from these data, which every doctor knows, is that low birth weight babies are much less likely to survive than normal weight babies.

America simply has vastly more low birth weight babies than other developed nations. Is this an indicator of poor health care? No, of course not. It is an indicator of cultural problems. Our culture has produced the conditions that cause thousands upon thousands of low birth weight babies. We also are much more aggressive in trying to save babies with marginal chances of survival. In many cases, what would be classified in the United States as a live birth would in other countries be called a fetal death, and not be included in these statistics.

Of live births in the United States, 1.15% are less than or equal to 1500 grams, compared to 0.39% in Japan and 0.59% in Norway.[25] This is the primary reason for the higher infant mortality in the United States. The question, then, is why do we have so many low birth weight babies?

The maternal risk factors for low birth weight include non-married status, race, extremes of age, drug use, "low socioeconomic status," lack of prenatal care, and some less frequent factors. These risk factors are in abundance in the United States. These are cultural issues, not measures of the quality of health care. If we want to address infant mortality, then we need to lower the out of wedlock pregnancy rate and the drug abuse rate, and convince women to go to a doctor when they are pregnant.

The Rhode Island Health Department tested women for recreational drugs while they were in labor in 1989. They tested for opiates, cocaine, marijuana, and amphetamines. Overall, 7.5% tested positive for at least one of these categories of drugs.[26]

Interestingly, while black race is a major risk factor for low birth weight, black women who immigrate to America fare better than do black women born in America. The infant mortality rate for the babies of black immigrant women is 19% lower than the rate for the babies of native-born black women. The causes would certainly seem to include culture and behavior.[27]

Like perinatal mortality, advocates of socialized medicine point to longevity data to support their cause. The United States was ranked 21st out of 30 OECD nations in lifespan.[28] This means, of course, that our health care is inferior, right? Again, our superior health care is not able to overcome the damage we do to ourselves through lifestyle.

Lifespan is heavily influenced by factors other than health care, such as obesity. The fatter people are, the more likely they are to develop diabetes, cancer, high blood pressure, high cholesterol, heart attacks, sleep apnea, kidney failure, severe arthritis requiring knee or hip replacements, and a whole host of other physical problems which lead to costly treatment and/or premature death. Our incredible affluence, unrivaled anywhere else in the modern world, has led to our becoming a very fat people. Even the so-called poor here are very likely to be fat, in contrast to the pictures of starving people that we see in the undeveloped nations.[29]

Here in the United States, our percentage of people with a body mass index over 30 is 26%, with Australia a distant second at 21%, England 19%, New Zealand 17%, Canada 15%, Germany 12%, France 10%, and Japan the slimmest at 3%.[30] It should be no surprise then that our longevity does not excel these other nations, in spite of having better medical care.

Aside from obesity, violence is another reason for people to die younger. Robert Ohsfeldt and John Schneider analyzed longevity in the OECD nations after accounting for violent death. It turned out that the Americans actually had the longest life spans after taking violent death out of the equation, even with our obesity.[31]

Doctors are simply not able to completely compensate for the behavior of the people. This is the reason infant mortality and lifespan are not better in America than in more socialist nations, in spite of better medical care. For given conditions, however, such as breast or colon cancer, or low birth weight, American medicine does a much better job.

Japan is sometimes upheld as a model of socialized medicine at its finest. After all, their life expectancy is estimated to be higher than ours, and their health care spending is lower. Yet again, looking at specific diseases gives a different picture. Japanese with cancer die off much more than American cancer patients do. Japan only started certifying cancer specialists, or oncologists, in 2006. A generalist will often carry out cancer treatment, without the assistance of a specialist. As a family practice physician, I would not want to do that. Certain cancer drugs have been delayed for years in getting approval by the Japanese government, beyond the time they came into use in the United States.[32] Again, the odds of dying from breast cancer for women who have been diagnosed with it are 17% for Americans, and 33% for Japanese.[33] For the reason for the difference in overall longevity, once again, look at the obesity numbers. Twenty-six percent of Americans are obese, as compared to 3% of Japanese.[34] Our drug use is also high. We cannot expect our superior medical care to overcome our personal behaviors, but it is coming close.

Probably the most damning indictment of socialized medicine is the decision that was delivered by Canada's own Supreme Court. In the case of Chaoulli v. Quebec, a physician without formal legal training argued in behalf of the huddled masses of Canada, and particularly the patient George Zeliotis. Dr. Chaoulli maintained that the waits imposed by government, by the prohibition on obtaining private hospital care and private insurance, violated the right of Canadians to life, liberty, and security as guaranteed by section 7 of the Canadian Charter. The Supreme Court agreed.

"We conclude, based on the evidence, that prohibiting health insurance that would permit ordinary Canadians to access health care, in circumstances where the government is failing to deliver health care in a reasonable manner, thereby increasing the risk of complications and death, interferes with life and security of the person as protected by s. 7 of the Charter."[35]

The minority opinion in this case agreed that the Medicare program of Canada sometimes interferes with life and security of the person, but they were satisfied with that as long as the intention was equal interference for everybody. "We accept the trial judge's conclusion that in some circumstances some Quebecker's may have their life or 'security of the person' put at risk by the prohibition against private health insurance."[36] "The enactment of s. 15 HEIA and s. 11 HOIA was motivated by considerations of equality and human dignity, and it is therefore clear that there is no conflict with the general values expressed in the Canadian Charter or in the Quebec Charter of human rights and freedoms."[37] So Canadian lives are sometimes put at risk, but that is fine as long as the intention was for equality. Ideally, the lives of everybody should be equally endangered. Intentions, of course, are more important than results in this style of thinking.

In essence, they affirmed what Winston Churchill said, that "The inherent vice of capitalism is the unequal sharing of blessings; the inherent virtue of socialism is the equal sharing of miseries." As long as people suffer equally, the more Marxist judges of the Canadian Supreme Court are happy.

The various nations are all looking to reform their socialized systems, by looking to other socialized systems as models. All these systems are very similar, however. The same situation exists everywhere socialized medicine is tried. Shortages, misery, death, and very high taxes always occur. This should be no surprise, as socialism always leads to the same result: "the equal sharing of miseries."

# What Turned Dr. Brook from a
# Socialist into a Pro-freedom Radical?

---

*"All people occasionally stumble upon the truth, but then they pick
themselves up, dust themselves off, and carry on as if nothing had happened."*

- WINSTON CHURCHILL

SOME PEOPLE MAY BE TEMPTED to dismiss my writing as the ravings of a hope-
lessly brainwashed right-wing radical. Before you jump to such a conclusion,
however, understand that I did not grow up with the sort of beliefs that you
are reading in this book. I came to them when I was partially through medical school, at about age 35. When I was young, I supported most of the leftist
causes. I even voted for Bill Clinton twice (but I repented). I supported the
Clinton plan for nationalized health care.

So what turned the leftist into the constitutionalist that I am today? A
harsh dose of reality caused the change. In medical school, I began to see the
results of our socialism. I saw what it did to people. I saw the dependence and
apathy that the welfare recipients developed. I heard the entitled attitude of
the people who claimed that other people owed them, while they did nothing
for themselves.

An example from my residency is the man who came from Pennsylvania to
North Carolina, and went to the emergency department when he became quite

ill. It turned out that his blood sugar was around 600 (normal is somewhere near 100, depending on when the last meal was). He had type 2 diabetes, and had not been taking his medicine. He had a Medicaid card from Pennsylvania, which was not honored in North Carolina. The medication cost somewhere in the neighborhood of $20 per month, and he said he could not get it because his Medicaid card was no good. When doing a social history as part of the history and physical, I calculated that he was spending about $150 per month on beer and cigarettes. I pointed out to him that he could get his medicine if he only spent a small part of his beer and cigarette money on it, at which point he berated me for my insensitivity. "What, is there a problem getting service here?" he asked. He demanded the best service that somebody else's money could buy, and if he did not get it, then I was going to be in trouble. While he demanded, and received, medical care paid for by somebody else, he did not realize that he could have died as a result of his negligence toward his own health.

There was also the woman who was admitted to the hospital for the fifth time in two or three years with chest pain due to high blood pressure exacerbated by cocaine use. She was single and had five children. When I asked what she did to support herself and children, she said "I get a check from the government." She would not even go to the pharmacy within a block of her house to get medication for her blood pressure, even though it was free for her with her Medicaid. She had developed a severe case of heart failure, and is probably not alive now.

There was the woman, who brought in her child to the family practice clinic for some trivial issue, and was reading ads for video camcorders during the visit. They cost about $800 at the time. She told me she was going to buy one of them for her eight year old son. It was not his birthday, or Christmas, or anything special. While she was so free and easy with her money, taxpayers were forced to pay for the visit through Medicaid.

These were just a few examples from my training. These are what most people think of as "welfare cases." Seeing them got me thinking about the less obvious forms of welfare also. I came to question the place of government in providing for people. Whereas I only listened to the sound bites and looked at the surface of issues before, I began to read more about matters of social and political importance. I researched the issues. What I discovered was quite different from what the mainstream media presented on the surface.

I also came to understand about our need to make choices, and be accountable for our choices, when I became Christian during medical school. I had no firm beliefs of any sort when I was younger, but it became obvious to me during my science studies that there had to have been creation. This led me to investigate the gospel of Jesus Christ, which I then accepted. Part of that gospel is moral agency, or freedom to choose, and personal accountability for the choices we make. Socialism is an attempt to force people to do right, thereby denying them their moral agency. People are not given the opportunity to choose whether or not they will give to a cause; rather, their money is taken from them to support it. People have their consequences removed from them. Buy your cigarettes and beer instead of your diabetes medicine, and demand that somebody else rescue you.

I went into medical school wanting to work for a state subsidized indigent clinic. Now I am as far removed as a doctor can be from that sort of clinic. I run a free market based medical practice. I receive no money that has been confiscated from other people to pay for my patients. In my practice, patients willingly pay for their own care. I believe that is the most moral way to practice medicine.

During residency I wanted to be a solo, privately practicing doctor. I was told by quite a few people that a doctor could not make it that way these days. The payroll and all the other overhead were just too much, I was told. Then I started hearing about doctors who were taking a low overhead approach. I read some of the information from the Association of American Physicians and Surgeons, an organization that defends free market principles in medicine, and joined them. I learned about doctors who had "opted out" of Medicare, and were not contracted with any insurance networks. People paid them directly, and their fees were much less than for typical doctors. An article by Gordon Moore, M.D., influenced me. He wrote in Family Practice Management of his low overhead practice.[1]

I decided to take that approach, and now I practice according to free market principles, in Idaho Falls, Idaho. I see patients in the office, in their homes, in their workplaces, and I have even gone out on a call to a ball field to see a patient for an injury. I charge by the time that I spend plus any significant supplies at my cost. I am able to spend the time that is needed without being hurt financially. My overhead is a small fraction of that of the typical family practice doctor, and so my fees are much less.

My average charge for 2014 was $58, including house calls, lab fees, and medications dispensed. Rather than collecting only 58% of my charges, like the typical family practice doctor does, I have collected 100%. I frequently receive tips. I simply do not need to charge a lot, because my overhead is low, and I actually collect what I charge.

I have seen some patients who have not seen a doctor in years, because they cannot get to one due to immobility. A family member hears that I do house calls, and they call me in. I generally see patients when they need to be seen, in the office in the evening or on Saturday. I see people promptly, usually offering a same day service. I have stitched up a scalp laceration for a child at midnight on the parent's kitchen table, with a sterile field that I set up. I can do anything in the home that I can do in my office - EKGs, nebulizer treatments for asthma, laceration repairs, etc. I have my equipment arranged into different portable toolkits, as well as the equipment in my office. Most of my visits are in my office.

When people hear about what I do, they wonder how I can do it. How can a fully trained physician offer this kind of service, for such low fees? The answer is in taking a free market approach. Most of the overhead that a doctor has, and most of the low collection rates, are due to Medicare, Medicaid, and insurance company hassles.

Regarding house calls, good luck trying to get paid by Medicare or insurance companies for a house call. You might as well address the claim form to Santa Claus, North Pole. When people pay a doctor directly for service that they appreciate, they do not have to clear it with any bureaucrat. They happily pay it, and sometimes even give a tip.

I have been happy with what I do, and my patients have been happy with me. Most of my business comes through word of mouth. Most are uninsured. These are the people the major media claim have "no access to health care." Some have conventional insurance, with preferred provider networks, but they prefer my service. They generally tell me it does not cost them any more to see me. Many tell me if it did cost more, they would see me anyway, because of the better service. People like having a doctor who will spend the time they need, respond quickly to them, call them, and generally be more available. I have patients coming from many towns away, bypassing a dozen doctors to reach me. They see me, thank me, and tell their friends.

I believe that if all doctors practiced this way, there would be no major problems with health care in America. It is time we saved American medicine and once again showed the world what freedom can do for a nation. We can keep America in its rightful place at the pinnacle of medical achievement, but only if we do not allow ourselves to be ruined by socialism. We have started down that road, but it is not too late to turn back. Why ignore the lessons of history? We have seen that freedom leads to prosperity, and socialism/communism leads to deprivation. Let us choose freedom, and continue to lead the world by our example, as a shining beacon on a hill.

# Damage Report – The Real Problems Identified

———

# Costs Are Skyrocketing

———

I HAVE EXPLORED THE SITUATION in health care in America before our government started interfering in the free market, and it seemed to be in pretty good condition. As we have seen, our economy in general has been the most powerful on earth. Our health care situation was second to none, in keeping with the rest of the economy. American health care was at the forefront of innovation, costs were reasonable, and service was excellent.

I next discussed the differences in principle between freedom and socialism. An examination was then undertaken of the socialized health systems of some other nations. Next I will discuss American health care today. Specific problems that we have will be examined in detail. Then causes for those problems will be uncovered, and solutions will be proposed.

First, there is the issue of cost. Most people would agree that costs are getting out of hand. We now spend much more of our resources on health care than in decades past. We do get more for our money, but not all that much more. The amount we spend on the same procedures now has gone up enormously from what they cost before the increased government control.

For example, I mentioned in a previous chapter that an appendectomy (taking the appendix out) cost $1,105 in 1960, after adjusting for inflation.

What does an appendectomy cost today? Good luck trying to get prices from hospitals or surgeons. They generally will not tell what their charges will be. In order to find out, people sometimes post on message boards on the Internet. One such board is ehealthforum.com. "Appendectomy Costs" is the name of a thread that was posted on February 11, 2004. The range was from $2,500 to $30,000. There were six replies, and the average cost was reported as $18,314.[1] This is roughly in line with what patients have told me. Not much has changed with the procedure. It is often done laparoscopically now (via thin tools introduced through very small cuts). That raises the cost of the surgery, but lowers recovery time and therefore hospital cost. There is not much net effect on cost. CT scans and/or ultrasound exams are often used now in diagnosis, but not always. Those tests are not responsible for an average increase of over $17,000.

What about the birth of a child? In a previous chapter, I quoted two cases in the neighborhood of $475, adjusted for inflation, for delivery fees in 1950. Now, the routine birth of a child costs somewhere in the neighborhood of twelve thousand dollars. Appendectomy and delivery of a baby have not changed dramatically in process, but they certainly have in cost. After adjusting for inflation, these procedures now cost about ten to twenty times what they did before the era of government intervention.

As I have laid out the case previously, there was no cost crisis in American health care prior to government controls. In spite of the lack of a problem, the government charged in to fix the non-problem with a set of solutions which, of themselves, created our current day problems.

Notice that I did not mention the costs of insurance premiums. Most of the writing on health care costs makes the mistake of equating the cost of health insurance with the cost of health care. They are nowhere near the same thing, although they are related. Canadians all have health insurance through the government, but it means nothing when they cannot get the health care they need.

To all this, there is a bright side. There is a way to fix the problem with high costs in health care. It does not require a complex formula, or complicated plans to be implemented at federal or state levels. The solutions will be discussed in later chapters, after discussing more of the problems and exploring their causes.

# What Happened to the House Call?

———

*"Ninety-eight percent of the adults in this country are decent,
hardworking, honest Americans. It's the other lousy two percent
that get all the publicity. But then, we elected them."*

*- LILY TOMLIN*

ANOTHER CASUALTY IN AMERICAN MEDICINE in recent decades is service. Whereas people used to expect good service, they now have come to expect much less. Insufficient time is spent with patients. "Providers" with much less training than physicians are being used to see patients. House calls are almost unheard of now. It can take weeks to get an appointment. As pointed out previously, the level of service was high, and patient satisfaction was high, earlier in our history.

One of the remarkable things about our economy as a whole is the catering, pandering service to which people have become accustomed. People generally hate to wait, and they usually will not. People demand what they want, when they want it, delivered to them where they want it. Service-oriented businesses have popped up throughout all sectors of the economy, which bend over backwards to deliver whatever the customer wants, just how the customer wants it. Like the sign in Jimmy John's says, "The Customer is Usually Right."[1]

This service economy contrasts sharply with health care. People have now come to expect long waits for their appointments, commonly for weeks and sometimes even months. People expect their appointments to involve lengthy waits in the office. The majority of time is spent in waiting rooms, and with staff that do not have much training or expertise. Time is spent filling out seemingly useless forms. Then, after all this time, there is a brief encounter with a "provider," who is sometimes a doctor. With increasing frequency that provider is now a "mid-level practitioner" - a nurse practitioner or physician assistant.

If you are too sick, in too much pain, or have too little mobility to get to the doctor, then you simply go without, unless you call an ambulance to take you to the emergency department. This opens up a whole new ordeal of expense and bureaucracy. In any case, it is wholly inappropriate in many cases to call for an ambulance. Somebody who has simply thrown his back out, and is in acute spasm, has an awful time getting into a car to get to the doctor. An ambulance would not be awfully comfortable either, and that type of response, with all the associated expense, is simply not needed. I have made house calls more than once for that type of issue, provided treatment, and the patients were quite satisfied with the outcomes. There are many similar cases that are simply not severe emergencies, yet the patient cannot get to a medical office, and cannot withstand the ordeal there.

House calls, however, are a thing of the past for the vast majority of doctors. We get pizza delivered within 30 minutes. We can order almost anything off the internet, and have it delivered the next day. We can get lobster, salmon, or fresh-cut flowers delivered to us without delay. Those are things we could usually go out and buy, when we are healthy. When we are sick, we simply do not want to go out. Yet, that is the time we cannot get, delivered to us, the one service we need most.

There is even a medical group that has a website which proudly proclaims that they will provide the next best thing to a house call, while admitting that true house calls are long past. They provide online basic health information, as if this is anything like the type of service they admit is no longer generally offered. I will not provide a reference to this, because I do not want to point blame specifically at an identifiable organization. It is really characteristic of the level of service we have grown to accept in recent decades in health care.

Waiting times for appointments have become much worse than we would accept in any other field, outside of government. "In surveying 1,062 physician offices in 15 major cities last year, consultants Merritt, Hawkins & Associates found that Boston had the longest waits for appointments for checkups and minor injuries and pain, from 24 to 50 days. A group of Massachusetts insurers that surveyed their members last year found that 60 percent of patients got in to see a doctor the same day when they 'needed care right away for an illness, injury, or condition,' similar to the national average. But for routine care, 72 percent of patients said they got an appointment within 14 days, compared with 84 percent of patients nationally."[2]

So the average for getting in to see a doctor the same day when a patient "needed care right away for an illness, injury, or condition," is only 60%! And this is supposed to be good enough? This number should be close to 100%. If you need care right away, do you really want to wait for another day? Of course not. If you have minor injuries and pain, do you want to wait from 24 to 50 days to see a doctor? For routine care, why should it take 2 weeks for an appointment? We have come to expect so much more from other providers of service. Imagine having a pipe spring a leak, and the plumber telling you it will be between 24 and 50 days to repair it. We would not accept a next day response. Plumbers want our business, and they act like they want it. They come to us, on the same day we call. That is the way it should be, and was in the past, in medicine also.

"Tufts-New England Medical Center also is tackling long waits for non-urgent care, which averaged three months in some specialties last year. 'My boss said, 'People are constantly complaining, saying their phone calls aren't answered and they can't get in,' Denise Schepici, vice president of clinical services, said.

"At Beth Israel Deaconess, a sophisticated computer system tracks wait times for all doctors. And in August, several nurses began 'mystery shopping surveys.' They call doctors' offices posing as patients with specific medical problems and write a summary of how they're treated. In the first survey, the nurses made 54 calls; in 13 of them, they did not get an appointment, mostly because receptionists promised to call back and never did. In addition, the survey found that some receptionists were rude or unhelpful."[3]

Again, we might accept this from school officials, driver's licensing agencies, or other government bureaucrats, but not from anyone else in the private sector except health care providers. But then again, as we shall see in later chapters, health care is not really in the private sector.

"Patient access to specialists has become increasingly problematic. This is most directly observed in hospital emergency departments, where patients are routinely diverted due to a lack of medical specialists willing or available to treat emergency patients. Through our continuous professional contact with thousands of physicians, Merritt, Hawkins & Associates has observed that the length of time patients must wait for a physician appointment also appears to be lengthening."[4]

For example, they found that, for "injury or pain in the knee," the average wait time nationwide for an orthopedic surgeon was 16.9 days. In Los Angeles, the average wait time was 43 days. The longest time, again in Los Angeles, was 112 days.[5] I expect most of us would not want to wait 17 days to see a knee specialist for an injury with pain. Imagine waiting 112 days! A knee pain can sometimes lead to serious problems if not addressed in a timely manner. Septic arthritis will lead to joint destruction within hours if not treated.

It is really not necessary to lay out examples of poor service in health care. Anybody who has been to a doctor much in recent decades can attest to this. As we have already seen, the situation is much worse in the more heavily socialist nations.

This type of service is unacceptable in any other area of our economy with the exception of government "services." We have simply grown accustomed to the hassles. In following chapters, we will see why this is so. As it turns out, medicine is not all that different from a government function, as it is heavily regulated and controlled by government. It should not surprise us, then, when the level of service is similar.

Again, on the bright side, it is very possible for us to restore that Marcus Welby type of service once again to American health care. Prompt delivery of health care can be as easy as calling the pizza guy. Same day service, flexible hours, and adequate attention to detail can be ours once again. All it takes is an understanding of the causes, and the willingness to change.

# Health Care Is Driving Our
# Economy Toward Collapse

———

*"The problem with socialism is that you eventually
run out of other people's money."*

- MARGARET THATCHER

ASIDE FROM THE EFFECTS OUR health care socialism has on individuals, it is also extraordinarily damaging to our economy as a whole. Health care now absorbs about 18% of the gross domestic product.[1] It has added trillions of dollars to the national debt.

According to the former Comptroller General of the United States, David M. Walker, our unfunded future liabilities amount to $70 trillion. Approximately $37 trillion of that liability is attributable to Medicare. This is the amount of money that needs to be in the bank now, earning interest, to cover shortfalls of revenue against future payments that have already been promised. This equals roughly $308,000 debt per household just for Medicare. This enormous amount of debt is increasing by leaps and bounds every year, with no slowing in sight. It can only be expected to accelerate. For comparison, the total unfunded liability in 2000 was $20 trillion. It has grown by over three times from 2000 to 2012.[2]

It is hard to comprehend how this kind of debt can ever be paid off, or how we can even keep up with interest payments. The consequences of such debt can be staggering. "The federal government issues U.S. Treasury bonds to finance its deficit spending. The largest holders of these Treasury notes-- our largest creditors-- are foreign governments and foreign individuals. Asian central banks and investors in particular, especially China, have been happy to buy U.S. dollars over the past decade. But foreign governments will not prop up our spending habits forever. Already, Asian central banks are favoring Euro-denominated assets over U.S. dollars, reflecting their belief that the American economy is headed for trouble. It's akin to a credit-card company cutting off a borrower who has exceeded his credit limit one too many times."[3]

If creditors decide to stop lending, our economy could be devastated. It is especially worrisome that much of the debt is held by nations, such as the People's Republic of China and Saudi Arabia, that could turn hostile to us at any time. A selloff of these bonds by our creditors would cause the value of the dollar to collapse. If creditors stopped buying our debt, then government would have to create massive amounts of dollars out of thin air to pay for ongoing deficit spending. That would cause further devaluation of the dollar. A situation like the Zimbabwean hyperinflation would ensue, with a complete collapse of our economy.

In a USA Today story on this problem, Dennis Cauchon and John Waggoner calculated that in order to keep up with our unfunded liabilities, one of three changes would have to be made. The first option is, "all federal taxes would have to double immediately and permanently." The second option is, "benefits for Social Security, Medicare and government pensions would have to be slashed in half immediately and permanently," and the Medicare Part D prescription drug benefit would have to be cancelled. The third option is a compromise between the first two - "such as a 50% increase in taxes and a 25% reduction in benefits." "Savings also could come in the form of price controls on prescription drugs, raising retirement ages and limiting benefits to the affluent."[4]

These types of drastic predictions also come from the highest financial officers of government. Former Federal Reserve Chairman Alan Greenspan has made similar statements. "'Tax increases of sufficient dimension to deal with our looming fiscal problems arguably pose significant risks to economic growth and the revenue base,' he said, adding that the government should seek to 'close the fiscal gap primarily, if not wholly, from the outlay side.' Mr. Greenspan also seemed to suggest a later retirement age. 'I fear that we may have already committed more physical resources to the baby boom generation in its retirement years than our economy has the capacity to deliver,' he said."[5]

In less obscure terms, David M. Walker said, "Current fiscal policy is unsustainable. The 'status quo' is not an option. We face large and growing structural deficits largely due to known demographic trends and rising health care costs. GAO's simulations show that balancing the budget in 2040 could require actions as large as: cutting total federal spending by 60 percent, or raising federal taxes to 2 times today's levels. Faster economic growth can help, but it cannot solve the problem. Closing the long-term fiscal gap based on reasonable assumptions would require real average annual economic growth in the double-digit range every year for the next 75 years. During the 1990s, the economy grew at an average 3.2 percent per year. As a result, we cannot simply grow our way out of this problem. Tough choices will be required."[6]

Another option, besides cutting benefits, is that we continue what we have been doing, which is to keep raising benefits and just wait for economic collapse. After all, why should the incumbent politicians try to fix a problem that will not become painfully obvious during their current terms? Their electoral chances, after all, are much more important to most of them than the economic devastation that will occur in the future, after they are out of office and would have probably already died. Most of them are fairly old, and will not still be here for the worst of it. It will be our problem, because we were gullible enough to elect them. It will also be a problem for our children.

A demographic time bomb has been described for years now, predicting a collapse of Medicare and Social Security. A collapse of Medicare would probably cause a depression worse than this country has ever seen, including

1929. With so much of the GDP tied up in healthcare, and the healthcare industry very dependent on Medicare, the consequences of Medicare going bust would be devastating. Taxes and deficit spending would continue to increase, in a futile effort to hold up the failing Medicare system and delay the inevitable huge decreases in benefits. Deficit spending of course leads to a diluting of the value of our dollars, so that each dollar is worth less. It is basically a hidden tax. When the tax increases are no longer able to keep pace with benefits, there will be failures of payments to health care providers for Medicare patients. Next will come failures of hospitals and clinics, and massive layoffs. The labor market will be flooded with people looking for jobs. With the voting power of seniors, can we really expect other welfare programs to remain undisturbed when Medicare and Social Security payouts fall? More likely, the "safety nets" for younger people will start crumbling also, just at the time when the layoffs and failures are happening in the healthcare industry. It is very sobering to consider what some younger welfare recipients might do when they start losing their benefits. Times may not be very tranquil when that happens. We will likely see looting and violence that will make the race riots of the sixties look peaceful.[7]

Another impact of Medicare and employer based health insurance on the economy is that of lower wages. With so much tax being taken to support Medicare, and with such high premiums being paid for health insurance, employers cannot pay as much in wages. There is only so much an employer can put out in compensation to have an employee. When taxes increase, the remaining portion must be less. This lowers the purchasing power of an employee, leading to a loss of activity in non-health care areas of the economy. This leads further to lowered employment in these areas. Lower net wages also lead to lower savings, fostering dependence on Social Security and Medicare in later years.

An ever-increasing share of our gross domestic product (GDP) is being spent on health care. It is now up to 18%. This is similar to one item taking a larger share of the budget of a family. As the share increases, it begins to crowd out other items. Only 82% of our productivity can now be spent on non-health care items. The government portion of health care alone is expected to reach one third of GDP by 2050, if we continue along our present trends.[8]

The largest element in state budgets now is Medicaid, even larger than elementary and secondary education combined.[9] Total Medicaid spending grew 10.8% during 2011 and 2012.[10]

Consider what happens to health when an economy is poor. In Zimbabwe, a country with many natural resources, the dictator-in-chief started printing money like crazy. Naturally, each dollar became worth proportionally less. In December 2008, a loaf of bread cost 500 million Zimbabwean dollars. They introduced a 10 billion dollar note, worth about 20 U.S. dollars.[11]

The Zimbabwean economy got so bad that basic necessities were no longer available. Cholera had become epidemic in Zimbabwe in 2008.[12] This is an infectious disease, spread by unclean water. Cholera was defeated in the developed world way back in 1853 by John Snow. He became known as the father of modern epidemiology for tracking cholera cases in London, finding that they were centered around the Broad Street water pump, and removing the handle from the pump. This stopped the cholera epidemic in London.[13] In 2008, cholera had come back in Zimbabwe due to unclean water resulting from the poverty that Robert Mugabe's regime had caused. If you want good health in a nation, you must have a sound economy.

The good news in the midst of all this alarm is that our country need not fall into economic ruin. If we develop the resolve to excise the malignant socialism that is threatening our future, health care can be restored to excellence, and our economy will be spared these life-threatening effects, for us and for generations to come.

# Ever Increasing Taxes

———

*"We could say they spend like drunken sailors, but that would be unfair
to drunken sailors, because the sailors are spending their own money."*

*- RONALD REAGAN*

A DEVASTATING EFFECT OF HEALTH care on Americans is high taxes. People
are paying through the nose, and many of them do not even realize it.
Medicare taxes consume 2.7% of the money that an employer pays in salary
and taxes to have a worker. The total for Medicare and Social Security is
14.2% (15.3 divided by 107.65). Think about how this affects you if you now
make $30,000 per year. If you actually were paid what your employer has to
pay for Medicare and Social Security, you would get a raise to $35,000.

This is just the direct tax. Try sometime to figure out all the different
taxes you pay. You cannot do it. There are so many different forms of taxation, both direct and indirect, that it cannot be done.

For the closest estimate of how much money is taken from the average American family in order to keep Medicare and Medicaid running, we
need to divide the annual expenditure by the number of families in America.
Medicare, in 2012, consumed $484.5 billion of federal money.[1] Medicaid
consumed another $398.4 billion in federal and state funds.[2] This total of
$883 billion, divided by 120 million households,[3] means that the average

household in America is having roughly $7,340 taken from it annually to pay for Medicare and Medicaid.

But that money is not taken from the people, it is taken from the corporations, you may say. Besides, it is all in the distribution (yes, somebody actually said that to me once). Most people are not paying that kind of money! Just think about this for a minute.

Too many people think that corporate taxes have no effect on them, or that they even help to lower their own taxes. Who pays corporate taxes? First of all, a corporation is merely a legal construct that people use in their businesses. The shareholders own the corporation, and therefore the shareholders are the ones who end up getting the tax bill. Shareholders include anybody who has a 401K or mutual fund that holds stock in the corporation. What do the people who run a corporation do to pay their taxes? They have to increase prices, lower wages, or decrease costs in some other way. Anything they do to raise the revenue to pay the tax bill will come from the people, whether customers, employees, or suppliers. It cannot be done any other way. They cannot just print money to pay their taxes.

Looking at it another way, where does Walmart get the money it uses to pay its corporate taxes? The same place it gets its other money, from selling products. If you want to raise taxes on Walmart, then someday take a trip to Walmart, and look around at the people there who are buying things. The corporate taxes will come out of the money those people are forking over at the cash register.

All taxes come from the people, whether directly, or indirectly. Every dollar government spends, whether federal, state, or local, comes from the people. Payroll taxes increase the amount an employer must pay to have a worker, so they also come out of decreased salary, increased prices of their products, or cutting costs in some other way. Customs and tarrifs are paid out of higher prices on those goods. When expenditures exceed taxes (national debt), treasury bonds are sold in order to pay for immediate expenses. Revenue gathered from treasury bonds is paid by future generations, with interest.

Sometimes the federal government prints more money to pay the treasury notes. This just makes each dollar worth less. Deficit spending is thus an important cause of inflation. It is a hidden tax.

Just to keep things in perspective, a rough rule of thumb is that every billion dollars that the Fed spends means about ten dollars being taken from the average family.[4] A hundred billion here, a hundred billion there, and pretty soon you're talking real money. If the average family simply got a bill for $7,340 for Medicare and Medicaid in 2012, we might have had another revolution. And the bill for these programs gets bigger every year.

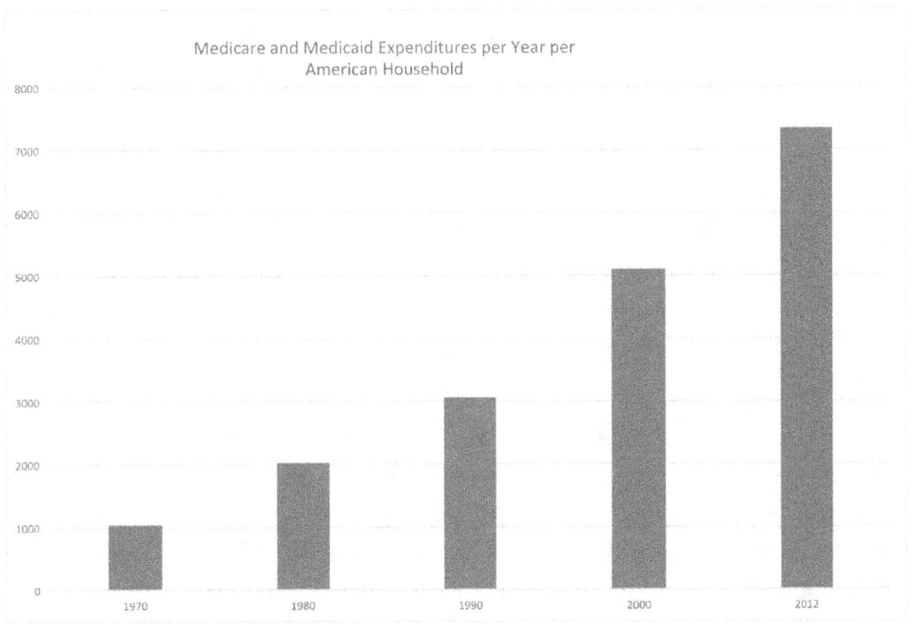

In 2012 dollars (adjusted for inflation). Source: US Government Office of Management and Budget,[5] and National Association of State Budget Officers[6]

So far we have been somewhat okay with the debt because the economy has been growing enough to be able to keep up payments on it. But what if it cannot keep up? The value of the dollar will plummet, and goods will skyrocket in price. This is already well under way. Most of our debt is just made up of welfare payments, or entitlements, that do nothing positive for the economy. They are simply a drag on our growth. Our economy is strong enough to withstand that drag, like fullback Earl Campbell crashing through defenders, and pulling them along, while he gains yardage. Eventually, even the strongest will be taken down, if enough weight is put on his back. Our economy cannot withstand infinitely increasing weights placed on it by the government.

Although employer based health insurance is tax deductible, the tax is simply shifted to other items, because the tax still needs to be collected. If an individual pays for health insurance, as opposed to being subsidized, that is also tax deductible now, although it was not prior to Obamacare. Those without health insurance have the higher taxes on the non-health items, and do not have the deductions for their health insurance. In 2007, it was estimated to be an annual tax subsidy of $246 billion for employer based health insurance, which needs to be made up with taxes on non-health items.[7] This works out to be $2,100 per household in increased taxes on non-health items.

Think about this for a minute. If you are the breadwinner of an average American family, and you do not have health insurance through your employer, you still have to pay about $2,100 per year in increased taxes to make up for people who do have employer-provided insurance. You pay for Medicare and Medicaid, bringing the total to $9,400. On top of all that, you pay higher fees at the doctor's office to support all the bureaucracy of third party payment.

If you have health insurance paid by you or your employer, you enjoy the financial gain of having that tax-free benefit. However, you still have to pay the offsetting $2,100 tax on non-health items.

The tax rates to support Social Security and Medicare have been increasing, almost since their inception.

Historical Progression of Tax Rates for Medicare and Social Security[8]

| Year | Social Security Tax | Maximum Taxable Income | Medicare Tax | Maximum Taxable Income |
|------|------|------|------|------|
| 1937 | 2% | $3,000 | | |
| 1942 | 2% | 3,000 | | |
| 1947 | 2% | 3,000 | | |
| 1952 | 3% | 3,600 | | |
| 1957 | 4.5% | 4,200 | | |
| 1962 | 6.25% | 4,800 | | |
| 1966 | 7.7% | 6,600 | 0.7% | 6,600 |
| 1971 | 9.2% | 7,800 | 1.2% | 7,800 |
| 1976 | 9.9% | 15,300 | 1.8% | 15,300 |
| 1981 | 10.7% | 29,700 | 2.6% | 29,700 |
| 1986 | 11.4% | 42,000 | 2.9% | 42,000 |
| 1991 | 12.4% | 53,400 | 2.9% | 125,000 |
| 1996 | 12.4% | 62,700 | 2.9% | infinite |
| 2001 | 12.4% | 80,400 | 2.9% | infinite |
| 2006 | 12.4% | 94,200 | 2.9% | infinite |
| 2013 | 12.4% | 113,700 | 2.9% | infinite |

Of course, there is no reason to believe these tax rates will not continue to escalate. How much tax can people bear to pay? Eventually there comes a point where tax rates become so great that the economy begins to crumble, people have a tougher time affording the basics, and overall tax revenue actually declines. Continually increasing the tax rates is an unsustainable policy. Unsustainable means that it *will not* be sustained, no matter how much we want it to be. At that point there is no possible way to keep increasing the expenditures. The money simply will not be there.

# Shortages of Doctors and Medicines

---

*"If you put the federal government in charge of the Sahara desert,*
*in five years there'd be a shortage of sand."*

- *MILTON FRIEDMAN*

THERE IS A SHORTAGE OF doctors, particularly in certain specialties and in certain locations. This is expected to worsen as many doctors reach retirement age, and our population ages. In 1985, 27% of doctors were at least 55 years old. By 2006, that number rose to 34%. [1] These physicians will start retiring soon, just as the baby boomers reach the age of needing more health care.

1,195 doctors responded to a survey in 2010 about what they would do if Obamacare was passed. Almost a third of them said they would "want to leave medical practice."[2] Imagine how long it would take to get in to see a doctor if this happens.

We are constantly hearing about how few doctors there are in certain areas, and how we need more of whatever specialty. We do not seem to suffer from that problem with other goods or services, however. Why should there be a shortage of doctors, if being a doctor is something that people would like to do? We do not seem to be running low on people intelligent enough to do the job. I will get into the reasons in a later chapter. For now, let us take a look at waiting times. Compare the following waiting times to the wait for, say, a computer repairman (maybe one day):

## Waiting Times for Various Specialists

| Specialist | Nationwide average wait (days) | Worst City's average wait (days) |
|---|---|---|
| Orthopedic surgeon | 17 | 43 |
| Dermatologist | 24 | 50 |
| Cardiologist | 19 | 37 |
| Obstetrician/Gynecologist | 23 | 45 |

Source: Merritt, Hawkins, & Associates[3]

During my residency in North Carolina, when I needed to refer a patient to a rheumatologist, the first appointment was typically two to three months away. That was even when I called Raleigh rheumatology groups, 60 miles away from the city I was in. A survey of waiting times for pediatric specialists in North Carolina revealed that it took almost two months to see an endocrinologist, three months for a gastroenterologist, and almost a year for a rheumatologist.[4] If someone has to wait for weeks or even months to get an appointment, then this is a pretty good indication of a shortage.

Medications are increasingly going into shortages. For several years as of this writing, I have not been able to buy doxycycline unless I am willing to pay about $600 for a bottle of 500 pills. That same bottle would have cost me about $22 before the shortage hit. It is a very commonly used antibiotic. Metronidazole is now over $200 for a bottle that previously cost $31. Manufacturers have stopped making these very useful medications. The number of drug shortages has increased by almost 300% from 2005 to 2012.[5] The drugs most often in shortage include cancer drugs and anesthetics. Some cancer patients end up dying because they have to use inferior treatment protocols due to unavailability of the preferred medication.[6]

I do not hear of books being in short supply. Nor do I hear this about pizza, or clothes, or pots and pans, or any other consumer item. I do not see news stories about the difficulty in finding a plumber, an auto mechanic, or a barber. This situation only exists in health care and other government controlled goods and services. If you do an Internet search for "waiting time specialist," it retrieves medical information sites. Waiting time for non-medical specialists (computer specialists, etc.) is virtually a non-issue.

On the bright side, we are much better off than the more socialistic health care systems of Europe and Canada. As we saw in the chapter "The Disasters of Fully Socialized Medicine," the waiting times are much longer there. Our situation can greatly improve, however. Our results will depend on which system we choose to emulate. We can follow the example of our heavily socialized neighbors, with their more dramatic shortages, or we can look to the free market with its relatively plentiful supply. We can choose either course. The results are very easy to predict. Those who cannot learn from history are doomed to repeat it.[7] We are in a wonderful position to profit from the example of other nations, and therefore avoid their problems. The experiment with socialism has been performed. The results are in, and they are as plain as day. Let us learn, and improve our situation.

# Causes of the Problems –
# Government Interference
# in Free Markets

---

# Don't Worry About the
# Cost – It's Covered

―――――

*"This country has come to feel the same when Congress is
in session as when the baby gets hold of a hammer."*

*- WILL ROGERS*

NOW THAT THE MAJOR PROBLEMS have been examined, it is time to look at
the causes of these problems. They are very easy to understand, by exploring
history, examining data, and applying a strong dose of common sense. Once
the causes are made obvious, the solutions will be equally obvious.

Many people attribute the skyrocketing costs in medicine today to the
increase in technology. They think our advancing technology is outstripping
our ability to pay for it. This is what I used to believe, also. If this was the
case, however, then why does increasing technology in other industries not
cause the same kind of inflation?

Sometimes the march of technology leads to slightly higher prices as the
product vastly improves. Automotive technology is an example of this. The
average new car price increased from $15,720 in 1970 to $21,007 in 2001
(adjusted for inflation).[1] This is only a 34% increase in 31 years, despite our
now having so many more features such as anti-lock brakes, airbags, and more
efficient engines that last longer.

The electronics industry is an example of tremendous advances occurring while costs plummet. Thirty years ago, a scientific calculator cost somewhere near $60, but I recently bought a new one for $5, which works just fine. It is El Cheapo brand, but there was also a Texas Instruments scientific calculator at Walmart selling for about $10 at the time. VCRs, CD players, and microwave ovens have gotten much less expensive. Prices for plasma and LCD flat panel television sets have been dropping like a brick for years. A 50-inch plasma TV sold for about $20,000 in 2000, had dropped to around $4,000 by 2005,[2] and by late 2013 a 51-inch plasma TV was advertised for $569 on Amazon.com. [3]

All these areas, and many more, have generated cost savings for consumers as a result of increasing technology. Only in the parts of our economy where cost is disconnected from the consumer do prices climb ever higher in inflation-adjusted dollars, while satisfaction decreases. This would include health care and schools, the two areas of our economy where cost is most disconnected from the recipient of services.

There are many causes of the high rate of inflation in health care, but technology is not one of the primary ones. Innovations must be coupled with a disconnection between cost and consumer in order to significantly raise prices. If somebody else is paying the bill, a more expensive new technique becomes attractive, because the customer does not care too much about the cost. If the consumer is paying the bill, then research is geared toward reducing cost while improving results, in order to attract those consumers.

One of the few areas of health care where a free market economy still prevails is Lasik eye surgery. Like other sectors of the economy, increasing technology has led to decreasing costs and high satisfaction. "Of the approximately 3 million Americans who underwent laser eye surgery since 1995, more than 85 percent said the surgery improved their overall quality of life and 93 percent of patients said they were satisfied with the results. 87 percent felt that the results met or exceeded their expectations and 73 percent of patients regretted that they did not have the surgery sooner."[4] In the late 1990s, the average price per eye for Lasik surgery, in 2008 dollars, was about $3,100.[5] In 2008, the average cost is reported at $2,100 per eye.[6] This is a decrease of 32% in cost. This one area of medicine that actually operates under free market principles, behaves exactly as one would expect of other areas of our economy. Cost decreases as technology improves.

One reason that we are spending so much now on health care is that we simply have more money to spend. So little of our earnings are needed to pay for the basic necessities of life, that we have enormous wealth that can be spent on things like health care. A high rate of spending on health care is in this respect an indication of our wealth, and is therefore not a bad thing. The average American spent $2,207 in 2004 on food, including eating out.[7] At a fairly low salary of $22,000 per year, a person is only spending 10% of earnings on food. There is simply a vast amount of money left that can be used for entertainment, luxuries, and health care. If much of this money is spent on medical costs, then hopefully that will leave us healthier.

While this may explain some of the overall increased spending on health care, however, it does not explain why the same procedures cost so much more today than in times past. It also does not explain why the same procedures can be done in free market economies for a small fraction of the cost that is typically charged in the United States, as we shall see in the discussion on medical tourism later in this book.

Although there are many causes of the high prices that we have today in health care, there is probably none that is more devastating than over-insurance. The problem began with employer-based health insurance. This may sound shocking, since so many erstwhile solutions center around getting more employers to provide health insurance, but nevertheless it is true. If employers did not provide health insurance at all, then our system would be in much better shape. Routine health care would be very affordable, and people would not feel a need to have everything "covered."

The beginning of this problem can be found in World War II. President Franklin D. Roosevelt, in an effort to keep vital wartime industries running, declared Executive Order 9017 on January 12, 1942. This established the National War Labor Board.[8] The purpose was to resolve disputes between labor and management, in order to keep such important industries as mining and railways operating.

This was meant to be a last resort for dispute resolution. "This Order does not apply to labor disputes for which procedures for adjustment or settlement are otherwise provided until those procedures have been exhausted."[9] However, government agencies have a tendency to take on more powers than were originally granted to them. Who ever could have guessed that? Soon, they were setting wage limits when there were no disputes to be resolved.

With a large part of the men off beating back the rampaging Nazis, this left industry with a shortage of workers at home. In order to keep running well, the managers naturally needed to be able to offer the compensation that would attract good workers. "As a result of wage restrictions, employers who needed to attract labor resorted to providing a growing range of fringe benefits, such as pensions, medical insurance, and paid holidays and vacations. These benefits ... did not violate the wage ceiling."[10]

Thus, business managers wanted to pay workers more. Workers wanted to be paid more. There was no dispute to be settled. The National War Labor Board said no, and that was that. Business owners therefore worked around the rules.

Governments have no more success in repealing the laws of economics than they have in repealing the laws of physics. People will still try to get what they need, in this case good workers. There are many unintended consequences of meddling with markets, including labor markets. If the wage could not be increased in a labor shortage, then other compensation would increase. That is how we ended up with health insurance becoming tied to employment.

The Internal Revenue Service then ruled in 1943 that health insurance payments made by employers were not taxable income of the employees. This was codified by Congress in 1954.[11] In other words, health benefits are not taxed as salary is. This has been the most important instigating factor in our health care woes until today.

Salary is subject to state and federal income tax, unemployment insurance, Social Security tax, and Medicare tax. These taxes are not paid on health benefits. The total is roughly 30 - 40% of employee wages that is taken away in tax. Since health benefits do not lose 30 - 40% in value to Uncle Sam, it takes about $143 - $167 in wages to equal $100 in health benefits.

With health care dollars worth so much more than salary dollars, people wanted to maximize their health insurance relative to wages. They started getting more and more routine things covered. Eventually, people came to expect every little thing to be covered by health insurance, paid for by their employers. "I have good insurance" now means everything, no matter how trivial, is covered.

Consider the effects of having low cost services covered by insurance. One effect of a routine charge being billed to insurance, is that it adds cost to the doctor. The effort of having to file a claim, wait for a response, file it again in many cases, wait for another response, and often not collect at all, adds tremendous cost to a service. Staff needs to be hired simply for insurance billing purposes. A larger office is needed for that staff to work. The average annual overhead for a family practice doctor without obstetrics in 2003 was $258,807.[12] This is what it costs to run a practice. Most of this overhead is due to billing somebody besides the patient for payment. The typical doctor only collects about 58% of his charges.[13]

Consider the difference in fees between a free market medical practice like that of the author, and a typical insurance-based practice. Suppose I charge $30 for something. The average doctor who collects his fees from a third party has about $218,000 more overhead per year than I do, averaged over about 7,500 patient visits.[14] This adds another $29 to the charge, bringing it up to $59. If only 58% of charges end up getting paid, then the doctor needs to charge $102. The $30 service now costs $102.

An insurance company has to collect more in premiums than it pays out in claims, or it cannot remain in business and continue to offer insurance. It is a fundamental truth in business that a company needs to take in more revenue than it pays in expenses, or it cannot continue to do business. Aside from the obvious expense of the claim itself, there are administrative costs, salaries, etc. that the insurance company has to pay. It therefore needs to collect more in premiums than the costs of claims plus these other costs. If a service would cost $102 to pay directly, then the insurance company would have to collect more than that, perhaps $140, in order to stay in business.

The insurance company does not charge its customer $140 directly, in order to collect the necessary revenue. It charges a monthly, quarterly, or annual premium that it calculates to be high enough to cover all the claims for that period, plus administrative and other costs, plus some profit. These premiums are calculated based on the aggregate risks of the population being covered. Nevertheless, the fundamental maxim of business is not ignored - that revenue must exceed expense. The average small claim must therefore be exceeded by a larger premium. People end up paying somewhere in the neighborhood of $140 in premiums to cover what would have originally been a $30 service if insurance was not involved at all.

People do not recognize the $140 in premiums that they are paying for a $30 service, because it is worked in to a regularly billed premium. What they do see is "their share" of the monthly insurance premium, which is often enough to shock them. Employers suffer from the much larger "employer share" of this premium. Employees usually do not realize that their paycheck suffers as a result of the employer having to pay massive premiums to cover their employees. An employer has to decrease salary, or raise prices on what he sells, in order to cover his insurance costs.

What the uninsured see is a $102 fee for something that could be costing $30. They cannot be billed any differently than the insured, or the doctor would be guilty of charging according to a "dual fee schedule," a form of insurance fraud. Charges have to be the same for everybody, although the costs incurred by the doctor are much lower if a patient pays at the time of service. Some doctors apply a discount for payment at the time of service, but that discount is just a fraction of the increased cost that is accrued because of insurance company involvement. The uninsured therefore end up subsidizing the cost of dealing with insurance companies.

Does all this mean that the insurance companies are committing some great evil? Are they "price gouging"? Actually, they are simply responding to the pressures that have been exerted by government intervention, which have skewed the free market far beyond recognition. They cannot continue to offer insurance without making a profit. They charge what they must in order to do that.

Consider an analogous situation that could result from automobile insurance becoming tied to employment through tax deductibility. This is not actually such a preposterous concept, considering the argument that could be made in favor of it. After all, people need their cars to get to work, just as they need to be healthy enough to work, which is an argument that has been advanced to support employer based health insurance. What will be explored here will simply be the inevitable results of such an ill-advised scheme.

First, people would want the most comprehensive automobile insurance that they could get, because it is not taxed. An auto insurance dollar would therefore be worth much more than a salary dollar. Maximizing auto insurance means getting more and more routine things covered, just as has happened with health insurance. Eventually, tire changes and even gas fill-ups would be covered. A gas station would send a claim in to the insurance company for the gasoline purchased. There would be no restraint in buying gas, and no shopping around for the best price. The price would not even be posted at the pump, as it would all be considered free to someone with insurance. The gas station would have to have a billing department, with several people hired just to collect claims. The costs of dealing with the insurance companies would drive gas prices way up.

Eventually, as premiums escalated in response to higher prices and wasteful driving habits, copays would have to be instituted as a partial deterrence. The copay might be $4 per gallon, whereas the actual price would be perhaps $12 per gallon. The uninsured would have to pay the full $12 per gallon. Deductibles would also be used to try to keep waste down. Then, people would avoid driving before they reached their deductibles. Then once the deductible was reached, people would take off on cross-country trips, with no restraint. Employers, who did not offer auto insurance, with gas covered, would be looked down upon as greedy exploiters of their workers. The outcry would be made for national auto insurance, covering gas, paid for with taxes.

Does this sound ridiculous? It is exactly what has happened with health insurance. Note the parallels. Workers need running cars, just as they need their health. Routine things like gas fill-ups, or the freezing of a wart, would be covered. Prices would not be posted, which is the case at the typical doctor's office. There would be wasteful use, like the person going to the doctor for a sniffle, or the Medicaid patient going to the emergency department for a rash of six months duration, which I have encountered. Copays would end up costing about what the original cost of the item was before the insurance fiasco started. For more discussion on this, refer to the $30 health care service discussed earlier in this chapter, as $30 copays are now commonplace in family practice. It is my actual experience that $30 is in the neighborhood of free market charges for a family practice visit. The outcry against exploitive employers, who do not offer insurance, is the actual scenario in health care today. Most of the solutions that have been discussed, including Obamacare, are pointing us toward a nationalized health insurance scheme.

The idea that an employer is responsible for an employee's auto costs including gasoline is no more preposterous than that employer being responsible for an employee's health. There is a simple exchange taking place, labor for wages. That is why it is called the labor market. The employer is not responsible for the well-being of his employee, in any way, outside of workplace safety and the payment of the wage.

The obvious result of such an economically unsound scheme in health care is runaway inflation in premiums, as well as much higher out-of-pocket costs. Health insurance premiums have risen by an average of 9.9% per year from 1988 to 2007, while workers' earnings rose an average of 3.3% annually and overall inflation was 3.2%.[15] This is what always happens when consumers are protected from costs. In the United States, as of 2003, only 14% of health costs are paid "out-of-pocket," or in other words, by the consumer of the services directly. This number has been steadily declining from 23% in 1987.[16] Consumers of health care in the United States are highly insulated from cost. This insulation rate of 86% is one of the highest in the developed world, even higher than in Canada.[17] Our problem is one of over-insurance, not under-insurance.

The other obvious example of consumers of a service being insulated from cost is found in government education. The inevitable result of this cost disconnection is that costs per pupil are skyrocketing in every state. The nationwide average expenditure per pupil in 2001 was 7.2 times the expenditure in 1945, after adjusting for inflation.[18] This kind of spending increase happens any time that people think they are getting something for nothing.

This argument does not mean that people should not have any health insurance. The reason for having insurance of any kind is to protect against the risk of a catastrophic loss. Insurance is purchased to protect individuals against very high cost problems that would otherwise be financially devastating. Our typical low-deductible policies that cover routine services are not insurance as much as they are pre-paid health plans. Catastrophic coverage, with high deductibles, is another matter entirely.

The lengths to which insurance companies resort in order to reduce their costs have become legendary. Since the patient is usually not their customer, they do not have to care about pleasing the patient. They can refuse to pay what they are contractually obligated to pay, and often seem to do just that.

Just one example of the kinds of things that insurance companies do, because the patient is usually not the customer, is the following. I have a friend who had a separate dental policy from her medical policy, with one of the biggest insurance companies in the nation. She sent in her premiums every month. The medical premium was misapplied, by the insurance company, to the dental policy. This resulted in dental overpayments and nonpayments on the medical policy. She was sent a cancellation notice for nonpayment. When she figured out what happened, the insurance company sent her a refund for her overpayments on the dental policy, rather than correcting their "mistake" by applying the premiums correctly and reinstituting the medical policy. She then was without coverage and her diabetes became a pre-existing condition so that any new policy would not cover it for a year. This is one way of getting rid of an insuree with diabetes.

This is not just one isolated report. An investigation was launched in California into Blue Cross of California for accusations of cancelling policies for sicker enrollees, in violation of state law. The chief HMO regulator of California investigated Blue Cross, and found that the insurer had cancelled coverage of its insurees inappropriately, and in violation of state law. The state Department of Managed Health Care found that Blue Cross had used "computer programs and a dedicated department" to cancel policies of people who were pregnant or had chronic illnesses.[19] In July 2008, both Anthem Blue Cross and Blue Shield agreed to pay a total of $13 million in fines and offer new coverage to over 2,200 people as a result of that investigation.[20]

State laws forbid insurance companies from adequately adjusting their premiums to the risk of the patient, so they must shift the cost of the higher-risk patients onto the lower-risk population by raising their premiums. This is called "community rating." If they can get rid of the higher-risk patients, like diabetics, then they can improve their bottom line. In a free market, a company does not try to drive customers away, but they will if state laws cause them to lose money on the customer. In the health insurance industry, the patient is usually not the customer, although it was in the case of my friend discussed above. The insurance company was forbidden from charging the premiums that would have been necessary to avoid a loss, so driving the patient away was good for business.

Refusals of insurance companies to pay claims have been frustrating doctors for years. Imagine sending a claim in by certified mail, receiving a signed receipt from the staff of the insurance company, and then when no payment comes, being told that they never received the claim. That is what happened to the Pediatric Alliance in Pittsburgh.[21] It is often possible for a doctor to get paid, but only after resubmitting the claim or other information that is either irrelevant or was already submitted. Many doctors will give up rather than have to relentlessly pursue an insurance company to finally collect a claim.

Another way of looking at our third party payment system is by looking at an option for neighborhood grocery purchases. Suppose you belonged to a neighborhood association that offered to buy all your groceries. You would not have to pay for any of your own food. The association would pay the bills. All you would have to do is pay a monthly bill that would not change depending on how much you ate. You could go to the grocery store as often as you want, and buy as much as you want, without changing your monthly bill. Each food item would cost three times what it does now, and your monthly bill to the association would be many times higher than what you pay now for food, but that would not be important because somebody else would be paying for each food bill. You also would not be allowed to choose certain foods any more, because they would all have to be approved by the association. This would be determined by the preferences of your neighbors, based on what they decide would be cost effective for the entire neighborhood. But don't worry, you get a vote in who is chosen to make those decisions. Of course, you do not need to join this food program, but if you do not your food will still cost you three times as much because that is what the grocery will be charging. It would be illegal for them to give anyone a better rate than the neighborhood association because that would be unfair and fraudulent. When costs start climbing out of control, copays would have to be introduced. Perhaps $3.20 for a gallon of milk, or $1.40 for a dozen eggs, would be appropriate copays.

Would you really want this kind of third party food purchasing? After all, as important as food is, we cannot leave food distribution to the free market! But wait, that is what Marx and Lenin said, before Soviet agriculture plummeted to a fraction of its previous production, and people began starving in what had previously been a food-exporting region.

Perhaps we should look at it another way. Food is much too important to allow interference that would destroy efficiency in the free market. So is health care. Perhaps it is time to stop allowing government intervention to hamper the efficient delivery of something as important as health care. Persuading people, through tax policy, to over-insure is one way that government intervention is harming health care delivery.

# Medicare and Medicaid

———

*"We're going to take things away from you on behalf of the common good."*

- HILLARY RODHAM CLINTON

ANOTHER WAY OUR GOVERNMENT INTERFERES with the efficient delivery of health care is through Medicare and Medicaid. Of all the reasons for high costs and poor service in health care, there are two that stand out above all the rest in importance. One is over-insurance, and the other is the Medicare / Medicaid system.

Health care costs began inflating when insurance became increasingly connected to employment in the 1940s, but it was in the mid to late 1960s when costs really started shooting through the roof. That was when Medicare was enacted.

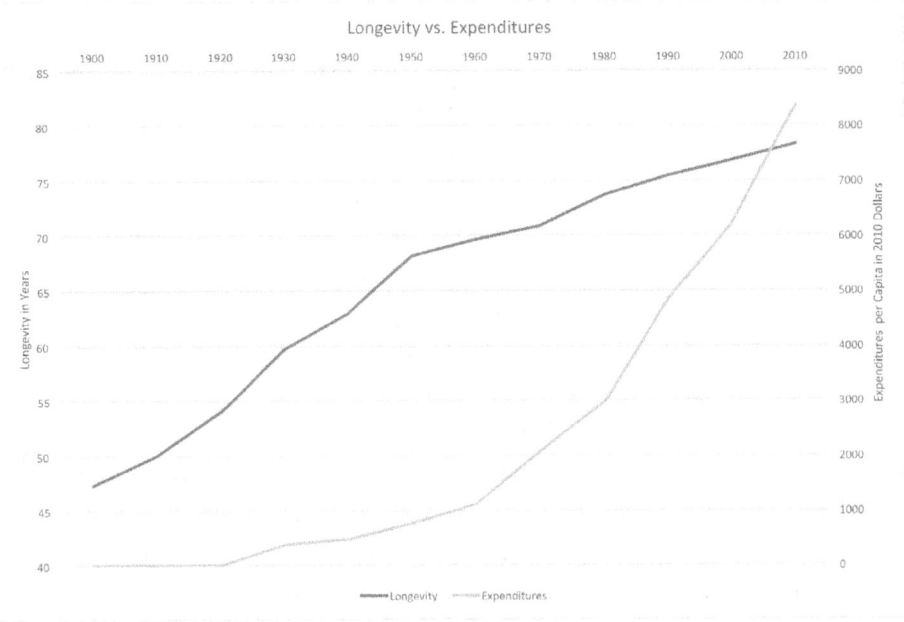

American longevity vs. average annual health care expenditures per capita, adjusted to 2010 dollars.[1,2,4,5] No data on expenditures available before 1930.

Even though there was not any major problem with seniors getting health care, government enacted a solution to our non-problem, thus creating a problem.

"The government used carefully doctored statistics to mislead the public into believing that nearly half of the senior population did not have medical insurance coverage prior to the passage of Medicare.

"These statistics, taken from a 1964 Department of Health, Education and Welfare report, didn't count an enormous number of people who were covered by a variety of programs including: indemnity policies that paid cash benefits, existing government programs such as the Veterans Administration, and welfare. It also didn't count those who could afford to pay their own way-i.e. lack of 'insurance coverage' is not the same as lack of access to medical care.

"The fact was that 77% of seniors were eligible for the Kerr-Mills program (Medical Assistance for the Aged), which had been passed into law a full five years before Medicare. The remaining 23%-if they couldn't afford to pay for their own care-could receive free care at their local hospital. Under the Hill-Burton Act, hospitals agreed to provide free care to anyone who needed it in return for government grants and loans."[5]

Medical care was not prohibitively expensive for the typical American, as we have already seen in the chapter "Crisis? What Crisis? Conditions before Government Interference." For those who did have unusually expensive problems that they could not afford, charity care was given, or friends, family, church, or other groups helped with payment. Health insurance was also possible for seniors to obtain before the enactment of Medicare.

The situation is greatly different now. If a doctor provides charity care, he is taking a chance on being prosecuted for Medicare fraud. Medicare stipulates that nobody can be charged less than the Medicare payment, unless the doctor does not participate with Medicare for any of his patients. Every patient must be charged according to the same fee schedule.

Seniors are having an increasingly difficult time finding a doctor who will take Medicare. This may not be a problem for a Medicare beneficiary who already has a doctor, but it is for someone on Medicare who wants to find a new doctor. I have had people, new to my city, who came to see me because they could not find any doctor willing to take a new Medicare patient.

There is no longer a market for those over 65 for primary health insurance. Only policies secondary to Medicare, or "Medigap" type policies are available. This refers to policies that kick in after a Medicare claim has been processed.

Over-insurance and Medicare have combined to drive costs up to the point where most people cannot afford to pay for it without health insurance or Medicare. This is like the auto insurance analogy in the last chapter, where the self-pay driver would not be able to afford gasoline because of the costs that directly resulted from the insurance effects. If not for the over-insurance and Medicare upon which people now depend, it would not be difficult to pay for our health care directly.

What kind of costs are associated with Medicare, to make health care unaffordable? This is what the American Hospital Association testified to the U.S. Senate about the effects of Medicare on staffing:

"The Mayo Foundation estimates that we are subject to 132,720 pages of rules that govern the Medicare and Medicaid programs... Some rural hospitals have almost as many billing clerks as they do beds. In Gonzales, Texas, Memorial Hospital has 33 beds and a billing staff of 20 employees. At Northwestern Memorial, our patient financial services department spends more than 3,200 staff hours per month, or 38,400 staff hours per year sorting through Medicare billing requirements alone. This year, Northwestern Memorial Hospital is adding 26 new FTEs solely to ensure compliance with regulations... Hospitals are drowning in this sea of government rules and regulations."[6]

Imagine the effects of this kind of a mess on your local grocery store. Can you just picture a grocery store that now has five clerks, needing to hire another twenty just to comply with government regulations, and to try to get paid? We would be hard-pressed to avoid starvation.

The typical doctor, whether in family practice or a multispecialty practice, has about five staff members per doctor.[7] This contrasts sharply to the one or maybe two that would be needed in a free market practice. This author has only one assistant. Most of the reason for having these extra employees is just to deal with getting paid.

"Every time the nurses, physicians and other health care workers care for a patient, a host of regulations and statutes govern their very actions, especially if the patient is a Medicare or Medicaid recipient. More than 30 agencies oversee some aspect of that health care delivery process – and that's just at the federal level. State agencies add yet another layer – or two. More than 130,000 pages govern the Medicare system – a sheaf of paper three times larger than the IRS Code and its federal tax regulations.

"Unfortunately, these regulations and statutes do not always enhance the patient care experience. In fact, quite the opposite. They absorb valuable time and resources – time that could be spent caring for the next patient to come through the emergency department doors."[8]

PricewaterhouseCoopers (PwC) performed a study on behalf of the American Hospital Association to determine how much time is spent on paperwork compared to patient care. They found that, in the emergency department, for every hour of care, an hour of paperwork is required. For an hour of surgery or inpatient acute care, 36 minutes was required. For an hour of home health care, 48 minutes of paperwork was done. For every hour of other skilled nursing care, 30 minutes of paperwork was needed.[9]

"While the PwC report did not evaluate the paperwork requirements placed on hospitals by the private sector, such as private health insurance plans, outside regulators, etc., we do know that these requirements mirror the paperwork burdens imposed by the Centers for Medicare & Medicaid Services (CMS). These numerous private sector payors and regulators add to the paperwork morass, since each typically has unique requirements with which hospitals must comply."[10]

Many of the rules and regulations that Medicare has promulgated have then become adopted by the private insurance companies, with some variations. These regulations are basically a result of the inherent difficulties in trying to eliminate fraud when somebody else is paying the bill.

What are the effects on doctors of all these regulations, and how are those effects felt by their patients? Many doctors have become fed up with their taskmasters. They are starting to feel like the Israelites making bricks for Pharoah, with the Egyptian overseers standing over them with whips.

Dr. Robert Schwartz published the following explanation to his community when he "opted out" of the Medicare program:

"The federal government, while possibly well intentioned, has now created such a complex maze of Medicare rules and regulations that compliance is practically impossible. By the time the physician figures them out, they have changed. By the time one realizes that they are not in compliance, they are audited...

"At this point, the federal government is not concerned that the doctor was not aware of the dynamic rules and regulations. To them, the doctor is committing fraud and will be fined up to $10,000 per fine (sic) item error...

"Every patient contact becomes an encounter with choice: Think first of the patient, or of the system? It has gotten to the point where only in a minority of cases can the two needs be met simultaneously...

"I, for one, am tired of honoring the Medicare system more than my patients' needs. I welcome the possibility of establishing and renewing physician- patient relationships that are not invaded by federal rules and regulations. There are few basic truths more fundamental than the belief that preservation of life and liberty also includes the right to unrestricted freedom when it comes to one's own health care. Opting out allows the physician to place patient care ahead of federal rules and regulations. It empowers him to practice medicine once again."[11]

This statement is similar to what many other doctors have publicly declared, such as Dr. John A Bennett, in his "Declaration of Independence from the Medicare Program."[12]

Respondents to a survey by the American Academy of Family Physicians found that 13% did not participate with Medicare in 2009, up from 8% in 2008, and 6% in 2004.[13]

Increasingly, doctors who have not opted out of the program are avoiding Medicare patients. Whereas seniors did not have a difficult time finding a doctor to see them before Medicare was enacted, now they often do have trouble. The American Academy of Family Physicians conducted a survey of family physicians in 2002 and found that "21.7 percent of FPs reported they could no longer take new Medicare patients, a significant increase from the previous year's figure of 17 percent."[14] In response to a 2012 survey, 25% of doctors across all specialties in America said they were not accepting new Medicare patients.[15] 46% of respondents to another survey in 2008 said that if planned pay cuts went into effect, they would limit or stop accepting new Medicare patients.[16]

Doctors who go to the extent of "opting out" of Medicare do so for much more than financial reasons. They do it to preserve the sanctity of the doctor-patient relationship. They do it because they believe in freedom. They do it because Medicare is a fundamentally immoral system. The moral aspect will be explored more fully in a later chapter.

It can be financially risky to opt out of Medicare. A doctor must send a signed affidavit to the U.S. government, promising not to send in any Medicare claims for two years. Nobody, patient or employer, can send in a Medicare claim for the work he has done. If a doctor does not make it financially after this big leap of faith, then there are few places in the United States where he can continue to work as a physician, outside of the military or the prison system. Yet, some doctors take this risk and opt out, because they feel that it is the right thing to do. I am one of those doctors who stands on principle.

Medicare and Social Security are violations of the United States Constitution. They have not been overruled by the Supreme Court simply because of political expediency. In 1935, the Supreme Court ruled the Railroad Retirement Act to be unconstitutional. It was a piece of New Deal legislation that would have taken a percentage of income from railroad workers, and twice that amount from the railroad companies that employed them. This money would have gone into a fund held by the U.S. Treasury. It would have then been disbursed to railroad workers when they retired. Does anything about this Railroad Retirement Act sound familiar? It is nothing but the Social Security Act in a slightly altered form, and limited to the railroad industry. Among other reasons for declaring it unconstitutional, the Supreme Court said, "the Act denies due process of law by taking the property of one and bestowing it upon another."[17]

The Supreme Court overruled many other New Deal programs as well. Roosevelt then got legislation introduced into Congress to appoint one extra Supreme Court justice for every one that reached 70 1/2 years old and did not retire. At the time there were six such justices. This would have increased the number of judges on the court from nine to fifteen, changing the balance of power. His new appointees of course would have been supporters of New Deal legislation.

With this court-packing legislation hanging over them as a threat to their power, the Supreme Court started to go along with Roosevelt. A scant two years after the Railroad Retirement Act was overruled, they ruled the very similar Social Security Act to be constitutional. Nothing about the Constitution changed. It was not amended to allow the property of one to be taken and bestowed upon another. The judges of the Supreme Court simply began to turn their backs to the Constitution, and have not looked back since.

Regarding the radical new idea that the federal government could take money from one person to spend on another, the Supreme Court simply said, "there have been great statesmen in our history who have stood for other views. We will not resurrect the contest. It is now settled by decision."[18] That those "great statesmen" included the ones who wrote the Constitution was of no consequence to the court. Without going through the amendment process, they simply decided to change the entire nature of the federal government.

I suspect, at least I hope, that most seniors would be opposed to Medicare and Social Security if they understood the basic facts about it. Most elderly people would not want to spend hundreds of thousands of dollars on the credit cards of their children and grandchildren, if they knew they were doing that. Most would not want to tax their grandchildren to the tune of 14% of their earnings. Most would not want to drive up the cost of health care for their grandchildren. They simply do not realize that their Medicare and Social Security are causing these problems for their own children and grandchildren. Most seniors would like to leave a better America for their posterity, not an economically devastated one. The truth needs to be made known.

# We Are Regulating Ourselves to Death

———

*"That's what governments are for - to get in a man's way."*

*- MALCOLM REYNOLDS*

THE ENORMOUS REGULATORY BURDEN IMPOSED upon doctors by the federal government extends far beyond Medicare and Medicaid.

These programs require bills to be submitted using Common Procedural Terminology (CPT) codes. Insurance companies have followed suit, and also require CPT codes. Because all patients must be billed according to the same fee schedule, uninsured patients must also be charged according to this enormously complex code set. In an attempt to describe everything that a physician will ever do, and standardize all those tasks, over 6,000 of these codes were created. Associated with the CPT code set is the International Classification of Diseases (ICD) code set, used in conjunction with it. A doctor must submit CPT codes to define what he did, along with ICD codes to describe the condition of the patient.

Of course, it is impossible to cover all possibilities for the condition of the patient and what was done, with numerical codes. There are many possibilities for which there is no adequate code. There is actually an ICD-9 code for "moron" (code 317).[1]

Enormous amounts of time are spent trying to find the right codes, in an effort to avoid being charged with fraud. Unnecessary exam items are done in order to check them off for payment. For example, in training I was taught to always get a complete set of vital signs (blood pressure, pulse, respiratory rate, and temperature), because it could increase the level of service, and therefore payment, from a coding perspective. With a simple rash, checking the respiratory rate and blood pressure is really irrelevant in most cases. All this wasted time increases the cost of medical care.

This CPT coding system is actually a copyright-protected work of a private corporation, the American Medical Association (AMA). Its use is mandated by government for every doctor who submits claims to Medicare or Medicaid. The AMA collects vast amounts of royalties on the use of the CPT system. It is, therefore, a government-enforced private monopoly, which generates money for the rights holders at the expense of those who are forced to use it. It is hard to imagine a worse case of corruption than this, in a supposedly free republic.

Senator Trent Lott wrote to Tommy Thompson, head of the Health Care Financing Administration (HCFA), concerning this abuse:

"It is my understanding that HCFA in 1983 granted the AMA what has been characterized as a 'statutory monopoly' by agreeing to exclusively use and promote the AMA's copyrighted CPT code for the purposes of reimbursing Medicare and Medicaid bills from doctors for outpatient services. As a result of HCFA's and the federal government's endorsement of the AMA's copyrighted outpatient code -- to the exclusion of all competitors -- private insurance companies and others were also forced to adopt the CPT as their billing standard as well. The CPT code has thus become a fixture in doctor offices around the country. This predictably led to a financial windfall for the AMA in the form of CPT-related book sales and royalties approaching $71 million a year according to a report by the Wall Street Journal.

"By using its CPT copyright aggressively in court, the AMA has also been able to control who uses the codes and who knows what about the cost of doctor services. For instance, the AMA has been able to impose on the entire nation the AMA's obviously self-interested policy against consumers comparison shopping for medical care based on price by suing web sites and others to prohibit them from posting comparisons of doctor and other medical fees on the Internet using the CPT code."[2] This is one of the reasons it is so hard to find out what a medical procedure will cost before having it done.

There are regulations called the Emergency Medical Treatment and Active Labor Act (EMTALA) that forbid doctors from turning away anybody that shows up in their emergency room. As a result of this, ERs in our southern states are being overrun with illegal aliens to the extent that they are going bankrupt. There is simply too much free care that they are being required to provide. We comprise roughly 5% of the world population, yet our federal government requires us to care for every person in the entire world, if they show up demanding that care. The federal government, while having the charge of enforcing our borders, does virtually nothing in that respect, except of course for trying to prevent states like Arizona from any enforcement activities. They allow thousands of people from other countries to cross our southern border every day. They then require us to care for their medical conditions.

"Undocumented persons cost border hospitals $189.6 million in uncompensated emergency medical costs during 2000...These figures do not represent the full cost incurred by southwest border counties and the healthcare providers serving them...Our scope was limited to emergency medical services only and did not include emergency medical services delivered by physicians when those physicians billed for their services separately from hospital charges. Both physician services and extended care arising out of a qualified medical emergency are substantial in cost."[3]

Hospitals cannot continue to provide care when they lose money in the process. People who work in hospitals must be paid, or else they have to find other jobs to feed, house, and clothe their families. Electricity and heating bills must be paid, or there will be no more heat and electricity to those hospitals. Supplies must be continually purchased, or there will be nothing with which to treat people.

"High-technology EDs have degenerated into free medical offices. Between 1993 and 2003, 60 California hospitals closed because half their services became unpaid. Another 24 California hospitals verge on closure."[4]

The same situation exists in all of our border states, and to a lesser extent throughout the continental United States.

Anybody who frowns on someone else who is not willing to provide a service for free, or at a loss, needs to ask himself these simple questions: "Would I go to work every day if I was not going to receive a paycheck (profit)? Would I be willing to pay (incur a loss) for the privilege of working full time?" If the answer to either of these questions is no, then why expect it of somebody else?

For a hospital to remain in business, it must spread the costs of treating unpaying patients onto those who do pay, raising their fees. EMTALA costs us all.

The result of EMTALA is not just the forbidding of emergency doctors from turning away true emergencies. They are simply unable to turn away any person presenting to the ER, for any reason. In all the time I have spent in emergency departments throughout my medical career, I have never seen anybody turned away. There may be some turned away, but I have never seen it. It does not matter how non-urgent or trivial the condition is. Hospitals have had to establish "fast-track" sections of their emergency departments in order to accommodate the huge volume of non-urgent cases. This is because turning anybody away risks an EMTALA lawsuit. A clever lawyer or a jury filled with people who lack economic sense could result in fines of tens of thousands of dollars, regardless of how trivial the case.

Stark laws are another form of federal regulations, which bar referrals to any entity in which the referring physician has a vested interest. This prohibition can create some very real barriers to obtaining the best care for the patient. I once had a patient who refused to go to the local large hospital,[5] because of a prior bad experience. Her condition required hospitalization for blood transfusion and urgent colonoscopy to find and correct the source of internal bleeding. There was a hospital that was affiliated with a surgical center in the area, where she could have gotten everything that she needed, but there would have been referrals between the two. I was informed by the hospital administration that this was not permissible under Stark laws, even though these affiliated centers provided what I believe is better care for a lower cost. Congressman Pete Stark and colleagues apparently felt that they knew what was best for this woman, and for everyone else in the country. It does not matter what the patient and the physician decide is best; our federal government will not allow it. What is done in Washington for supposedly good intentions does not always produce good results.

The Kennedy-Kassebaum bill of 1996 is another boondoggle of federal regulations that is costing Americans plenty. It forbids insurance companies from excluding people with pre-existing conditions or charging them higher premiums, if they have had coverage for the past year. While this may sound well and good at first, it can cause some serious problems.

According to Lambda Legal, Kennedy-Kassebaum "prohibits discrimination in health insurance based on health status (e.g., companies cannot refuse to insure, or provide equivalent insurance to, people with HIV)."[7] If people choose to engage in those incredibly risky behaviors[8] that Lambda Legal is dedicated to protecting, insurance companies just have to suck up the costs. Of course, this means that people who avoid high-risk behaviors also have to pay higher premiums to make up the losses.

Kennedy-Kassebaum therefore increases the incidence of risky behavior by removing one of the consequences for the individual, and distributing that consequence onto the rest of society, that of higher insurance premiums. If people who built houses in flood plains could buy flood insurance at the same rate as everybody else, they would have the deterrent value of higher insurance premiums removed from them. More people therefore would build in flood plains than if insurance premiums provided that deterrence.

Suppose you had a car whose steering became irreparably damaged, so that every once in a while it would swerve out of control. If the Kennedy-Kassebaum bill applied to auto insurance, then any insurer would have to sell you a policy at the same premium as everybody else if you applied for it, as long as you already had a policy. They could not charge you a higher rate than anybody else because of your pre-existing steering condition, even though your car had become a road hazard.

Overall, the costs of regulation are staggering. "The total cost of health services regulation exceeds $339.2 billion. This figure takes into account regulation of health facilities, health professionals, health insurance, drugs and medical devices, and the medical tort system, including the costs of defensive medicine. Moreover, this approach allows for a calculation of some important tangible benefits of regulation. Yet even after subtracting $170.1 billion in benefits, the net burden of health services regulation is considerable, amounting to $169.1 billion annually. In other words, the costs of health services regulation outweigh benefits by two-to-one and cost the average household over $1,500 per year."[9]

To discuss all the forms of regulations that are imposed upon doctors and an unsuspecting public would take volumes. This chapter just provides a brief overview of some of them. The compliance industry is very large and lucrative, just to help doctors in their futile efforts to remain compliant with this morass of regulations. Books and lecture tickets are sold to doctors who are trying to avoid the penalties of noncompliance with federal and state regulations.

It is hard to imagine how we got ourselves into this quagmire, given our constitutional protections against federal interference in matters of state or individual jurisdiction. I carry a copy of the United States Constitution in my wallet, with all 27 amendments, printed on a single sheet of paper (both sides). This simple document describes the framework and functions of our entire federal government. Consider how far we have progressed by comparing that to the over 130,000 pages of Medicare regulations that we now have. This could only be considered progress in the same way that fungal decay, or rust, can be called progress. Our regulations are like hobbles around our ankles, weighing us down, and slowing true progress.

# Controls on Price and Physician Supply

*"There can be no liberty unless there is economic liberty."*

*- Margaret Thatcher*

There have been shortages of many things in America, resulting from government interventions into the free market. Shortages occur when people are willing to pay the prevailing price, but cannot find the item available. By this definition, it is impossible to find a shortage of an item, which is possible to produce, when there is no interference in free markets. The price changes in response to supply and demand. If a person wants something badly enough, he offers more money than a competing buyer.

If one defines a shortage as happening when the price for an item is higher than he would like, then everything is in shortage. The price of an item is merely a reflection of what other things must be foregone in order to obtain that item. All of our resources have a finite supply. We need to choose how to use them. Prices provide a mechanism of doing this. If supply decreases, then price increases. This way, the proper amount of importance is placed on different items. In other words, consumers prioritize the things that they want producers to supply, by being willing to pay different prices.

Gasoline was in shortage during the times of price controls in the 1970s, initiated by President Nixon, but continued during the administrations of

Presidents Ford and Carter. People waited in long lines to buy gasoline, when many would have much rather paid more, rather than waiting. A higher price would have reduced demand to match supply. Instead of gasoline being rationed through prices, it was rationed through waiting lines and governmental decrees on how much could be purchased.[1] People wanted gas at the posted prices, but were unable to obtain it.

Electricity shortages developed in California during the government controls of the 1990s. The state put into place numerous interventions into the free market, including price caps. They impeded the production of new power plants to keep up with demand. They had a state-run power broker. Power companies were forced to sell some of their production plants. The state forbade certain types of contracts, which had been in use.[2] Oddly, advocates of those regulations called the process "deregulation." It was actually a more onerous set of regulations than they had previously. The result was, predictably, rolling blackouts.

In 1994, the Vaccines for Children program, a federal program to buy vaccines at reduced prices for children, was instituted. It was the brain child of then First Lady Hillary Clinton.[3] Through it, the federal government "buys vaccines at a discount,"[4] and then distributes them to providers. Government purchases now comprise over half the vaccine market in the United States.[5] The Vaccines for Children program has reduced the revenue of vaccine makers, by pushing prices down. Profits have decreased considerably, and with profits gone, so went incentive to make the vaccines.[6]

Most American vaccine manufacturers stopped making vaccines after this federal feel-good program was started. Since the early 1970s, there were over 25 companies making vaccines for use in the United States, but in 2003 only 5 remained.[7] Shortages became chronic as we became dependent on one or two manufacturers for each vaccine.

In 2004, there were two flu vaccine suppliers, both British, and one developed a problem, cutting the supply in half. In 1998, an American manufacturer of influenza vaccine had shut down its production, because of the difficulties and costs of compliance with federal regulations. They sold their plant, and the buyer also determined that meeting regulations would be too costly.[8]

The same principles apply to all pharmaceuticals. The results of the new Medicare Part D program for prescription drugs can be easily predicted, if price controls are put into place. Shortages of medicines will likely become more severe, as they have with vaccines, because the same incentives will be at work. The goals are the same.

Medicare prescription drug coverage is touted to make medicines more affordable, so that more seniors will be able to obtain them. The Vaccines for Children program was supposed to make vaccines more affordable, so that more children will be immunized. Scarcity of many vaccines has resulted. Likewise, there will probably be a scarcity of many medications. Without the profit motive, we will see the American pharmaceutical industry dwindle, just as the vaccine segment of that industry has dwindled. Why will the results be any different, when the incentives are the same?

Do we really want to stop research and development into new medicines? Are we satisfied with what we have now? Would we want innovation to "grind to a halt,"[9] as Harvard University economist Kenneth Rogoff predicts would happen if we become more socialist in health care? A scholarly paper points out the obvious, after a lengthy evaluation of the economic forces at work: "Clearly, price regulation provides a disincentive for pharmaceutical innovation."[10] If the United States were to regulate drug prices down by 40-50%, a study estimates that between 30-60% fewer research projects would be undertaken.[11]

Medicare Part D could of course lead to such price regulation. Some believe such controls are likely.[12] Others think they are inevitable.[13] Others say that government will, and should, only negotiate prices, without applying undue force.[14] Currently, the law does not allow price negotiations or controls, but forces are at work to remove this prohibition.[15] H.R. 4, which passed the House January 12, 2007, would provide for "negotiations" of drug prices for Medicare Part D. As of this writing, follow-up bills are in committee in both the House and in the Senate.[16]

Medicare was not supposed to influence medical decisions, but it certainly has. The U.S. Code concerning Medicare still reads, "Nothing in this subchapter shall be construed to authorize any Federal officer or employee to exercise any supervision or control over the practice of medicine or the manner in which medical services are provided, or over the selection, tenure, or compensation of any officer or employee of any institution, agency, or person providing health services; or to exercise any supervision or control over the administration or operation of any such institution, agency, or person."[17] What an absurd notion! Every doctor now practicing in the United States who is paying attention is painfully aware of a great deal of supervision and control over the practice of medicine, by Medicare regulators. The very bill referred to above, which would bring about government price negotiations on medicines, violates that Medicare code.

Judging from history, it seems very likely that Medicare Part D will lead to government price controls. What government pays for, it ultimately ends up regulating and controlling, just as it has with the practice of medicine for seniors. A likely outcome of setting Medicare drug prices as some percentage of the average retail price, is that the average retail price will rise so that drug manufacturers can still make some profit. That would mean higher prices for everybody who is not on Medicare, and relatively unchanged prices for drugs covered by Medicare.[18] This has already happened with Medicaid. It was found that for every 10% increase in Medicaid market share of a drug, the average price of that drug increased by 10%, which is what non-Medicaid purchasers had to pay.[19]

The population in the United States has been increasing, but the number of graduates of U.S. medical schools has barely budged. From 1980 to 2000, the number of Medical Doctors (M.D.s) and Doctors of Osteopathy (D.O.s) increased by only 12%,[20] while the U.S. population increased by 24%, as the population has also been aging.

M.D.s and D.O.s are the two types of fully trained physicians in the United States. Both graduate from four-year postgraduate colleges, then attend residencies in the specialties of their choice. They often mix in the same residency programs. For example, I completed a family practice residency that was affiliated with Duke University. In it, roughly 30-40% of the residents were D.O.s, and the rest were M.D.s. D.O.s go into all specialties and subspecialties, surgical and otherwise, but the majority practice in primary care - family practice, pediatrics, and internal medicine.

In Wyoming, an attempt was made to establish a medical school in the 1990s, to ease the shortage of doctors in the region. Wyoming has no medical school. Ross University School of Medicine, a school in the Carribean, had interest in opening another campus in Wyoming, to graduate M.D.s. They had the approval of many in the local economy. The Liaison Committee on Medical Education (LCME) would not consider their application for accreditation of a U.S. campus. The LCME will not consider accrediting a medical school that is for profit.[21]

This refusal to consider Ross happened in spite of their reputation for quality graduates. The Massachusetts College of Pharmacy and Health Sciences has established a combined program with Ross. They described Ross as having a "technologically advanced campus, exceptional faculty and rigorous U.S. style curriculum."[22] Ross graduates attend U.S. residencies. Nevertheless, they would not be considered for accreditation of a new U.S. campus, and the shortage of doctors continues.

There has not been a for-profit medical school in the U.S. in about 90 years, until Rocky Vista University College of Osteopathic Medicine opened in Colorado in 2008.[23] This school trains D.O.s.

"Non-profit" status is simply a designation in tax law. It does not mean that the staff and executives of non-profit institutions are not making money. They often make a great deal of money. It does, however, mean that there cannot be shareholders of stock who make money. They need to be engaged in a "public interest" as the IRS defines it, such as education, environmental quality, etc. There are some specific organizational requirements. If an organization can get classified by the IRS as non-profit, then they get out of paying taxes. Interestingly, the economists Malani and Choi "find support for the profit-in-disguise model" in their study of salary and turnover of executives in non-profit nursing homes.[24] In other words, "non-profit" status is often just a racket for avoiding taxes.

The profit motive has brought more goods and services to more people than any other system. With the physician shortages that we have, it is about time we had more for-profit schools.

The academic leaders are finally starting to recognize a shortage of physicians. In 2006, the Association of American Medical Colleges called for a 30% increase in medical school enrollment.[25] It would seem that they are way behind the times in this call.

The LCME is recognized by the U.S. Department of Education as the only accrediting authority for medical schools granting the M.D. degree in the U.S. (this does not apply to the D.O. degree). A student cannot get a student loan to help pay for an M.D. degree in the U.S. unless the school is accredited by the LCME. Thus, the federal government indirectly exerts control over medical schools in the U.S, through the exclusive recognition of one accrediting agency, and the requirement of accreditation through that agency for the financial aid on which students depend.

The funding of residency positions is mostly through the Medicare program.[26] This results in the allocation of physicians to various specialties being done through central planning in Washington, D.C. Congress has limited the residency positions they fund to roughly 85,000 per year from the late 1990's through 2012.[27] Just like the Soviet Union experienced shortages because of their central planning, our long waits for various specialists are a result of our federal control over residency training.

# Uncivil Law

———

*"The market economy involves peaceful cooperation. It bursts*
*asunder when the citizens turn into warriors and, instead of*
*exchanging commodities and services, fight one another."*

*- LUDWIG VON MISES*

SOMETHING THAT SERIOUSLY UNDERMINES A free market is the power of the
courts to take away the fruits of someone's labor, and indebt him for years,
through malpractice awards. Liberty includes the right to benefit from your
own labor, without having the results of your efforts taken from you.

Some people, like Amitai Etzioni, writing for the Los Angeles Times, say
we need to sue much more often when things go wrong medically.[1] He says
that since bad things happen frequently in medical care, we need to have
many more lawsuits, in order to keep doctors in line. This chapter will examine what would happen if people sued whenever they had a bad outcome
with a doctor. First, I will describe how tort law came to be, and what the
purpose of it was.

Common law developed in England, as a set of "laws" that became law
through precedent. That is, when there was no law that had been enacted
through legislation, but a judge made a ruling on a case, that was taken as
precedent in similar cases. Common law, then, is the "unwritten law."

The concept of tort is a subset of common law. Tort describes injuries committed on others outside of criminal offenses. Because it is based on precedent, not statutory law, tort has grown to include more and more actionable causes throughout history. Earlier in history, willful actions or gross negligence were required to sustain a tort case. Essentially, when blameworthy conduct resulted in another person sustaining a loss, the person who was to blame was forced by the courts to compensate the injured party for their losses. It expanded ever more, beyond financial losses, into areas of pain and suffering and such things as the years went by. Tort has now expanded to the point where reasonable actions, if they result in unexpected bad consequences, can be punished under tort law, even if no blameworthy conduct is found.

For example, it would seem reasonable for McDonalds to sell coffee that is hot. When someone sustained a burn from that hot coffee, McDonalds was punished. People who do reasonable things are often punished under tort law. Doctors are often punished when they do reasonable things but bad outcomes happen, as is the nature of human health.

A look at simple probabilities, regarding medical malpractice, is quite ominous indeed. Medicine is all based on probabilities. It is not exact. Its outcomes are not entirely predictable. Doctors are trained to do what is most likely to result in a good outcome, given the information available.

The medical literature is filled with statements on the incidence and prevalence of whatever disorder is being discussed. When relating the signs and symptoms of any illness, they are given in percentages. In other words, lists of the findings of a disease are given, with each symptom having the percentage of patients that have the disease who have that particular symptom. If a classic combination of symptoms is discussed, a good medical book will often state the percentage of patients who have that disease who also have that combination of symptoms. No illness has any set of physical findings that is 100% accurate for the disease. It is all based on likelihood, or probability. Even lab testing is not 100% accurate for whatever is being tested.

Suppose that a patient has a one in a thousand probability of having some serious condition that should not be missed. Consider a headache patient.

Most patients coming in with what seems to be a fairly typical tension head-ache or migraine have at least a one in a thousand chance of that headache being an intracranial bleed, a tumor, or meningitis (a life-threatening infec-tion). It would take a CT scan, lumbar puncture, and/or MRI to rule out those conditions.

To tell an uninsured patient that two thousand dollars worth of testing should be done to rule out a one in a thousand chance of something serious would be ridiculous. Patients cannot afford that, and they would not get it done. To order that kind of testing for every insured patient for a typical headache would get the doctor fired from his group practice for overutiliza-tion. If he is in solo practice, but is on a preferred provider network, that network would drop him for overutilization. If it is a Medicaid or Medicare patient, he would be denied payment for unnecessary testing, and might be investigated for fraud charges if the habit persists. In any case, whoever is get-ting the bill for this kind of testing, would shun the doctor.

A stomachache, that appears for all the world to be viral gastroenteritis (stomach flu that should clear up on its own), has a small chance of being ap-pendicitis. Typical heartburn or costochondritis (harmless chest wall pain), has a small chance of being coronary artery disease (life-threatening heart pain). A garden variety joint or bone pain could be a malignant case of osteo-sarcoma (cancer). Any sick baby might have meningitis, as the signs can be very nonspecific. Most patients have a small chance of something very serious that should not be missed, but would require expensive testing to rule out the dangerous disorder.

Yet, if a doctor sees several thousand patients per year, each having a one in a thousand chance of something serious that should not be missed, those odds are going to turn up on the wrong side of the coin several times per year, with possible lawsuits resulting. So unless a doctor orders expensive testing for most patients whose clinical picture is classic for minor disorders, he is go-ing to miss serious problems at an unacceptable frequency.

What, then, is an unacceptable frequency of missing serious problems? From a financial perspective, if the doctor is forced by the courts to pay more than he can bear, and is therefore unable to support his family and pay his debts, then that is an unacceptable frequency. From a moral viewpoint, some people say that any bad outcome is unacceptable, and should be punished.

If a doctor expects to make a living, he is compelled to observe the financial perspective. How often, then, can he be sued, and still make a living? This, again, is a mathematical argument. This author just loves math. A few assumptions need to be made. Let us assume that a doctor needs to pay $25,000 per year for student loan and/or startup loan debt, and that he needs to make $50,000 per year to support his family, a fairly paltry amount. That adds up to $75,000 per year, in after-lawsuit income. Suppose that his pre-lawsuit income is $150,000, which is near the national average for family practice. If a mistake or bad outcome costs a doctor half a million dollars on average, then it takes 6.7 years to make that half a million dollars and still have the necessary income to continue. This comes from the following:

$$500,000 + 75,000*y = 150,000*y, \text{ where } y = \text{number of years}$$
$$y = 6.7$$

Suppose that he sees 6,250 patients per year. That means that a typical doctor would need to see 41,667 patients, with one serious bad outcome, to make the money to pay for that one bad outcome, and still support his family and pay his debts.

Ordering tests, to make sure he does not miss a serious disorder, therefore needs to be done for any condition that is estimated to have at least a one in 42,000 probability of occurring. Any less testing would result in a frequency of misses that is financially unacceptable to the doctor. Testing based on a one in 42,000 threshold, however, is financially unacceptable to whoever is paying for the testing. It is thus a catch-22 situation. Testing cannot be ordered frequently enough to avoid lawsuits that would financially cripple a doctor, because to do so would financially cripple patients and insurance companies.

Some people think that doctors should be able to make the correct diagnosis without expensive testing. This is usually true. However, no doctor is so close to perfect that he makes the right diagnosis 99.998% of the time based on history and physical exam. That is what would be required if he is to continue to support his family, if people sued whenever there was a bad outcome. That 1 in 42,000 missed diagnosis rate translates into a 99.998% rate of being right. We do not even have lab tests that are that good.

Most emergency physicians practice "defensive medicine," which is simply the ordering of more tests to try to catch more of the low-probability serious diseases. This raises ER costs to levels that most people cannot afford. Even ER doctors, however, do not order tests at a threshold of anything approaching the 1 in 42,000 probability. They end up getting sued frequently, because even they do not order tests often enough to keep up with the odds. I once attended a meeting of doctors lobbying the North Carolina legislature, in which an emergency physician I knew stood up and said that 80% of the tests he orders are just "defensive medicine." Of course, while this raises the costs of ER visits, it is still probably not enough to protect himself from lawsuits, when the actual probabilities are considered, as above.

Basically, doctors just hope that patients will not sue them if there is a bad outcome. They are often sued even if no mistake is made; there was just a bad outcome even though the doctor did everything right. Jurors simply feel sorry for the patient or the loved ones of the patient, and even though they might recognize that the doctor did nothing wrong, they feel that the patient deserves something.

Not all, perhaps not even most, bad outcomes are a result of bad medicine. Every procedure has an expected rate of complications which is not zero. The procedure is undertaken if the probability of benefit exceeds the probability of risk. Even diagnostic tests carry risk. For example, a lumbar puncture (spinal tap) occasionally causes nerve damage, spinal headache, or infection. Yet in many cases, not doing the lumbar puncture carries a much higher risk of untreated fatal meningitis. The procedure is done because the perceived benefits outweigh the risks.

I personally know a surgeon who had the following experience. He was sued when the patient had a bad result, and he ended up getting hit with a

$300,000 judgment. He heard about the jury deliberations later. The jurors did not find that he did anything wrong, but they felt that the patient deserved money because they felt sorry for her, since she suffered.

But doctors do not need to pay for lawsuits; malpractice insurance companies do, you might say. Then where do the insurance companies get the money to pay for the lawsuits? Mostly from the doctors, of course. They have to collect enough money through premiums, and return on investments of those premiums, to pay for the jury awards, settlements, costs of defense, administration, and still have some profit. Doctors therefore have to make enough money on average to pay the costs of the lawsuits. The insurance only distributes the risks among doctors.

Fortunately, the typical patient that has a bad outcome does not sue. "The percentage of patients injured by medical negligence who actually bring suit is very small. Estimates range from one-in-eight to one-in-ten."[2] This is what prevents the whole system from falling apart. If this changes, then the probabilities discussed above will crush us. Doctors will simply not be able to make a living. When people cannot make a living being doctors, then we will not have doctors.

So what is the average monetary effect of someone filing a lawsuit? In 2002, the nationwide average jury verdict in a medical malpractice lawsuit was $6.2 million. The percentage of jury verdicts that were awarded to the plaintiff was 42% in 2002. The median (not the average, but the median) settlement in 2004 was $1,000,000.[3] This means that 50% of settlements were for less than $1,000,000, and 50% of settlements were for more.

What the average result is of a patient initiating lawsuit actions is very difficult to say. It is not simply a matter of the average jury award, multiplied by the likelihood of winning the case. That figure in 2002 would equal $6.2 million times 0.42, or $2.6 million. Adding the cost of defense to that would give the average for cases that go to trial. Then there are all the cases that do not go to trial. They get settled or dropped. The average amount of cost to a doctor when a lawsuit is initiated varies tremendously by state. Assuming half a million in the earlier probability analysis is probably going a bit low for the nationwide average. It is probably reasonably close for one of the better states, such as Idaho, where I practice.

The cost to society of our lawsuit, or tort, system is very high. This includes the cost of defensive medicine. PricewaterhouseCoopers estimates that a total of 10% of the cost of health insurance premiums is consumed by medical liability and defensive medicine, which they define as "where doctors, in order to mitigate the threat of lawsuits, order tests and procedures they believe are not medically necessary."[4]

Pacific Research Institute did an exhaustive study of the effects of our litigation system on Americans, including all industries rather than just healthcare. They find that the total annual cost, to a family of four, of excessive litigation is an astonishing $9,827.[5] This includes indirect costs such as loss of innovations, productivity, and jobs.

Many malpractice insurance companies have simply left the market. They have pulled out of certain geographical areas, or stopped insuring certain specialties. Some have gone out of business completely. This is because they have been losing money.

In insurance terms, the "combined ratio" is the ratio of operating expenses and losses to premiums. This tells how much of a loss is made before investment income. A combined ratio of 123 means that $1.23 is paid for every $1 of premium taken in, for a loss of 23 cents. Anything over 100 represents a loss on the premium dollar. The combined ratio that is needed to break even in medical malpractice is estimated to be 114.5.[6]

Insurance companies invest their premiums, so they end up with more revenue than if they just let the money sit, waiting for claims to pay. Investment income can only compensate for so much loss, however. This investment is one of the reasons that the break-even point is not at a combined ratio of 100. Note in the following graph that the combined ratio has climbed to 165 by 2002.

Annual Combined Ratios[7]

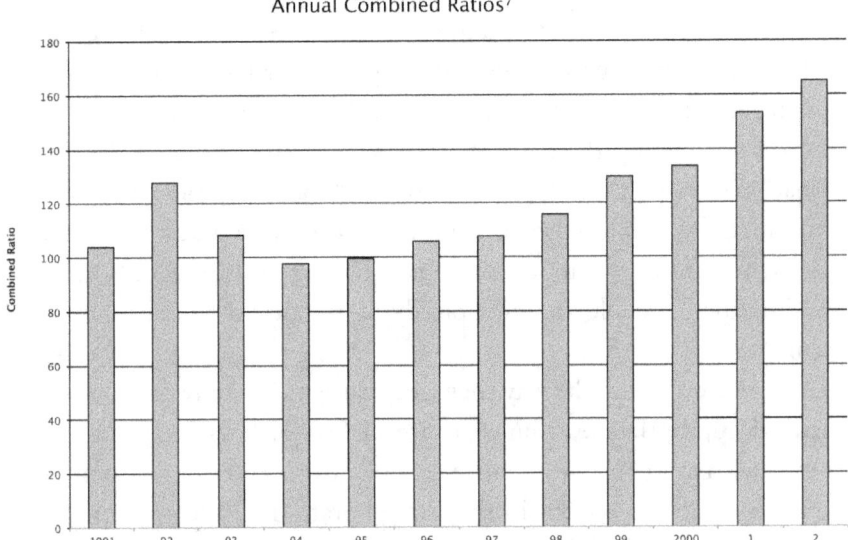

The insurance industry realized that they were underpricing, and had to start dramatically increasing their premiums to keep up with their outlays. Yet, the increases in premiums have not been able to keep up with higher claims. Why were their outlays so high? Lawsuits, of course. The only way to keep insurance premiums down is to keep lawsuit payouts down. This would seem to be common sense.

I have spoken to the executives of two different medical tourism companies. Medical tourism will be explored further in a later chapter. The salient point to the malpractice discussion is that both of them, when asked if they would open a United States facility, cited litigation first among their reasons why they would not.

Litigation, and the fear of it, often keeps good products off the market or prevents people from using them. For example, automated external defibrillators (AEDs) can be lifesaving in a case of ventricular fibrillation, commonly referred to as cardiac arrest. The devices are virtually idiot-proof. They have clear, simple instructions on how to apply them, they verbally tell you what to do, they analyze the heart rhythm for you, and they tell you if you should push the button to deliver a shock. Yet, fear of a lawsuit deters their use. A fitness center would seem to be a great place to keep an AED. People occasionally have heart attacks while exercising. A journal that is geared toward the managers of these facilities said in 2005 that many owners of these facilities are not buying the devices. The article further stated that "IHRSA [International Health, Racquet, and Sportsclub Association] has concluded that the adequate liability protection is not yet in place that would allow businesses or their employees to feel safe about having or using AEDs in an emergency situation."[8] People are therefore dying because of lawsuits and the fear of them.

Doctors are altering the way they treat patients in many cases, not because of medical appropriateness, but because of fear of lawsuits. Many doctors have stopped practicing in certain areas of health care for the same reason. The rate of cesarean sections in the United States in 2006 was up to 31% of births.[9] A great many of these are done for fear of lawsuits being filed if anything is wrong with the baby and a c-section was not done quickly enough.

A leader in his field, John Edwards won tens of millions of dollars from doctors, claiming that they caused cerebral palsy because of lack of timely c-sections. One case brought an award of over $23 million in 1997.[10] He "pioneered the art of blaming psychiatrists for patients who commit suicide and blaming doctors for delivering babies with cerebral palsy."[11]

Of course, if somebody really wants to commit suicide, there is nothing a doctor can do to stop that from happening. He can only decrease the risk in many cases. A person cannot, and should not, be kept locked up indefinitely to protect him from himself. That is what would be required to ensure that somebody does not kill himself.

John Edwards argued some of the cerebral palsy cases after scientific studies showed that what happened during the birth period had very little to do with cerebral palsy. It was usually a problem that occurred well before delivery.[12] Increasing rates of cesarean sections resulted in no decreases in the rates of cerebral palsy.[13] These things were known to doctors before many of the cerebral palsy cases were argued by Edwards.

I cannot imagine that John Edwards was unaware of the scientific evidence that ran contrary to his arguments. It certainly appears that he was just in it for the money and power. In his final year of practicing law, 1997, his adjusted gross income was reported as $11.4 million.[14]

North Carolina doctors feared Edwards' tremendous courtroom charisma. "'The John Edwards we know crushed [obstetrics, gynecology] and neurosurgery in North Carolina,' said Dr. Craig VanDerVeer, a Charlotte neurosurgeon. 'As a result, thousands of patients lost their health care.'"[15]

Only about 15% of new family physicians now deliver babies. Fear of litigation is the most commonly cited reason. During my residency in North Carolina, I even met a veteran obstetrician/gynecologist who changed to gynecology only. This is someone specially trained to deliver babies, who has stopped doing it, and confined himself to other female-related care. This phenomenon is not isolated. Nationally, one in seven members of the American College of Obstetricians and Gynecologists (ACOG) has quit practicing obstetrics because of fear of lawsuits.[16] Is their fear justified? It would seem so. Over three quarters of ACOG fellows had been sued at least once, and almost half had been sued at least three times.[17]

Neurosurgeons are hit especially hard by lawsuits. Neurosurgery is a high risk field. As a master of the painfully obvious, I point out that performing surgery involving the brain, spinal cord, or peripheral nerves is usually done on people who are at high risk for death or disability. Yet, that subtlety seems to be lost on our judicial system. Nationally, neurosurgeons are sued an average of once every 18 to 24 months.[18] Every year, about half of the neurosurgeons in the United States is sued.[19] In New York State, 70% of neurosurgeons have been sued in the five years ending in 2004, at an average of three suits each.[20]

Can it be that most neurosurgeons are incompetent fools? Not likely. They are generally very intelligent, skilled, and caring people. Otherwise, they would not brave the treacherous field of neurosurgery. To restate the obvious, a person is not going to undergo surgery involving his brain, spinal cord, or peripheral nerves unless he is at high risk of death or disability without the surgery. Many of these surgeries are inherently dangerous, some more so than others. They are performed when the risk of not having them done is greater than the risk of having them done.

If we, as a society, sue neurosurgeons out of existence, then what will we do? Well, we can always sue the hospital for not being able to find a neurosurgeon to perform an emergency surgery. When somebody died from a brain bleed, that is what her family did. The hospital faced a lack of neurosurgical emergency services because the doctors were afraid of lawsuits.[21] What if this becomes a trend, and our hospitals have to shut down emergency services? Who will we sue then? How does this help bring us better health care?

This is the legacy of John Edwards and others like him. Fees have been forced to increase. Doctors alter their treatment decisions, often to the detriment of their patients, to guard against lawsuits. Doctors also avoid doing certain procedures due to their well-justified fear of lawsuits. They are leaving certain areas and high risk specialties.

It has been said of our "civil" law system, "Every time you get involved with the legal system, the way it is ... you feel like you're walking through a hog lot, barefoot."[22] I hesitate to use the word civil, when discussing "civil" law. It is anything but civil.

# Food and Drug Administration

———

*"When buying and selling are controlled by legislation, the*
*first things to be bought and sold are legislators."*

*- P.J. O'ROURKE*

IN AMERICA, THE OLDER GENERIC drugs are generally quite affordable, but we pay extremely high prices for the newer, brand name drugs. Once again, if there is some area of the economy that does not seem to make sense; i.e., that does not seem to follow normal market principles, look for some sort of government intervention that is distorting the free market. As a general rule, free markets work, leading to increasing quality in goods and services at affordable prices. Government intervention typically leads to high prices, shortages, and declining quality. An exploration of the problems with pharmaceuticals leads the honest evaluator clearly to the Food and Drug Administration.

The FDA distorts the free market, bringing in enormous political and financial pressures that drive prices up and keep good drugs out of the American marketplace. The FDA demands such lengthy and expensive trials that it costs an astonishing amount of money to bring the average new drug onto the United States market. Tufts University, with information supplied from drug makers, estimated the average cost to be $802 million.[1] This is probably the most widely quoted study. An often cited, more recent study, by Bain & Company, finds the cost to be approximately $1.7 billion, up 55% from 1995 to 2000.[2] This $1.7 billion obviously needs to be paid for, by profits on the drugs that survive FDA scrutiny.

The Bain study also determined that the annual return on investment has dropped to 5%.[3] This is a measure of the profitability of an industry. 5% is well below most industries, and makes pharmaceuticals an unattractive place for investment. Only one of every thirteen drugs that have reached the pre-clinical testing phase now reaches pharmacy shelves.[4] The average time for a new drug to get from the lab to the consumer is 12 years.[5] Only one of every 1,000 drugs that begin laboratory testing reach human studies.[6]

So what? What's the big deal about making "Big Pharma" spend money? They have too much money already! This is the big deal: If $1,000 for a one month prescription of a medicine apalls you, then realize that it takes 1.7 million of those prescriptions to be bought and paid for in order to pay the $1.7 billion in research for the average drug. This is just the research cost, not including production cost or any profit. So do not blame "Big Pharma" if they charge you so much for medications. Blame whatever it is that is making them spend so much money to get a drug to market. Blame the FDA.

A major FDA market distortion is the pressure to keep drugs off the market. Many drugs are available in Europe that cannot legally be purchased in the United States. There is no "pro-choice" mentality at work with regard to pharmaceuticals in America. If two mutually consenting adults want to conduct a transaction, medicine in exchange for money, based on the informed choice of the individuals involved, they cannot do it without the permission of the U.S. federal government. An analysis of risk versus benefit, by the person whose body will be affected by the drug, is of no relevance without FDA permission. "I can do what I want with my own body" holds no weight with the FDA.

The reason that good drugs, which are available elsewhere, are not available in the United States, has to do with incentives that influence FDA regulators. If a drug would save a thousand lives, but cost one life, then that one death has by far the most political influence. The drug must therefore not be allowed, or heads will roll at the FDA. There is a great deal of press, and even congressional hearings, associated with negative outcomes of FDA approved drugs. There is no meaningful public reaction to the loss of lives caused by drugs not being allowed to be sold. Because of this, an FDA regulator is under tremendous pressure to not allow a drug onto the market that might have negative consequences, even though the positive effects might outweigh the risk a thousand fold. Consumers are not allowed to make the decision of risk vs. benefit themselves, or in consultation with a doctor or pharmacist, and are often left to die or suffer needlessly because that choice is taken away from them.

There have certainly been cases when the FDA has kept unsafe drugs off the market. These cases are celebrated as proof that the FDA is proper and good for us. However, the times when they prevent Americans from obtaining life-saving medications do not receive much attention.

Many times, drugs finally do make it to the United States marketplace, after being available in other countries for many years. The suffering and death that occurs in America during that time of delay is often enormous.

The FDA delayed approval of propranolol, a beta-blocker type of cardiovascular drug, until 1968, 3 years after it was available in Europe. They did not approve it for the treatment of hypertension and angina (heart related chest pain) until 1978. Because of delays in approving beta-blockers in the United States, the loss of life was probably in the tens of thousands.[7]

Approval of lovastatin, the first "statin" type cholesterol lowering drug, was delayed for 3 years after its introduction in Europe. It is estimated that 1,000 people may have needlessly died from heart attacks during those 3 years.[8]

Tissue Plasminogen Activator (TPA) is a drug that breaks down blood clots that cause strokes and heart attacks. In 1985, a study on TPA was stopped prematurely because it was proving to be so much more effective than the comparison drug, that the researchers could not ethically continue to treat the control group with the comparison drug. In spite of this, FDA regulators hemmed and hawed for over two years, rejecting the application, and then finally granting approval.[9] The list of delayed approvals of life-saving and life-improving drugs goes on and on. No matter how much a physician and patient want to use a drug, they cannot do it if the regulators at the FDA say no.

Dr. Mary Ruwart, a veteran pharmaceutical researcher, estimates that about half of potential innovations are thwarted by FDA regulation. Many drugs that could be very beneficial never reach the market at all because of this. She cites, as an example, a drug to treat fibrotic liver disease that could not be developed because of the regulatory morass. There is very little to offer these patients. Research on the drug had to be dropped because patent protections could expire before the drug was approved. She estimates that millions of lives have been lost due to unavailability of drugs, as a result of FDA regulations. This dwarfs, in her opinion, the number of lives that have been saved by the FDA.[10]

A medication called colchicine has been used for many decades to effectively treat painful attacks of gout. Until 2009 it was available for about ten cents per pill. Suddenly the price jumped to five dollars per pill.[11] Why did it suddenly increase to fifty times its original cost? It must be those darned greedy drug companies! Colchicine is "an ancient remedy," used as early as "the first century A.D." for joint pains.[12] The problem is that the FDA granted URL Pharma, since bought by Takeda, the exclusive right to sell colchicine in 2009. They did this because URL Pharma ran a study that showed what doctors have known for a very long time, that colchicine is relatively safe and effective. URL Pharma did not develop this medication, but they now have what amounts to patent protection on it in the United States.

Perhaps this author should do a study on water, and show it to be safe and health-promoting. Would I then be able to get a monopoly on all the fresh water in the United States? How can the federal government imagine up to itself the authority to prohibit companies from selling a medication once it has been proven effective? A company cannot patent something that has been in common use for many years.

If congress needed a constitutional amendment in 1920 in order to have the authority to prohibit alcohol, then how does our federal government hallucinate unto itself the authority to prohibit the sale of colchicine, or any other drug, without a similar amendment? They do not have the authority. They simply have the armed enforcers to see that their demands are met.

If you do not believe that the FDA sends gunmen to people who do not comply with their demands, then watch the Youtube video of officers with guns drawn raiding the Rawsome Foods facility for the "crime" of selling unpasteurized milk.[13] They have also raided Amish farmers for selling raw milk. They conducted a raid with guns drawn in the office of Dr. Cal Streeter and arrested him while he was in the midst of treating patients.[14] His "crime" was treating cancer patients who had been told they were terminal, without hope, by using non-FDA approved remedies. None of his patients had complained. Even if his treatments were a bit hokey, so what? The decision whether or not to use them should not be made by some bureaucrat and enforced by gunmen. It should be made by the patients and their doctor.

Dr. Ron Paul, retired obstetrician/gynecologist and former congressman from Texas, told Congress, "The FDA prohibited consumers from learning how folic acid reduces the risk of neural tube defects [such as spina bifida] for four years after the Centers for Disease Control and Prevention recommended every woman of childbearing age take folic acid supplements to reduce neural tube defects. This FDA action contributed to an estimated 10,000 cases of preventable neural tube defects! The FDA also continues to prohibit consumers from learning about the scientific evidence that glucosamine and chondroitin sulfate are effective in the treatment of osteoarthritis; that omega-3 fatty acids may reduce the risk of sudden death heart attack; and that calcium may reduce the risk of bone fractures."[15]

The Competitive Enterprise Institute commissioned a nation-wide poll of cardiologists (heart specialists) and oncologists (cancer specialists) on the issue of FDA interference, and its effect on patients' lives. Among other questions, they asked the doctors about their agreement with the statement, "The additional time it takes for the FDA to approve drugs and medical devices costs lives by forcing people to go without potentially beneficial therapies." 57% of cardiologists and 47% of oncologists agreed with the statement. On the statement "The FDA is too slow in approving new drugs and medical devices," 65% of cardiologists and 77% of oncologists agreed.[16]

This is the result of allowing government regulators to make life and death decisions concerning our medical treatment. They do not just help us to make an informed decision. They make the decisions for us, and enforce those decisions with the police powers of the state.

While the FDA drives the cost of research and development through the roof, the drug companies cannot recoup their costs in other countries. They need to recover their R&D costs primarily in the United States. This results in name brand drugs being much more expensive for Americans than, for example, Canadians.

Drug companies cannot increase their prices in Canada and other similar countries, thereby allowing a lowering of prices in America, because the socialist nations tell the drug companies what they are willing to pay. If the drug companies do not agree, there is nothing to stop other countries from ignoring patents and making the drugs themselves.

Regarding the increasing number of generic medications that are becoming unavailable, a congressional investigation laid the blame for that largely at the feet of the FDA also. According to the report, "the widespread shortages are causing inferior treatment regimens, higher health care costs, and even premature death ... information obtained by the Committee on Oversight and Government Reform shows that the crisis was largely sparked by actions of the Food and Drug Administration (FDA). The Committee has learned that FDA regulatory activity has effectively shut down 30% of the total manufacturing capacity at four of America's largest producers of generic injectable medications ... 58% of the drugs on the shortage list were produced by at least one facility undergoing FDA remediation."[17] They found that the FDA was not shutting down drug makers as a result of any actual harm caused by negligent manufacturing processes. "Among shuttered manufacturing lines that occurred over the previous two years, the committee's review did not find any instances where the shutdown was associated with reports of drugs harming customers."[18] The shortages are primarily the result of the FDA being overzealous in their regulatory activities.

Along with their other impacts on drug availability, the regulatory difficulties caused by the FDA have driven the producers of the ingredients out of the United States, in order to escape that burden. According to the New York

Times, "the crucial ingredients for nearly all antibiotics, steroids and many other lifesaving drugs are now made exclusively in China."[19]

For our desire for safety and security, we are paying a very high price. By turning our personal decisions over to a federal regulatory agency, we end up with extremely expensive drugs. We delay the use of beneficial medications for years. In many cases, we never obtain the use of potentially life-saving medicines. Even when medications have been used effectively for decades, many are now becoming unavailable. We are regulating ourselves to death.

# Licensure – Protecting Ourselves From Our Own Decisions

───

*"The worst thing in this world, next to anarchy, is government."*

*- HENRY WARD BEECHER*

ANOTHER AREA OF INTERFERENCE WITH the free market is licensure. Nearly everybody in health care needs the permission of government to practice his craft. Doctors, pharmacists, nurses, optometrists, respiratory therapists, etc., all need government permission to practice.

Some would argue that we have to have a government permission process for highly skilled professionals, in order to protect society. Yet, automotive specialists, computer specialists, and many other highly skilled craftsmen have managed to ply their trades for years without destroying society, in spite of the lack of a government permission slip.

It is obvious to most people that government workers are not shining examples of competence and dedication to service. They are usually thought of, often correctly in my estimation, as functioning at the height of ineptitude. One need look no further than the rollout of Obamacare as an example of this. The launching of Obamacare has been compared to the launching of the space shuttle Challenger. Why, then, should we turn to government bureaucrats to protect us from the ineptitude of highly trained professionals?

Professional associations and boards do a much better job of ensuring proper skills than government bureaucrats do. Much more importantly, the court of public opinion would see to the success or failure of someone who is practicing a skilled trade. A practitioner's reputation of skill and knowledge would become known, and lead to that person's level of success. If people want to go to a quack, then that should be their choice. More likely, as with other tradesmen, a good reputation would bring the business to a good doctor, and those who do a poor job would not get much business.

"Preferred provider" networks and licensure now limit the number of doctors who a patient is able to see, which leads to a steady flow of patients for bad doctors as well as good ones. The criteria for choosing a doctor now are not quality and service, but whether a doctor has the permission of government to practice medicine, is on the patient's insurance network, and is not booked up for the next month.

A doctor getting onto a preferred provider network is not a measurement of quality. It is just a matter of being willing to accept the contracted payment, after meeting minimum qualifications.

From a moral perspective, we should be able to choose for ourselves how to care for our own bodies. It is not the place of government to protect us from ourselves. That is contrary to the principles of proper government. People can choose to lay around and drink beer all day if they want to. I do not agree with that choice, but it is right that people are able to make the choice for themselves. How odd, that in a society that calls itself "pro-choice," people cannot choose the health care that they want.

Licensure leads to a decrease in competition and choice. It leads to shortages and increased waiting times. By limiting entry into a field, people have fewer practitioners from which to choose. Those who are licensed therefore become overbooked.

Board certification is dependent upon completion of a residency in the specialty. This would probably work just fine, if not for government control of residency positions, through the Medicare program.[1] There is no free market at work in residencies when federal bureaucrats decide how many residents, and in what specialties, get trained.

If not for government control, specialties with longer waiting times for patients would soon have increased residency positions, as those fields would begin to have more appeal. That happens much more quickly in a free market, where individuals respond to market pressures. Changes like that lag by many years under central government control.

That is one reason that shortages were so severe in the Soviet Union. Factory managers could not decide to change production to meet changing demand. They received orders from central planners, who could not possibly efficiently respond to all the changing demands of an entire economy. The results were shortages that would astonish ordinary Americans.

Physician licensure reminds me of the clever article I once read about the dangers of "home feeding." I do not remember where I saw it. In a satire about the concern over the safety of allowing home schooling, someone addressed the dangers inherent to allowing unlicensed parents to feed their children. All manner of health risks were present. Food borne illness, malnutrition, obesity, and injuries from sharp kitchenware were all possibilities, when we allow people who are not properly trained and certified, to feed their own children.

It may seem absurd to talk about licensing parents to feed their children. Yet, we carry it another step when we not only will not allow parents to medically care for their children, but we will not even allow adults to care for themselves without a government permission slip.

Barbers, beauticians, "nail technologists," and morticians must be licensed in Idaho.[2] Our fingernails will thus be kept safe, and dead people will be protected from dangerous morticians. Safe from what, I am not sure. In the attempt to keep us safe from incompetent providers of service, in Louisiana they license the highly dangerous practice of professional floral arrangement.[3] There will be no reckless and irresponsible florists at large down in the Bayou.

Aside from the obvious loss of freedom, the question of whether licensing of professionals improves quality is open to debate. There is no solid body of evidence that licensing protects us. Rather, there have been several studies, with contradictory results. This is a very difficult subject to study.

Measurements of quality in these studies of licensure have been very questionable. Criteria such as type of equipment, or whether or not practitioners advertise have been used. Often used, as quality measurements, are self-reports or peer reviews, or attendance of continuing education. It can certainly be argued that these are not true measurements of quality of care. Some studies have shown that when licensing is more restrictive, people more often substitute care from other types of professionals, or go without care. Stanley J. Gross of the Cato Institute summarized this body of research and concluded that the case has not been made that licensing improves quality, in order to justify the attendant loss of freedom that licensing produces. Indeed, he concludes, because of substitution and lack of availability, quality of care often suffers.[4]

I have a patient who almost choked to death as a child because of a licensed dentist who had narcolepsy. He fell asleep while working on the patient, and dropped a tooth down his throat. He now needs sedation every time he gets dental work done, because of the resultant anxiety. This patient agrees with me that in the absence of government licensure, that dentist would probably not be able to get the patients he does, because there would be more competition. Especially in this age of social media, reputation would become very important to the ability of a doctor to get business. With licensure, options are much more limited. A narcoleptic dentist is able to stay in business, because there are not enough dentists from which to choose.

What seems obvious is that licensing limits the entry of people into a field, thereby decreasing the availability of practitioners in that field. This has the potential to lead to shortages of skilled professionals, with the inevitable waiting times and higher prices that shortages bring. A seven-month waiting time to get in to see a rheumatologist would result in more people learning the skill of rheumatology, in a free market. In a market controlled by government allocation of residency slots, and licensing restrictions, we just continue to wait.

# State Insurance Mandates

———

A PROBLEM THAT DRIVES UP the cost of health insurance is mandatory coverage. Certain specified services have to be covered in order to legally sell an insurance policy. If two consenting adults want to conduct a transaction, health insurance in exchange for money, government force will be applied to prevent that transaction unless those things that government specifies are covered. A person wanting insurance might not want coverage for, say, alcohol treatment, because he does not foresee a reasonable possibility of becoming addicted to alcohol. An insurance agent might be perfectly willing to sell that policy to him, avoiding the cost of the extra coverage. Yet, if they attempt to make that transaction, the force of government will be deployed against them. We have given government bureaucrats the power to decide what should be left up to the individuals involved. This drives up the cost of insurance, because a great many coverage specifications are forced upon the consumer.

Suppose a Jehovah's Witness does not want to pay for coverage for bone marrow transplantation. Georgians and others have empowered their rulers to say that bone marrow transplantation must be covered or an insurance policy cannot be sold.[1] It does not matter if the consumer does not want it, and an insurer would be willing to sell the policy without it. It is illegal.

A Mormon bishop in Utah could not purchase health insurance without alcoholism being covered. A marathon runner in Indiana could not get insurance without coverage for morbid obesity. A Catholic nun could not buy health insurance without contraceptive coverage in 31 states. Hair prosthesis coverage is mandated in 10 states.[2]

Somebody might realize that while it is possible to develop a mandated condition, it is extremely unlikely and therefore wasteful to spend money to insure against it. The marathoner may become disabled or just get lazy, and put on a couple of hundred pounds. Suppose he does not want to spend money to insure against that possibility? Is it really the place of government to employ deadly force to prevent him from obtaining an insurance policy without that coverage? Remember, a government mandate does not mean gentle persuasion. It means men with guns enforcing their mandates.

Insurance mandates drive up the cost of health insurance, by not allowing us to tailor our policies to what we decide is best for us, based on the risks that we want to guard against. How much do they drive up costs? It was found that mandating chemical dependency treatment raises premiums by an average of 9%, psychiatric hospitalization raises premiums by 13%, routine dental services by 15%, and psychologist visits by 12%.[3]

While a 9% increase may not seem like much, when all the mandates are taken into account they become very expensive. The Council for Affordable Health Insurance has counted 1,961 mandates nationwide, for an average of 38 per state.[4] It has been estimated that between 20 and 25 percent of those who lack health insurance do so because of insurance mandates.[5] That was the case before Obamacare, which has made the situation worse.

Even politicians who call themselves conservative often jump on the bandwagon of trying to protect people by legislating their personal priorities onto them. Senator Jesse Helms, for example, wanted to force everybody who buys health insurance to pay for colon cancer screening.[6] I heartily recommend colonoscopies every ten years for people over 50, or earlier if there is a greatly increased risk, for people who can afford it. However, to be forced to pay increased premiums to cover the expected expense of routine screening would raise the cost.

The purpose of insurance is to spread risk, so that an individual does not bear the full risk of devastating conditions. A small number of people develop very expensive conditions, and it is unknown beforehand who those people will be. Large numbers of people pool their risk by purchasing insurance. Then those who do incur large costs have those costs absorbed by the larger group of people, through their premiums.

Pre-paying for expected services is not insurance at all. It does not pool risk. It merely causes people to pay for the service through their premiums, plus administrative costs and profit for the insurance company. Some people would still choose to do this, but those who would avoid wasting their money on such foolishness should not have it forced upon them by politicians.

There are large differences in insurance premiums from state to state, largely because of different levels of mandates. In 2004, the average cost for a single person for an individual policy in New Jersey was $4,080 per year, when just across the river in Pennsylvania that cost was $1,656 per year.[7] Why would any fairly healthy person in New Jersey buy a health insurance policy, under these kinds of costly rules?

People who argue for specific mandates often do so because a loved one suffered from the specified condition. However, that does not mean that everybody has the same risk, or would even welcome the mandated treatment. Not everybody would accept a hair prosthesis even if it was free. The Mormon bishop might not want to pay an additional 9% for chemical dependency treatment. He may instead choose simply to live according to his faith, avoiding any need for such treatment. People may want to simply pay out of pocket for certain things, instead of having to pay more through increased premiums.

Liberty suffers when government is put in charge of writing insurance policies through mandated benefits. Individuals are more suited to make their own decisions, and should have the freedom to do so. Premiums increase, and people go without health insurance, when bureaucrats make those decisions.

Advocates of mandates say that evil insurance companies would not cover certain things if not for government force. What they fail to realize, is that if the patient was the customer, then insurance companies would compete with each other to attract their business, by offering more attractive policies. Instead, the employer is usually the customer now. This problem stems not from a lack of insurance mandates, but from tax incentives that bind health insurance to employment.

Then there is the moral issue of allowing people to conduct business the way they see fit. It is hard to see the morality behind preventing two mutually consenting adults from conducting a transaction, health insurance in exchange for money. Health insurance is not something which is inherently illegal or immoral. When someone wants to offer such a product, and another wants to purchase it, why should government define the terms of the transaction? Using government to protect us from ourselves is not the solution to health insurance problems. It is in many ways the cause of those problems.

# "Privacy" Regulations That Will Disclose Your Health Information

─────

*"We've got the NSA getting logs of every call you make.*
*The IRS is weaponized like Richard Nixon could only have dreamed of."*

- CONGRESSMAN LOUIE GOHMERT

ANOTHER WAY THAT WE TRY to use government to protect us, and end up worsening our situation, is through the Health Insurance Portability and Accountability Act (HIPAA). This was passed ostensibly to protect the privacy of patients, but actually has the opposite effect. It opens up patient records to many people without patient consent. It costs doctors a great deal of money, which of course ends up costing patients money.

Most patients do not realize that their privacy protection has actually been lost due to HIPAA. Under these current regulations, if a representative of the federal Department of Health and Human Services wants the records of a doctor's patients, the doctor has to turn them over. A patient cannot refuse the request. A doctor cannot refuse to disclose the medical information.[1] The patients do not even need to be told if their information has been released.[2]

Most doctors are very good about protecting the confidentiality of patients. There was not really a problem to begin with. There were occasional indiscretions, but nothing of any large scale. But now, by providing for federal health information collection from doctors, the framework for a national health information database has been established.

If a doctor avoids certain activities, including not submitting electronic insurance claims, then he can avoid being covered by HIPAA, and then he is able to protect patient records.[3] This is called the "country doctor escape clause." Either specific patient authorization or a search warrant would be needed for government agencies to get records from a doctor who is not covered by HIPAA. No reason, no warrant, and no permission is needed for any or all patient records to be seized from a HIPAA covered doctor, pharmacy, lab, insurance company, or anybody else involved with a patient's records. If one of those "privacy notices," with which most people have become familiar, is given to the patient, then that means that HIPAA has jurisdiction there, and the sanctity of patient records is at risk.

There are penalties of up to $250,000 and possible imprisonment of up to ten years for HIPAA violations.[4] Fear of HIPAA prosecutions has caused a huge compliance industry to spring up, with seminars, software, and expert consultations, which are quite costly. Compliance officers are now a part of medical practices. The American Medical Association estimated that the cost of complying with HIPAA would be about 445,000 hours and $6 million in both 2007 and 2008.[5] Of course, if doctors are forced to cough up money for compliance officers, encryption systems, seminars, etc., then patients will end up having to pay. In typical government fashion, this new regulatory mess is referred to as "administrative simplification."

For hospitals of over 400 beds, the 2003 budgets for HIPAA compliance were:

16% of hospitals:  > $1,000,000
17% of hospitals:  $500,000 - $1,000,000
47% of hospitals:  $100,000 - $500,000
20% of hospitals:  < $100,000[6]

Apparently it costs a lot of money for administrative simplification.

Patient care sometimes suffers as a result of HIPAA. I was personally told, by a member of an ambulance crew, of a lengthy delay they had in finding a patient. The dispatcher felt, correctly or not, that she could not reveal certain information to the crew, which would have helped to locate the patient.

In another case, a patient under the care of Dr. Glenn Treisman at Johns Hopkins University almost died because emergency physicians could not discuss his case with Dr. Treisman. Maria Blackburn of Johns Hopkins Magazine interviewed Dr. Treisman. "'Nobody contacted me, so we didn't collaborate on his care,' Treisman says. 'As a result, they gave him a bunch of benzos [valium class medications that are often abused] that he shouldn't have gotten, and he went out and started using them again. He relapsed into drinking and then relapsed into using cocaine after being sober for months. And then he had a very serious suicide attempt. Now it's going to cost maybe $10,000 or $15,000 to detoxify him.'"[7]

HIPAA also harms research efforts. A study conducted at the University of Michigan, comparing pre-HIPAA methods to the methods required after the implementation of HIPAA, found it very difficult and costly to obtain consent for follow-up questionaires. Their consent rate was 96% under the pre-HIPAA methods, but only 34% under post-HIPAA methods, as well as thousands of dollars of extra costs.[8] The researchers conclude that although "maintaining privacy is a laudable goal, the HIPAA Privacy Rule may create a substantial burden and prohibit the development of valuable research."[9]

Dr. Kim Eagle, senior author of the research paper, and clinical director at the University of Michigan's Cardiovascular Center, said "'We won't solve safety, quality and cost issues in health care unless we do quality research, and our findings show that HIPAA, as currently written, has the potential to hinder that effort."[10]

As Kara Gavin of UMHS Public Relations explains of the pre-HIPAA rules, "Post-hospitalization surveys are crucial to helping quality-minded hospitals like U-M assess and improve care. Patients' names and other identifying details are removed before their information is entered into a database. Doctors can use the database to find out what treatments and preventive measures help patients most, and what factors worsen their chances."[11] HIPAA can greatly harm those efforts toward improving care.

HIPAA paves the way for a national health information database. It allows for government acquisition of all health information of all patients. The next step, the framework for that database, was passed into law in 2009. The so-called "stimulus bill" of 2009 provides for a "nationwide health technology infrastructure that allows for the electronic use and accurate exchange of health information" containing "each patient's health information," and a "certified electronic health record for each person in the United States by 2014."[12] In other words, everybody in the United States was to have their health records on the internet in a government database by 2014, although the government is behind schedule on implementing it.

So, why would an internet-based national health information database be a bad thing, some might ask? It would only be bad if somebody wants to keep their privacy. If someone does not mind having their personal health information available to just anybody, then it is not important. Or, if you are a computer hacker, then this could be good news for you. Most people would be concerned.

The Fourth Amendment to the United States Constitution reads: "The right of the people to be secure in their persons, houses, papers, and effects, against unreasonable searches and seizures, shall not be violated, and no warrants shall issue, but upon probable cause, supported by oath or affirmation, and particularly describing the place to be searched, and the persons or things to be seized."[13]

Now, not only can the federal government take a person's medical records, they can do it without consent, and even if the person tries to refuse that access. It would be hard to find a more blatant violation of the Fourth Amendment protection against seizures of a person's papers or effects. Then, if the new law embedded in the stimulus act gets implemented, those health records will all be on the internet, just waiting for computer hackers to crack the system. Even if you do not have a problem with the federal government seizing your health records, are you confident in their ability to protect your privacy, or what they themselves might do with the information?

The Veterans Administration had data on 26.5 million veterans stolen from its computer systems in May 2006.[14] Tricare is another government benefits program connected with the military. In 2002, computers containing the medical records of Tricare beneiciaries were stolen from the corporate offices of TriWest. They contained personal and medical information, and Social Security numbers.[15] If you believe your government can and will protect your privacy, you are being naive. Computerized health information is obviously not safe from thieves. It will only be easier for hackers once it is on-line.

So why, then, would we trust government with our personal health information? It becomes more vulnerable to theft. Research efforts are hampered. It is not really the business of government to track the health histories of its citizens. It costs us a great deal of money. For all these reasons, HIPAA is a major setback to freedom and health care in America.

# Fraud – Inevitable When Somebody Else Pays the Bill

———

*"When one gets in bed with government, one must expect the diseases it spreads."*

*- RON PAUL*

PART OF THE REASON FOR high costs is the fraud, and the risk thereof, that is inherent to the third party payment system. Anytime someone who is far removed from the scene of the transaction gets the bill for that transaction, the potential for fraud exists. There is really no way that a third party such as a government regulator or insurance company clerk can know what happened in the exam room. They have to trust in the truthfulness of the claim, to some extent. Because they cannot legitimately trust in the honesty of everybody making claims, extensive efforts are made to catch the dishonest ones.

These efforts sometimes result in catching a miscreant who has been engaged in fraudulent billing. They also often result in chasing doctors who have been doing their level best to comply with the immense array of Medicare regulations. Either way, the cost to doctors of doing business with any third party is always high, because of regulations which are put in place to decrease fraud.

It is not just the effort to catch fraud that costs money, it is sometimes actual fraud. The General Accounting Office in 1999 reported an estimated $12.6 billion in "improper payments" for Medicare alone.[1] This does not include Medicaid, SCHIP, or private insurance companies.

What is an "improper claim?" Claimants can bill for services that had never been provided. They could be for patients who do not exist or are dead. Charges can be inflated. Services can be medically inappropriate. Facilities can be just front operations, existing only for the billing process.

In New York, Dr. Dolly Rosen billed for 991 dental procedures on a single day in September 2003. For all of 2003, Dr. Rosen and her associate collected $5.4 million from the Medicaid program.[2] 991 procedures in one day? There is no way a dentist could accomplish that. Only after the New York Times brought Dr. Rosen's practice to the attention of the state, was Dr. Rosen prosecuted.[3]

Former New York Medicaid fraud prosecutor John M. Meekins said of Medicaid, "It's like a honey pot."[4] Just like a honey pot attracts bears, Medicaid and Medicare attract crooks.

The Senate Special Committee on Aging heard testimony in 1995 of $300,000 in bills for dead patients. After questions arose, only $20,000 was deducted from the payments.[5]

The Office of the Inspector General conducted unannounced site visits to 1,581 medical equipment suppliers in south Florida. The criteria that they were checking were that the suppliers: (1) maintain a physical facility, (2) be accessible during business hours, (3) have a visible sign, (4) post hours of operation, and (5) maintain listed telephone numbers. They found that 31% of suppliers to whom Medicare had been paying money did not meet the first two criteria. Sometimes there was another business at the site, or it was vacant. Only 55% of the suppliers met all five criteria that reflect being an actual supplier of medical equipment.[6]

These types of fraud add to the taxpayer bill. Fraud against private insurers increases premiums. The regulations that are enacted to try to prevent fraud increase costs to doctors, and therefore increase fees to patients. Fraud is extremely difficult, if not impossible, to eliminate in a third party payment system.

In a free market, with the recipient of service paying the fee, an attempt at fraud would be quite obvious to the customer. In my office, I charge patients directly, at the time of service. If I were to charge a patient for substantial supplies that I did not use, the patient would know it immediately. If I run labs, I need to discuss their justification with the patient at the time I order them. If my fees seem way out of line for what I did, the patient would immediately know it. And how in the world could I charge a nonexistent or dead patient?

These immediate checks against fraud do not happen when some clerk gets the bill in some distant land, weeks after the alleged patient visit. There is no way for the clerk to know that the patient was actually there, what was done in the office, or how appropriate it was. Relatively untrained clerks often have to guess, or apply rigid rules that often do not fit exactly. This leads to con artists getting away with fraud. It also leads to problems with getting paid for completely legitimate medical care, provided by honest doctors trying to do their best for their patients. It sometimes leads not only to lack of payment, but to prosecutions of honest doctors.

Edgardo Perez-Leon was the office manager for his wife, an internist. He was sent to jail for a year because he coded patient visits which did not involve a physical exam as "office visits." These codes did not exactly match criteria for Medicaid codes. However, they were the closest match for what was done. A physical exam is not always necessary in a patient encounter. For example, some things in the psychiatric realm are like that. I often manage blood pressure by phone follow-up of patients' home blood pressure readings, without a physical exam every time. Some things are just done by history, with no physical exam being useful. To Medicaid regulators, it did not matter. The codes did not meet their criteria. The children of this unfortunate couple were sent back to Puerto Rico, to live with extended family, because their parents could no longer support them.[7]

The case of Mr. Perez-DeLeon is by no means an isolated instance. There are many more examples of fraud investigations ruining the lives of decent people who had the misfortune of running afoul of Medicare investigators. Sometimes the fraud prevention mechanisms are used maliciously to get even with honest doctors.

The office of Dr. Danny Westmoreland was invaded by federal agents who held patients, staff, and even his nine year old son at gunpoint. They then proceeded to ransack his files, in search of evidence of Medicaid fraud or drug diversion. After the case ended up in his courtroom, Judge Joseph R. Goodwin threw it out in disgust. He commented, "It is one of the most outrageous things I've ever heard of ... And if I have to call for an investigation from Washington ... I will do that because that will not happen in this district ever again. There is not justification for it." Dr. Westmoreland later learned that he had been set up by a vengeful former employee.[8]

These types of problems are inherent to any system wherein somebody else is getting the bill. The system invites fraud. The extremes to which the agencies who get the bill must resort in order to prevent fraud will always cause problems for the honest, decent people who are only trying to work within the system. With third party payment comes fraud, and with fraud comes inflated cost to everybody. Also with fraud comes imprisonment for both the dishonest charlatans and honest providers of care as well.

# False Solutions –
# Trying to Fix the System
# with More Regulations

——

# HMOs – Washington's Attempt to Rein in the Cost of Medicare and Medicaid

---

*"Government does not solve problems. It subsidizes them."*

*- RONALD REAGAN*

OUR HEALTH CARE PROBLEMS AND their causes have been explored. It is time now to look at a few solutions that have been posed, and see why they are not true solutions. After that, beneficial solutions will be put forth.

One false solution is the Health Maintenance Organization (HMO). Many people point toward HMOs as evidence that the free market does not work. After all, an HMO is an example of the free market run amuck, is it not? This could not be further from the truth. An HMO is not a free market mechanism. It is just another layer of government intervention, on top of the other layers. HMOs existed to a small extent before the HMO Act of 1973, but that legislation made some changes to them and greatly expanded their market share.

The administrators of HMOs were protected from damage lawsuits. The Employee Retirement Income Security Act (ERISA), passed in 1974, accomplished this. It preempted state courts, taking jurisdiction into federal courts, leaving as the only legal remedy, to grant the care that was denied, but not the damages that resulted from the lack of care.[1] HMOs are still tied via the tax code to employment, because premiums are not taxed if they are paid by the employer. Power to make decisions was taken away from doctors and patients and transferred to administrators, to an extent previously only seen in Medicare and in the socialized systems of other countries.

To understand what HMOs are all about, it is important to look at how they came into being. There were a few scattered HMOs in the early twentieth century. They promised care to their members for a prepaid fee. One of the most famous was run by Henry Kaiser for the workers on the Grand Coulee Dam project in 1938.[2] Henry Kaiser went on to found Kaiser Permanente, one of the largest HMOs in the United States. HMOs continued to remain a fairly small part of the insurance market in the United States up until the early 1970s.

The big event that brought HMOs into the mainstream was the creation of Medicare and Medicaid. Starting in 1965, an all-you-can-eat medical buffet opened up for beneficiaries of these programs. Of course, restraint went completely out the window, and costs began to soar.

Congress then faced the dilemma of how to control those accelerating costs, before they crushed the federal budget. They could not just start explicitly rationing care, or they would be thrown out of office. Since the one overriding issue of concern to most congressmen is staying in office, they had to find a way to limit care without being too obvious.

Senator Edward (Teddy) Kennedy and President Richard Nixon advanced a solution.[3] It was finally passed as the HMO Act of 1973. "Sometimes referred to as the father of the modern HMO movement, [Paul] Ellwood was asked in the early years of the Nixon administration to devise ways of constraining the rise in the Medicare budget. Out of those discussions evolved both a proposal to capitate HMOs for Medicare beneficiaries (which was not enacted until 1982) and the laying of the groundwork for what became the HMO Act of 1973."[4]

HMOs were a response to the rapidly escalating costs of Medicare and Medicaid. They were a small part of the health insurance industry, but in order to be able to absorb millions of Medicare and Medicaid beneficiaries, their capacity had to be increased. They were therefore forced upon the private sector, and subsidized with tax dollars.

The Act took $375 million in taxpayer money[5] ($2 billion in 2013 dollars) and put it toward strengthening the market share of HMOs. That money subsidized the creation and expansion of HMOs. This addressed the problem of start-up cost for the fledgling organizations. There were some HMOs, but they did not have the capacity to start absorbing millions of enrollees as the administration desired. So taxpayer money was fronted to meet those costs.

One of the problems with HMOs, that had to be overcome, was that employers often did not want to offer them. That was solved by requiring all employers with 25 or more employees to offer an HMO if they offered any other health insurance plans.[6] This requirement remained in place until 1995.

Another problem was that it was illegal in most states to pay a doctor to ration care. So federal law preempted state law, making it legal.[7] That way, the rationing that is so fundamental to the operation of an HMO would be allowed. Primary care doctors could be gatekeepers to care. This means they could close the gate as well as open it.

An HMO works by an enrollee paying a monthly fee in exchange for the promise of health care when it becomes necessary. The enrollee is assigned to a primary care doctor, who then makes decisions about what is necessary, provided that the administration allows it. If care costs more than the monthly fee, then the HMO loses money. If care costs less than the monthly fee, then the HMO makes a profit.

The incentive, obviously, is to withhold care, to the extent that employers would still be willing to enroll their employees. The less care provided, the greater the profit. The administrators of an HMO apply these same incentives to their gatekeepers. The more a primary care physician can hold cost down, the greater will be his financial reward. If financial incentives are not sufficient to restrain an unruly doctor who is trying to provide too much care, then there are other ways to keep costs down. Boards of review sometimes need to approve more expensive treatments. Care is also rationed by waiting times, as they do in Britain and Canada. If the waiting time for the only neurologist is six months, then a lot of neurology appointments will vanish.

Many people will go to a neurologist out of their plan, or recover, or die. Either way, the HMO will not have to pay.

Preferred provider organizations (PPOs) are a sort of a hybrid between HMOs and fee for service medicine. The doctors are not salaried employees of the organization, but they are paid by them. Most doctors are part of several different PPOs as well as Medicare and Medicaid. These organizations pay them, although not directly through salary. They also heavily manage the care that doctors provide. That is why it is called "managed care." Patients can go out of network, but it is costly for them to do that. There are utilization review managers in managed care organizations. The clout that these managers can exert is to drop a doctor from a plan. Also, through preauthorizations and other means, coverage can be denied as it is in an HMO.

The amount of people enrolled in HMOs skyrocketed beginning with the HMO Act of 1973. Soon, tens of millions of people were enrolled. In 1978, Senator Teddy Kennedy said, "As the author of the first HMO bill ever to pass the Senate, I find this spreading support for HMOs truly gratifying. Just a few years ago, proponents of health maintenance organizations faced bitter opposition from organized medicine."[8] In more recent years, he lambasted the very organizations he helped to create.[9]

It became possible for HMOs to start absorbing the Medicare and Medicaid populations next. By 2001, Medicaid had 11.9 million of its beneficiaries in HMOs, up almost a million from 2000. This growth occurred while HMO enrollment was declining in the private sector.[10] Millions of Medicare beneficiaries are also enrolled in HMOs. In 2000, a high of 15.3% of Medicare beneficiaries were enrolled in HMOs.[11] In 1998, over half of Medicaid beneficiaries were on some form of managed care.[12]

When people use the HMO example as evidence of a failure of free markets, they are clearly misdirecting their angst. HMO abuses are not proof of a market failure. They are the result of government interference in free markets. After congress drove health costs through the roof with the creation of Medicare and Medicaid, they then created HMOs in an attempt to rein in the runaway costs. In so doing, they just foisted another problem on the American people.

In essence, the Canadian health care system is a huge government-run HMO. It uses primary care physicians as gatekeepers to care. It also rations by means of shortages and waiting times. Bureaucrats decide what is medically necessary and for what they are willing to pay. Appointments disappear when the patient goes out of network (to another country), recovers, or dies while on the waiting lists. The difference is that the HMO premiums in Canada are paid in taxes, and there is no legal way to avoid enrollment. If we want the worst kind of HMO for all Americans, one with government bureaucrats making the decisions, then all we have to do is enact a national mandatory health system like Canada has.

# State Attempts at Providing Health Insurance

---

*"The more corrupt the state, the more numerous the laws."*

*- TACITUS, FROM THE ANNALS OF IMPERIAL ROME*

SEVERAL STATES HAVE HAD A go at health care "reform" recently. The Hawaii legislature tried "universal health care" for children. They called it "Keiki Care." They did this by offering a government health insurance policy to any child up to age 18 who did not have one.

Naturally, large numbers of parents dropped the private insurance policies that they already had for their children. They then got onto the state program. Dr. Kenny Fink, administrator of the program at the Department of Human Services, said that "People who were already able to afford health care began to stop paying for it so they could get it for free. I don't believe that was the intent of the program."[1] Once again, incentives matter more than intentions.

Within a mere seven months, the Hawaiian government had to throw in the towel. The costs were so high that they could not keep running the program.

In Massachusetts, the state legislature commanded all of their subjects to purchase health insurance under penalty of law. "Thou shalt purchase comprehensive health insurance. Thus saith the state." This is the latest fad in government schemes in an effort to make health care affordable and available to all. The Massachusetts plan was later overridden by Obamacare.

In a plan such as the one in Massachusetts, the state ordered businesses to provide health insurance to their employees. This applied to businesses with 11 employees or more. If employers did not comply, then the police powers of the state came down on them. Any individuals who were not provided with health insurance by an employer were then ordered to buy health insurance policies. Those who refused were penalized.

In Massachusetts, the penalty to an employer for refusing to comply with the directives of the Commissar of Health initially was a fine of $295 per employee per year.[2] Big deal. That is a lot less expensive than the premiums would be. If an employer chose this alternative, however, he was taking a huge risk. If any employee cost the state over $50,000 in health costs in a year, then the state could charge the employer anywhere from 10% to 100% of those costs.[3] This could run into huge amounts of money. Many small businesses in Massachusetts took this risk, and dropped health insurance coverage of employees, encouraging them to get on the state dole. The premiums simply became too costly for them.[4]

Individuals, if not provided health insurance by an employer, were commanded to purchase it themselves. The maximum penalty for noncompliance amounted to only $219 in 2007,[5] a paltry sum compared to the premiums. In an effort to rein in health insurance scofflaws, the Massachusetts Department of Revenue increased the penalty to a range from $228 to $1,212 per year as of 2012.[6] Also, if an individual was deemed to be "low-income," he could get the state to pay for his health care, through the Health Safety Net Trust Fund,[7] or the state-provided free or subsidized insurance programs.

Massachusetts insurance policies were required to cover 43 specified conditions.[8] The state determined what deductibles will be allowed, what must be covered, and many other specifics of the policies.[9] The Commonwealth Connector, an agency of the state government, had placed themselves as the overall manager of the insurance companies. The insurance company executives were then mere underlings of the Commonwealth Connector. People were required to buy one of these approved policies, ensuring a hefty volume of business for the companies that sell them.

Predictably, insurance premiums had become quite expensive in Massachusetts. I shopped for insurance through the Commonwealth Connector in early 2009, for a family of 4 including a 46 year old, a 50 year old spouse, and 2 children, and the lowest monthly premium it showed me was $866. For the same family size and ages, on the same day, I researched ehealthinsurance.com in New Hampshire and found a monthly premium of $487. For Pennsylvania, there was a premium of $203 available.

These are greatly different plans, but that is the entire point. The $203 plan had a $10,000 deductible per person, up to $20,000 for the family. The cheapest Massachusetts plan, at $866 per month, had a deductible of $2000 per person, or $4,000 for the family. If somebody wants to save $8,000 per year by choosing a higher deductible, then that should be the decision of the individual. The difference in individual deductible is equal to just one year's premium savings, and the family deductible can be saved by banking two years of premium savings.

Even choosing a policy that was fairly comparable in details, there was a policy in Pennsylvania for $655 monthly. The biggest difference was that it had only half the deductible of the cheapest Massachusetts policy, but it cost only 76% as much. So much for making health insurance affordable.

Another predictable outcome in Massachusetts was that large numbers of people went onto the government rolls. When shopping for insurance through the Commonwealth Connector, identifying myself as a single 25 year old, I was told that I might be eligible to get on the state dole if I made up to $31,212 per year. When I entered that I had a family of four, I could belly up to the state bar up to an annual income of $63,612.

57% of the newly insured people in Massachusetts have gotten the state insurance paid for by other taxpayers since the new program went into effect.[10] With such high premiums, and the state determining that people with such high salaries need assistance paying those premiums, it is no surprise that so many have taken the offer.

Another predictable outcome was a shortage of doctors to treat the upsurge in demand. Once the insurance is obtained, a person would perceive health care as free, or close to it. Doctors therefore had become swamped with demand. It can take months to get into an appointment. In late 2008, Holyoke Health Center had over 1600 people on its waiting list, and it took four months to get an initial appointment.[11] One practice even resorted to group appointments, with strangers lumped together into an appointment.[12]

In 2008, The Massachusetts Medical Society released a detailed report on the worsening shortage of physicians in the state. Waiting times for a first appointment with a family physician averaged 36 days, obstetrics/gynecology 44 days, and internal medicine 50 days.[13] 44% of doctors were planning or considering changing careers.[14] 18% were planning or considering moving out of the state if the environment did not change.[15]

The cost to the state, of course, was much higher than the original appropriation of $472 million for the first year. The actual cost for the first year was $625 million.[16] The Boston Globe, using projections obtained from the Massachusetts government, estimated that by 2011 the cost to taxpayers would be $1.35 billion, or almost double original predictions.[17] This means that not only were people in Massachusetts required to buy costly insurance policies, but by 2011 they also had to pay $550 per household annually in taxes to support the system.[18]

I have already used a car analogy with health insurance. The Massachusetts plan puts it in a different light. It is as if the state required everybody to buy a car, from a list that they approved. The choices range from a new, fully loaded Lincoln Town Car to a Rolls Royce. Anybody who refused to buy one would be punished through the tax code, with armed agents to enforce that as necessary. A new Ford Focus would not qualify to protect somebody from the tax man. Anybody who could not afford one of the approved cars, as the state determines affordability, would have one bought for them and paid for by other taxpayers.

# Obamacare – It Must Be Affordable, It Says So in the Title

---

*"State intervention in economic production arises only when private initiative is lacking or insufficient, or when the political interests of the state are involved. This intervention may take the form of control, assistance, or direct management."*

*- BENITO MUSSOLINI*

NOW BARACK OBAMA HAS GOTTEN his "Affordable Care Act" passed to do essentially the same thing to the nation that the Massachusetts legislature and Mitt Romney did to its citizens. The crux of Obamacare is to require people to purchase health insurance, to require employers to offer it, and to define what those policies have to include. It does not include an offering of government insurance policies (the "public option") yet, but that is to be expected to follow. An expansion of Medicaid, and taxpayer-funded subsidies, fill that role anyway.

We have already seen how affordable health insurance is under the Massachusetts plan. We have seen the shortages that have developed. We have seen the cost to the state skyrocket. The same plan, put into effect by Barack Obama, however, will "make health insurance affordable and accessible for all," and "lower health care costs,"[1] or so the President says.

As the Massachusetts experience showed, accessible health insurance is quite a different matter from accessible health care. Like Canadians, everybody has first-rate insurance coverage for imaginary visits with doctors that they cannot get in to see, while paying through the nose in taxes.

The Lewin Group estimates that Obama's plan would increase federal spending by $1.2 trillion from 2010 - 2019.[2] It also estimates that the number of governmentally insured people would increase by 48 million, while the number of privately insured would decrease by 22 million.[3]

The Congressional Budget Office (CBO) analyzed Obamacare, and estimated that "the ACA's coverage provisions will result in a net cost to the federal government of $1,487 billion over the 2015 - 2024 period."[4] This is roughly $12,000 per family in America. Imagine what the real cost will be, if even a federal agency predicts such high costs. Government programs generally end up costing much more than originally predicted. For example, in 1965, federal estimates were for Medicare Part A to cost $9 billion by 1990. The actual cost was $66 billion.[5]

As far as "making health insurance affordable," the exact opposite appears to be the result. As early as mid-2013, I already had patients come to me after losing their health insurance because it became unaffordable to them. Some have told me their premiums have gone up by 50% because of changes their insurance companies have had to make because of the new law. I hear the same theme from patients repeatedly.

The CBO "projects that, as a result of the ACA, between 6 million and 7 million fewer people will have employment-based insurance coverage each year from 2016 through 2024 than would be the case in the absence of the ACA."[6] The CBO report also forecasts that "about 31 million nonelderly residents of the United States are likely to be without health insurance in 2024, roughly one out of every nine such residents."[7]

Stories in the news from Tennessee and California have described the sticker shock that many families have been getting from the new law. Their insurance companies have cancelled their plans, and offered other plans that cost hundreds of dollars more per month, sometimes even $1000 more per month.[8,9] Some people will be paying less for premiums, but usually because of shifting their cost onto others through subsidies.

Other requirements of the law force insurers to lose money on sicker patients as they shift that cost to their healthier patients. Insurance companies are required to charge older patients no more than three times as much for their coverage as they charge younger patients, even though their costs average six times as much. That means that younger, healthier patients have to pay much more for their insurance than would make economic sense in their situation. They balk at having to pay those premiums, leaving a higher proportion of sicker patients in the pool. That drives premiums still higher, causing more young people to drop out. Eventually, the insurance pool is comprised almost entirely of older, much more expensive patients. This "death spiral" becomes an economically nonfeasible situation, unless the government can make it painful and expensive enough on the healthier patients to force them into the system.[10]

On a nationwide scale, a study was done on the average impact on health insurance premiums as a result of Obamacare. The study was done by the Society of Actuaries. Actuaries are the best source of information that could be found on this subject. They are the statisticians that are relied upon by insurance companies for the information they need to set premiums. The study estimated a 32% average increase in premiums for individuals purchasing health insurance, compared to what they would be without the new law.[11]

In 2015, "health insurance companies around the country are seeking rate increases of 20 percent to 40 percent or more [for 2016], saying their new customers under the Affordable Care Act turned out to be sicker than expected."[12] This is exactly what was predicted in the "death spiral" scenario described by John Goodman.

If you could not afford to buy health insurance before, it is now becoming one third more expensive. President Obama's signature achievement is that he can now have IRS agents penalize you for not buying it.

We cannot reduce our spending on health care by making everything more expensive, and then just shifting the cost onto other people. Taxes go up to cover the costs. According to data released by the Department of Health and Human Services, 5.6 million of the first 6 million people signing up for Obamacare are to have their plans subsidized, as of January 2014.[13] It is, as Frederic Bastiat says, "that great fiction by which everyone tries to live at the expense of everyone else."[14]

The "Patient Protection and Affordable Care Act," a.k.a. Obamacare, is simply corporatism at it fullest. It drives up the price of a product, and then forces everybody to buy that product. The big insurance companies, the ones that are favored by government, will have massive amounts of money flowing into their coffers. Some will be paid directly by their insurees, but vast amounts will be sent to them from the United States Treasury in the form of taxpayer subsidies. Just like the bailouts of the large financial institutions, this sends government money (taxpayer money) to government-favored health insurance companies. If you do not like the big insurance companies, then how could you be in favor of forcing everybody in the country to buy their products at higher fees than previously? Even if some people pay lower premiums because of subsidies, the insurance companies still collect higher premiums because the U.S. government sends the remainder to them. The marriage of big business and government, benefitting both at the expense of the peasants, reaches new heights in Obamacare. Benito Mussolini would have been proud.

Blue Cross and Blue Shield of Massachusetts filed an amicus brief to the federal circuit court arguing in favor of the "Affordable Care Act,"[15] as did the American Hospital Association.[16] It only makes sense that the biggest insurance companies would have supported a law forcing people to buy their product.

Companies are dropping full-time workers in favor of part-time workers in order to avoid the penalties of Obamacare. Now who could have predicted that? There was even a call center being set up in California for people to call with questions about working through Obamacare, and half of their employees ended up being part-time. During the recruiting, a job posting said that the positions would all be full-time.[17] Then the people running the call center apparently realized that they cannot afford the high costs of Obamacare, and changed to part-time. The call center is funded by a state whose electoral votes went to Obama twice, and is being administered by a county whose votes went overwhelmingly to Obama twice.[18] They just got a taste of their own medicine.

The Congressional Budget Office projects "a decline in the number of full-time-equivalent workers of about 2.0 million in 2017, rising to about 2.5 million in 2024,"[19] as a result of Obamacare.

20% of physicians who responded to a survey said they would quit if an Obama type plan is implemented.[20] The same shortages that have developed in Massachusetts would likely hit the entire country. We will have all the attention to detail that we can expect from four minute appointments or group appointments. The waiting times for doctor appointments will grow. We will have the kind of shortages that prompted the Canadian Supreme Court to declare "interferes with life and security of the person."[21]

Why did the U.S. Supreme Court rule that Obamacare is constitutional? As Chief Justice John Roberts wrote, he saw it as his duty to find some way to read the constitution, and the Affordable Care Act, to uphold that act. He considered it his job to twist either the constitution or the law to make it constitutional. He said in his written opinion on Obamacare, "every reasonable construction [interpretation] must be resorted to, in order to save a statute from unconstitutionality."[22] He further stated, "as between two possible interpretations of a statute, by one of which it would be unconstitutional and by the other valid, our plain duty is to adopt that which will save the Act."[23] He then goes on to say, that "the most straightforward reading of the mandate is that it commands individuals to purchase insurance. After all, it states that individuals 'shall' maintain health insurance ... the Commerce Clause does not give Congress that power."[24] Therefore, the court changed the law to be a tax, not a penalty, and Roberts claimed that the constitution gives the federal government the power to tax non-activity. The law was defended many times by the Obama administration saying it was not a tax. Taxing non-activity has now become a new revenue source for our government.

Putting a federal appointee in charge of determining what powers the federal government has is like putting someone from the home team in as the umpire in the game, and then telling him he can make up the rules as he goes. It should be no surprise that we get these kinds of rulings.

It is assumed by many who back plans like those in Massachusetts or Obamacare that the uninsured use a disproportionate amount of emergency department resources. This is simply not based on reality. An analysis looked at several studies on emergency deparment use and found that "publicly insured patients use the ED substantially more often than uninsured patients."[25]

These "publicly insured" patients, such as those on Medicaid, are precisely the group that is enlarged by plans like Romneycare and Obamacare. These types of programs thus should be expected to result in more, not less, emergency department crowding.

During the first few weeks after the Obamacare exchanges opened, the state-run exchanges (the ones that worked), were having a large majority of their new enrollees going into Medicaid. In Washington state, that figure was 84% Medicaid, in Kentucky 82%, and in New York 64%.[26] As of 2011, 31% of doctors nationwide did not accept new Medicaid patients.[27] That percentage is likely to increase as Medicaid becomes more onerous to deal with. We are likely to experience much more E.R. crowding. Where else will all those Medicaid patients be able to go? A survey of New York doctors revealed that 44 percent said they would not participate with Obamacare.[28]

Update: The previous paragraph was written in 2011. Note that I predicted that Medicaid acceptance rates would go down. It turns out that by 2014, 54% of doctors do not accept Medicaid. The same study showed that 24% of doctors do not accept Medicare patients.[29]

It is also assumed by many that uninsured patients are subsidized by those with insurance. Former governor Arnold Schwarzenegger of California cites figures of $1,186 per family, and $455 per individual, that the insured are paying to subsidize the uninsured.[30]

Let us look at which patients are actually subsidizing whom. As has already been discussed, approximately $2,100 per family is paid in tax on non-health items to pay for the health insurance tax subsidy.[31] Add to this the average of $7,340 per family that is being confiscated to pay for Medicare and Medicaid.[32] This total of $9,440 is far more than the $1,186 per family that the Governator says is subsidizing the uninsured. This does not even address the large overhead that must be paid by the uninsured to subsidize the third party payment processing in most doctor's offices. As I explained in a previous chapter, for something that costs $30 at my office, I would have to charge $102 if I worked through insurance.[33] Clearly, the uninsured are subsidizing the care of the insured, not the other way around.

Another issue concerning the vast increase in Medicaid beneficiaries resulting from Obamacare is that state governments can seize assets from a person's estate to repay Medicaid costs. If Medicaid payments were made for a person at least 55 years old, then when they die, their assets can be taken before children inherit.[34] Put everybody on Medicaid, then take their property when they die. This is like inheritance tax on steroids.

People are rightfully alarmed at the prospect of having government agents so heavily involved with their health care. After all, we keep hearing of abuses of power by government agents that are completely callous to the safety and needs of ordinary Americans. They lie to us, and then say it was "the least untruthful"[35] thing they could have said, and get off scot-free.

The recent scandal about the staff of governor Chris Christie closing lanes of the George Washington Bridge, just to exact revenge on a political enemy,[36] is a much bigger issue than many people have made of it. That is because it demonstrates the damage that government workers can do to ordinary people, seemingly without a care. This is a huge story not because it is so unusual, but because they got caught. How many times have government workers done nasty things to people they do not like? We will never know. Awful things happen to the peasants at the hands of government workers commonly. We usually just chalk it up to incompetence, or grinding bureaucracy. Perhaps it is often actually motivated by just plain meanness.

It does not take a head of an agency to wreak havoc. Mid-level bureaucrats can cause enormous harm on their own accord, without their managers even needing to know about their actions. Whether Chris Christie knew what his agents were doing or not is irrelevant to the larger point, which is the amount of damage that government agents can inflict on ordinary people, if they choose to do so. This is the result of giving them too much power.

Some people go into government because they think they can do some good there. Others go into it because they have a lust for power. Normal people do not want to control the lives of other people. That desire can be considered a psychiatric pathology. Actually, many politicians match the textbook definition for narcissistic personality disorder, as described in the Diagnostic and Statistical Manual of Mental Disorders. There are plenty of people with that kind of pathology who are attracted to government in order to satisfy their drive to control and be above others.

These are just the kinds of people that have now been put into positions of power over the health care decisions of ordinary Americans. Now, just imagine the kinds of damage these kinds of government workers can inflict on people they do not like. It does not take a Kathleen Sebelius to do it. Just typical mid-level bureaucrats in the government health care machine can be awfully creative about the ways they exact revenge on the people who are subject to their whims.

If somebody wants to abuse and pillage people, there is only so much he can do in the private sector. In a free market, people are free to do business with him or not. If he wants to abuse people on a much larger scale; if he wants to join the big leagues, he needs to get into the government business. Then people have no choice but to deal with him. Or he can have the government force people to do business with him, like with the new mandate on buying health insurance.

The public response to the looming threat of Obamacare is growing increasingly negative. There was a huge outcry against it at its passage, and now large majorities are against it. A Rasmussen poll even showed that a majority of Americans would prefer a partial government shutdown if that is what it takes to cut the funding of Obamacare.[37] The Teamsters union has even turned against Obamacare recently. Their leadership sent a letter to congressional leaders, talking about "perverse incentives" and "nightmare scenarios" that "will destroy the very health and well-being of our members."[38] It seems that just about everybody that is being forced into Obamacare wants to be exempted from it. This even includes the IRS agents that are being tasked with forcing it on the rest of us. The leadership of their union was asking their members to send a letter to their congressional members, opposing a bill that would require IRS agents to be under the mandates of Obamacare.[39]

Volunteer fire departments across the country were being threatened with crippling penalties that would shut many of them down, as volunteer fire-fighters are classified by the IRS as employees that then have to be covered with health insurance.[40] Our government passed yet another exemption to resolve that problem. Extended travel, such as going south for the winter as many Americans do, could become financially risky for the average American. This is because most of the Obamacare-certified insurance policies would leave people uncovered out of network in other states for non-emergency issues.[41] Non-state American territories such as Guam have been thrown into turmoil because some of the requirements of Obamacare are in effect there, and some are not, leaving Guamanians in a confusing quandary.[42]

As it turns out, Nancy Pelosi was right. We needed to pass the bill to find out what is in it. Like a stool sample.[43] We just keep finding more pathogens in the bill. Again, incentives are more important than intentions. Whenever government undertakes to regulate and mandate human behavior and economy, they cause all manner of unintended consequences that are usually harmful.

The purpose of this book is not so much to go into the details of Obamacare as it is to lay out the roots of our current woes, and therefore how to fix them. Obamacare is on the minds of many Americans these days. Their fears are well founded. The solution is not to find some other, smarter, more friendly government program to solve our health care crisis. Just imagine if the government jumped in to solve the electronics crisis. No, there is no electronics crisis. There would be one if the government tried to control that industry, however.

Since the causes of high cost and low service in American health care are largely over-insurance caused by tax incentives, and excessive government regulation, the solution is not to exacerbate those causes. That only makes the situation worse. There is not even a remote possibility that Obamacare can decrease health care costs or improve service, since it only increases the pressures that have caused those problems. The solution is to reduce regulations and mandates, and remove the interferences in the free market which lead us to over-insure. Specific ideas on how to do this will be discussed in later chapters.

# Health Savings Accounts –
# One Step Forward and One Step Back

———

*"If you want government to intervene domestically, you're a liberal.*
*If you want government to intervene overseas, you're a conservative.*
*If you want government to intervene everywhere, you're a moderate.*
*If you don't want government to intervene anywhere, you're an extremist."*

*- JOSEPH SOBRAN*

HEALTH SAVINGS ACCOUNTS (HSAs) CONSTITUTE one step forward and one step backward. Because they are more consumer directed, with the consumer of health care benefiting from restraint in his health care expenditures, they are a big step toward individual fiscal responsibility. They are simultaneously a step in the wrong direction in that they extend the tax preference of health care spending over other types of spending such as food and clothing.

HSAs eliminate the disparity between employer-purchased health insurance and individual-purchased insurance. Since they are available to individuals, they "even the playing field" by extending the health care tax deduction to individuals, thus cutting the strings that tie health insurance to employment.

Patients have a certain amount of money that they can spend, tax preferred, toward the health care of their choice. The health care chosen must be of an approved type, although the list is quite extensive. If people are efficient with their account, they get to roll it over to the next year, potentially accumulating quite a bit of money toward their later years for retirement, or even bequeathing it to an heir. HSAs provide quite an incentive to people for conserving money in their health expenditures. Patients are theoretically incented to choose doctors who are cost-effective in their approach, but in actuality that incentive is very limited.

The incentive to choose cost-effective doctors is limited because 95% of HSAs work in conjunction with Preferred Provider Organizations (PPOs).[1] This limits the range of doctors from which to choose. Below the deductible, when money is being spent out of the account, there is no PPO requirement. Once the deductible is reached, however, there is a strong financial incentive for the patient to stay within the network. Because of this, most people will stay within the network below the deductible as well. That way, the same doctors are caring for them. So HSAs partially drive people toward doctors who have all the costs of working through insurance. HSA enrollees do not tend to go to doctors like me, who are much more cost-effective. I run an HSA transaction just a few times per week. These people usually go to doctors who are geared toward working through insurance, with all the cost that incurs. It is also very difficult in our current health care marketplace to shop around for deals. Finding out beforehand what a procedure might cost can be a futile attempt.

HSAs are only available if they are coupled to a modestly high-deductible insurance policy, to cover high health costs. That is, after all, the purpose of insurance in the first place. Unforeseen very large costs are insured against, so that they do not devastate the individual. Routine things are just paid for, without any insurance claim. Those out-of-pocket costs are paid for out of the tax-preferred account.

Unfortunately, HSAs do have a defined range of acceptable deductible amounts. The allowable range of deductibles is from $1,250 to $5,000 for an individual, and from $2,500 to $10,000 for a family, in 2012. A person could not get a $20,000 deductible in order to further lower the premiums. Because of this, the premiums are still high, though not as high as more traditional health insurance policies.

The higher the deductible, the lower the premiums should be, enabling people to save more money. Those savings could be saved over the years to go toward the deductible if needed, or put toward retirement. For example, the deductible might hypothetically be $5,000 with an annual premium of $4,000, and $1,000 is spent annually toward routine health costs. Or the deductible could be $20,000 with a $1,500 annual premium and the same $1,000 in routine annual costs. In 6 years, the extra $15,000 deductible would have been saved through lower premiums.

It should be up to the individual, as to the level of risk that he is willing to take for different savings. Somebody young might not be as able to bear a $20,000 cost, but he might also decide that it is not very likely that he will have a costly expense because he is young and healthy. A bureaucrat in Washington, D.C. is the last person who should be making that choice.

By allowing more consumer choice, we might now start to see more doctors who practice medicine with cost in mind. Doctors could use older, generic medicines when appropriate. Often, the older medicines are still best. More emphasis could be placed on the history and physical exam, to save on costly tests. Service could return, including even housecalls. Doctors will look for innovative ways to please the customer, which will once again be the patient, rather than the insurance company.

Given the current frenzy of so many socialists to establish nationalized health care in America, HSAs are actually quite an advance in restoring some freedom to the health care marketplace. Any progress toward connecting the consumer to cost is quite an achievement now.

HSAs are catching on fairly quickly. By 2010, 10 million people had HSAs. This was up 25% since 2009. Then by 2011, the total went up another 14%.[2] The premium cost of the best-selling HSA in the large-group market was 73% of the cost of more traditional insurance.[3] A 2007 report shows that 27% of new individual HSA enrollees were previously uninsured. This means that HSAs are bringing health insurance to the uninsured, a goal of many advocates of health reform. 46% of enrollees were at least 40 years old, so they are not just limited to the young and healthy.[4]

Critics say that HSAs do not help those with chronic health problems. Unhealthy people do not choose HSAs. They therefore leave other insurance plans with more unhealthy individuals, driving their premiums up. The critics complain that this is unfair. That is like saying that it is unfair for someone who owns a house in a flood plain to pay higher premiums for flood insurance than one who builds on high ground. Healthy behaviors will lead to lower out of pocket costs for people with HSAs. This should be considered a good thing, for people to adopt healthier lifestyles.

Even those with chronic health problems could benefit from HSAs by managing their health problems more efficiently. Diabetics are a perfect example. Ideally, they manage their own care, with doctors acting as consultants. They can do so while realizing cost savings through an HSA. This is especially true if they are fortunate enough to have a doctor in their community who practices according to free market principles, and therefore provides better service for a lower fee.

Critics of HSAs also charge that they shift more of the cost of healthcare from employers onto employees. Oh, no! Say it ain't so! Shifting the cost of a service onto the person receiving that service! Why is that a bad thing? As we have already seen, shifting the cost of health care away from the patient is one of the biggest reasons for our accelerating costs and our decline in quality. Shifting it back would be a good thing, as it would restore fiscal sanity, and lead to better service.

Another criticism of HSAs is that people will skimp on their health care. Actually, this would be true for minor ailments, but a study concluded that people are less likely to forego care for conditions that they describe as very serious if they have consumer directed health care than traditional insurance.[5]

HSAs are a step toward getting people to resume an active role in their own health. They are helpful in getting cost reconnected to the consumer. They do not, however, address many of the causes of our health care problems, as they have already been outlined in this book. Since the problems are caused by tax preferences and the market distortions that those preferences cause, the solution is not to extend those tax preferences. There are many more direct solutions, and those will be explored in the following chapters.

# True Solutions – Based on the Causes,
# We Must Restore Freedom

———

# Restore Free Markets

———

*"Capitalism needs neither propaganda nor apostles.*
*Its achievements speak for themselves. Capitalism delivers the goods."*

- LUDWIG VON MISES

NOW THAT THE CAUSES OF our health care problems have been diagnosed, and some faulty solutions have been reviewed, true remedies can be discussed. People may be alarmed at the severity of the problem, but the only thing we need to be worried about is whether or not we are willing to remove the causes of the problems. When it comes right down to it, the fixes are as easy as falling off a log. If a person is standing on a log, and stops putting forth any effort, he will fall. Likewise, we are expending effort on governmental regulations and solutions to health care. If we simply cease those efforts, and get government out of the way, our problems will resolve themselves.

The first principle to follow in healing American health care is to restore the free market. When considering any change to be made, the ultimate question that should be answered is: will the proposed change increase or decrease freedom? Changes that increase freedom will lead toward greater patient and doctor satisfaction, lower costs, and greater availability. Changes that reduce freedom by increasing government control lead toward higher cost, lower patient and doctor satisfaction, and more shortages.

Specific changes that should be made are directed at fixing the specific causes of our problems, as outlined in the previous chapters. Ideally, these include eliminating the tax incentives that skew the perceived cost of health care and tie health insurance to employment. They would reduce regulations, eliminate the compulsory nature of the FDA, licensure, and HIPAA. They would stop insurance mandates. They would restore civility to the courts, so that civil law would once again be an instrument of justice rather than of social engineering. They would eliminate price controls and other government interventions.

Restoring free markets means restoring choice. A true pro-choice environment gives choice to all the individuals who are significantly affected by the decision being made. To the extent that an individual is affected by a choice, that individual would have a say in that decision.

In a pro-choice society, people could decide to buy or sell their goods or services with no coercion by government. Permission of bureaucrats would not be needed, and people would make the choices that they feel serve themselves best, based on their knowledge of their own situation. Consultation with experts would be sought and valued to the extent that an individual chooses.

If somebody says he is "pro-choice," it would be amusing to ask if he supports choice in how you use your property. Or ask whether you should be able to have and carry a gun for defense of innocent life. Or ask whether you should be able to choose what to do with the money you earn, or if you should be forced to give it to Social Security, Medicaid, etc. Most people who claim to be pro-choice are actually very much against most choices, and would deny the rights of defenseless victims who do not yet have a voice.

What is the feasibility and practicality of such free market reforms in health care? Would it cause great hardship if the government was not protecting us? Would the level of suffering and dying increase as a result of unrestrained capitalism? I contend that suffering and dying would decrease dramatically. Americans of all classes would benefit, but I believe that those who would benefit most would be those at the lower economic levels. These are the very people who have the most difficulty affording health care now. Subsequent chapters will explain this, and describe real modern day examples of how this is true.

There are plenty of people who think that capitalism is terrible for the lower economic classes, leading to big industrialists exploiting the common people. Karl Marx and V.I. Lenin made such statements, right before they proceeded to cause incredible hardship to the common people of the Soviet Union. They did this even while the "poor" in America were reveling in unprecedented luxury.

It is true that the actions of some capitalists have led to some suffering also. It is not a perfect system. However, if you want to really cause a lot of hardship to a lot of people, you need to stop being a piker, and get into the government business. Free markets are not the place for people who really want to develop their lust for power. Capitalists need the voluntary cooperation of people. Rulers of government can force everybody to do their bidding.

Some people point toward the big industrialists of earlier American history, as proof positive that a free market is bad for the common people. They call these captains of industry "robber barons," a term coined to describe their exploitive depravities against the people. The truth is that men like Andrew Carnegie, Henry Ford, John D. Rockefeller and other industrial giants raised the standard of living for the common people, in the process of acquiring their tremendous wealth. The Myth of the Robber Barons by Burton W. Folsom, Jr.[1] makes this case very well.

There were some monopolies established, but these were made possible by government intervention into the free market. Some of these men saw the potential for buying the influence of politicians, which enabled their monopolies. Rather than government, through the leadership of the noble Teddy Roosevelt, being the great savior of the people, government was actually the means of creating many of the problems of that age in the first place. The overall effect of the industrialists on the common people, however, was of increasing prosperity. More goods became available to the common people, at prices they could afford.

While capitalism has been advancing the interests and prosperity of all it touches, socialism/communism has had the opposite effects. People in the fertile agricultural regions of the Ukraine starved to death by the millions. People in socialist France lost jobs and became accustomed to the very mediocre lifestyle of the French welfare system. America surged forward, while others slowly plodded on.

The same socialist result is seen in health care, as has been thoroughly explored in preceding chapters. The only difference is that there is not a large American free market in medicine to make the contrast to socialism more obvious. Considering how much better the free market performs in other economic areas, it should be obvious that the same value would result in a health care free market, if we had one. The same principles apply. There is no reason to suggest that after socialism has produced shortages and poor quality in every other economic realm, that it would produce prosperity in health care. This simply makes no sense. A study of history reveals that it does not happen.

A careful look will show, however, that there are examples of free market activity in health care, and that they produce exactly the result that would be expected: value, service, and prosperity. In following chapters, some of these examples will be given. First, specific solutions will be offered to the specific causes of our problems in American health care. Throughout the discussion, the overriding principle is reducing government interference and restoring free markets.

# Restrict Government to Governing

———

*"A wise and frugal government, which shall restrain men from injuring*
*one another, which shall leave them otherwise free to regulate their own*
*pursuits of industry and improvement, and shall not take from the mouth*
*of labor the bread it has earned.  This is the sum of good government."*

- THOMAS JEFFERSON

IN ORDER TO HAVE FREE markets, government must be restricted to govern-
ing.  As the purpose of governments is to secure people in their rights, government has no business attempting to provide for citizens or to protect them
from themselves.  "We hold these truths to be self-evident, that all men were
created equal, that they are endowed by their Creator with certain unalienable
rights, that among these are life, liberty, and the pursuit of happiness, and
*that in order to secure these rights*, governments were instituted among men."[1]
(emphasis added)

Government generally has the reverse Midas touch - whatever it touches
turns to rust.  Distant bureaucrats are completely incompetent when it comes
to micromanaging the affairs of individuals.  They cannot possibly set prices
and allocate resources in efficient ways, as happens in a free market economy
where millions of decisions are made every day by individuals.  These millions of decisions about priorities are what set prices and allocate resources.
Government is good at maintaining armies and police, to uphold law and

protect the rights of individuals. That is what it should stick to, and leave the managing of individual affairs to the individuals concerned. Ideally, armies protect us from foreign attack, and police protect us from individuals who commit violent attacks or fraud against other citizens. These protections, as well as things like patent protections and contract enforcement, are what secure our rights and provide a lawful society in which individuals can pursue happiness and prosper.

Forcing us to make the right decisions for ourselves, such as wearing seatbelts, preventing us from buying the wrong medicine, or preventing us from consulting someone on health matters, is not for government to decide. It should be left to individual choice, with the individual bearing the consequences of his decision. More importantly, government has no moral or constitutional authority to make those decisions for individuals, even if it was any good at it.

James Madison said, "I cannot undertake to lay my finger on that article of the Constitution which granted a right to Congress of expending, on objects of benevolence, the money of their constituents."[2]

Thomas Jefferson said, "A wise and frugal government ... shall restrain men from injuring one another, shall leave them otherwise free to regulate their own pursuits of industry and improvement, and shall not take from the mouth of labor the bread it has earned. This is the sum of good government."[3]

Grover Cleveland said, when vetoing legislation to provide welfare assistance, "I can find no warrant for such an appropriation in the Constitution, and I do not believe that the power and duty of the General Government ought to be extended to the relief of individual suffering which is in no manner properly related to the public service or benefit."[4]

Franklin Pierce said when vetoing a bill to help the mentally ill, "I cannot find any authority in the Constitution for public charity. [To approve the measure] would be contrary to the letter and spirit of the Constitution and subversive to the whole theory upon which the Union of these States is founded."[5]

James Madison said, "It is sufficiently obvious, that persons and property are the two great subjects on which Governments are to act; and that the rights of persons, and the rights of property, are the objects, for the protection of which Government was instituted. These rights cannot be separated."[6]

The United States Supreme Court said the very same thing in 1795 concerning property rights. Protection of property was one of the main reasons that people formed governments. There is no moral authority for governments to take property from one person and give it to another. The majority decision said, "The right of acquiring and possessing property, and having it protected, is one of the natural, inherent, and unalienable rights of man. Men have a sense of property: Property is necessary to their subsistence, and correspondent to their natural wants and desires; its security was one of the objects, that induced them to unite in society. No man would become a member of a community, in which he could not enjoy the fruits of his honest labour and industry. The preservation of property then is a primary object of the social compact... The legislature, therefore, had no authority to make an act devesting one citizen of his freehold, and vesting it in another, without a just compensation. It is inconsistent with the principles of reason, justice, and moral rectitude; it is incompatible with the comfort, peace, and happiness of mankind; it is contrary to the principles of social alliance in every free government; and lastly, it is contrary both to the letter and spirit of the Constitution."[7]

The U.S. Constitution has never been amended to allow the federal government to "expend, on objects of benevolence, the money of their constituents," or in other words, to take the property of one person to give it to another. Any welfare programs, including Medicaid and Medicare, are outside of the proper authority of government. It has also never been amended to grant the federal government the authority to remove people's "freedom to regulate their own pursuits of industry and improvement," or to protect them from themselves, as the FDA does.

It is not the place of government to provide for the material needs of anybody, by taking away from somebody else. That is the province of private, voluntary charity. Again, government is completely inept in deciding to whom, and how, support should be given. Individuals can make much better decisions about these things, because they can better understand the situation. Charity is simply not the place of government. As Walter Williams said, the government needs to "get out of the miracle business."[8] We need to restore government back to its proper place and purpose.

# Eliminate Tax Incentives

---

*"A liberal is someone who feels a great debt to his fellow man,*
*which debt he proposes to pay off with your money."*

- G. GORDON LIDDY

PROBABLY THE MOST IMPORTANT THING that needs to be done to improve American health care, and restore fiscal sanity to the health care marketplace, is to remove the tax incentives that lead to third party payment of routine health care. The tax code favors health care over food, clothing, student loan payments, and most other expenditures. As long as health care dollars are worth substantially more than other dollars, then a disproportionate amount of spending will go into health care. The true value of health care is distorted.

The laws of supply and demand still apply, but in a very warped manner. These laws can no more be repealed than can the laws of physics. Insulating consumers from cost only drives demand up, causing prices to rise.

The federal government exerts a great deal of pressure, through the Internal Revenue Code, on Americans to adopt certain behaviors. The tax man does not just collect taxes, he entices us to act the way he wants in order to get our tax bills changed. Among the favored behaviors is purchasing health insurance through employment.

This has led to some outrage by people who feel that it is unfair for them to have to pay for their health care with after-tax dollars while others pay with pre-tax dollars. Others do not like that the federal government should be zapping us with the cattle prod of the tax code for any type of behavior modification. They feel that the tax code should not be used to change the way we live; it should only be used to collect necessary revenue.

There are a number of proposals that would eradicate the extensive social engineering that the federal government implements through the Internal Revenue Code. Among these are the Fair Tax, a flat tax, and a national sales tax coupled to the elimination of the income tax.

What would happen if health care was not tax deductible? What if we kept the income tax and eliminated the tax deduction for health care altogether, whether purchased by the employer or the individual? Or, in the event that some type of consumption tax replaced the income tax, if health care was taxed in the same way that building supplies were taxed? Would this help or harm the quality, service, and affordability of health care?

The first thing that needs to happen if we eliminated the tax incentives is to make the change neutral on overall revenue. In other words, this should not be just an excuse for the federal government to confiscate more of our money. When deductions are removed, the overall tax rates should be reduced, to keep overall tax revenue roughly equal. The various proposals to replace the income tax do try to accomplish this.

What would happen as a result of these changes is that health care would assume its true value to people. Instead of preferring health care expenditures to home building or investment into education or food, there would be no distortions of value. As we have seen in the chapter entitled "Don't Worry about the Cost - It's Covered," health care costs have risen dramatically because of these value distortions.

You may say that health care actually is more valuable than homes or education or food. It is not that simple. It would all depend on what health care we are talking about, what quality and quantity, etc. It is hard to make the case that removing several nonpainful skin lesions that have no cancerous potential is worth more than a month's worth of food. Yet that is the case with our current cost distortions. I had a patient with about 12 seborrheic keratoses, benign skin blemishes without any significant cancerous potential. I froze them off for $18, as it really did not take much time. She told me that she was quoted $89 per lesion, for a total of $1068, by one of the local dermatologists. Perhaps the dermatologist would have knocked the price down to several hundred dollars if he did them all at once. Either way they would have cost her far more than a month's worth of food to remove them in a financially typical practice, even though they are nothing but unsightly annoyances.

So what is the true value of health care? Only supply and demand in a free market, unshielded by the distortions of the tax code, would reveal that. Prices are really only a measurement of what must be foregone in order to obtain the item in question, since our resources are finite. We use prices to prioritize things by their relative value. With the elimination of the tax incentive and other market distortions, health services would assume their true value.

Quality and service would have to rise if health care assumed its true value in pricing. Doctors would once again have to please their customers, as other tradesmen must do. Rather than insurance companies being the customers of the doctor, patients would resume the role of customer. In order to keep those customers, then, the doctor would need to please them.

Insurance companies would also have to start treating the patients with some respect. The patients would more often be the customers of the insurance companies, instead of the employers being the customers. This would lead to competition for those patients, through more value and service being offered by the insurance companies. An insurance company that violated its contracts with patients would lose business to one who honored its contracts.

If health services assumed their true value, they would be much more affordable to the average American. Like the appendectomy that cost $1105 in 1960 (inflation adjusted),[1] things would again be within our financial reach. Eliminating the tax incentive is just one of the steps that needs to be taken to restore a free market and achieve quality, service, and affordability in health care. The following chapters describe other steps toward this worthwhile goal.

# Reduce Regulations – Phase Out Medicare

―――――

*"To argue with a person who has renounced the use of reason
is like administering medicine to the dead."*

- THOMAS PAINE

ASIDE FROM THE ELIMINATION OF tax distortions of medical costs, the other
major step toward improving our health care is getting rid of the overabun-
dance of regulations that plague doctors. With regulations and paperwork
eating up so much patient care time, and causing doctor's offices to be jobs
programs for clerks, it is no wonder that health care has gotten costly and
inefficient. The chapters "Medicare and Medicaid" and "We Are Regulating
Ourselves to Death" detail the effects of this regulatory quagmire.

The reason the regulations sprang up is Medicare. What government
funds it must of necessity regulate. It is inevitable that if our federal government is going to be the biggest payer of health care dollars, it will promulgate
layer upon layer of regulations, to control the delivery of those dollars. This is
necessary to try to eliminate fraud, because the United States Treasury is to a
scam artist like a giant honey pot is to a bear.

I have arrived now at the point where I must discuss the unthinkable.
Brace yourself. Take some deep, calming breaths. The only way, really, to

get the regulations down to a reasonable and efficient level is to phase out Medicare. Although there are proposals to reduce regulations and streamline the bureaucracy of Medicare, that truly would be impossible while leaving the Medicare program intact.

There was even a recommendation by a task force of the Department of Health and Human Services to scrap the Evaluation and Management (E&M) code sets, a large part of the CPT coding used by Medicare.[1] These are used to define the complexity of the care provided. Eliminating the codes is really not practical, however. There has to be a way to quantify the work being done by a physician anytime payment for that work is requested from a leviathan bureaucracy. The bureaucrats must have some way to determine the amount of payment. There is no good way for a distant third party to determine the value of a service that a doctor provides for a patient.

Since the Medicare clerks cannot be in the exam room monitoring the doctor, they need some sort of code set to work from, in order to achieve some semblance of appropriateness in amount of payments. Considering the lack of knowledge of the bureaucrat about what medical care is being provided, that code set inevitably grows more complex as years pass. Any system that replaces the current system would quickly become just as cumbersome.

Any other streamlining of Medicare runs into the same problems. It is completely impossible for central planners and bureaucrats to achieve any sort of efficiency when overseeing an entire segment of a national economy. The Soviet experience bears strong witness to this.

"During the days of the Soviet Union's centrally planned economy, a recurrent problem was a piling up of unsold goods in warehouses at the very time when there were painful shortages of other things that could have been produced with the same resources. Like oil company executives in the United States, the executives who ran Soviet enterprises had no way to keep track of all the thousands of local conditions and millions of individual desires in a country that stretched all the way across the Eurasian land mass from Eastern Europe to the Pacific Ocean. Unlike American executives, however, their Soviet counterparts did not have the same guidance from prices or the same incentives from profits and losses. The net result was that many Soviet enterprises kept producing things in quantities beyond what anybody wanted, unless and until the problems became so huge and so blatant as to attract the attention of central planners in Moscow, who would then change the orders they sent out to manufacturers. But this could be years later and enormous amounts of resources would be wasted in the meantime.

"The wastefulness of a centrally planned economic system translated into a painfully low standard of living for millions of Soviet citizens, living in a country with some of the richest natural resources in the world."[2]

The same type of central planning exists with Medicare, with its fee schedules and lists of covered services and conditions. Because doctors have more autonomy than Soviet factory managers, they are able to partially overcome that drag on their efficiency. However, to the extent that Medicare rules influence what doctors do, we lose efficiency in our health care and lower our results.

Thus, in order to decrease the regulations that are doing immense harm to the quality, service, and affordability of health care in America, it is necessary to phase out Medicare. Many people who read this will be automatically repulsed at the thought. They will not listen to any amount of logic, regardless of how sound it is. Data, historical perspective, and moral arguments are meaningless to such people. Yet, certain things are simply true, and need to be said. Leaving Medicare in place only continues its immoral abuses of Americans.

The effects of Medicare on America have already been examined. I will again briefly summarize some of the damaging effects. Medicare causes health care to be much more expensive for all Americans, even for seniors. It contributes $37 trillion to our unfunded liabilities, or $308,000 debt to the average American family,[3] inexorably leading to an economic depression of staggering proportions. It targets doctors for prosecution. Many, if not most, of these are simply trying to honestly do their best to provide a service. It creates a huge potential for true fraud. It is an unconstitutional and immoral theft of the fruits of one person's labor to give to another. It hampers the quality of service in health care.

On average, Medicare takes money from those who have less in order to pay for those who have much more, a perverted sort of "reverse Robin Hood" scenario. The median net worth of people in their sixties is $168,200. The median for people in their seventies is even higher, at $173,500. The median for people in their twenties is only $7,800.[4] Money is being confiscated from people in their twenties to pay for people in their sixties and seventies. If those people in their twenties withold payment, then just like Robin Hood, armed men will force it from them, imprison them, or shoot them if they resist sufficiently.

Medicare is destructive to families by encouraging people to depend on government rather than family for assistance. This is true of all government welfare programs.

People quit working at younger ages now than they did decades ago, even though their health and ability to work is on average much better now. In 1960, 45.8% of men aged 65 and older worked. By 1998, that number had dropped to 16.5%.[5] In spite of better health, people are just quitting working, and kicking back in easy chairs, for many years. A lot of seniors enjoy their time on luxury cruises, while taking money from the paychecks of younger Americans. Some seniors have physical disabilities, but a large number are quite capable of working.

I am not saying that people should not retire and enjoy luxuries. They should get to enjoy the fruits of their labors. However, so should younger people. When physically capable people take the earnings of others by force in order to pay a part of their retirement bill, I call that wrong.

I cannot begin to understand how people can say that Medicare and Social Security are good things, if they realize these effects that they have on our future and current state. To emphasize the damage that Medicare causes, I now repeat what recently retired Comptroller General David M. Walker said. "Saving our future requires tough choices today... Current fiscal policy is unsustainable. The 'status quo' is not an option. We face large and growing structural deficits largely due to known demographic trends and rising health care costs. GAO's simulations show that balancing the budget in 2040 could require actions as large as: cutting total federal spending by 60 percent, or raising federal taxes to 2 times today's levels. Faster economic growth can help, but it cannot solve the problem. Closing the long-term fiscal gap based on reasonable assumptions would require real average annual economic growth in the double digit range every year for the next 75 years. During the 1990s, the economy grew at an average 3.2 percent per year. As a result, we cannot simply grow our way out of this problem. Tough choices will be required."[6] Most of this problem is attributed to Medicare. Our Comptroller General has made clear just how much Medicare has to do with the problem. He flatly stated, when discussing the contribution of Medicare alone to our unfunded liability, "If there's one thing that could bankrupt America, its health care."[7]

How can people support such a damaging program? Are people really willing to let America fall into economic ruin just to try to save Medicare? Are people willing to bankrupt America to save a program that takes from those who have little and transfers it to those who have more, which invites fraud, harms families, and hurts the quality and affordability of health care for everybody?

Do you want the federal government to be able to do anything besides transferring money from younger workers to older retirees? Is government to be nothing but a perverted sort of pension fund administrator?

That is what we will get if we steadfastly cling to Medicare and Social Security as they get closer to the failing point. On our current course, by 2050, almost 75% of federal revenue will be needed just to maintain these two retirement programs, and eventually, all federal revenue will be needed, leaving nothing for anything else.[8] We will not be able to sustain an effective military, or do any of the other things that the federal government does. The money will not be there.

If we cannot defend our nation, because we cannot fund the military, then there will be no point in even discussing Medicare and Social Security. These programs will not continue if our federal government, and our entire nation, collapses. If you are worried about national defense, then you need to think about the economic security of our country first. Without a vibrant economy, we cannot have a powerful military. This requires righting the horrible wrongs of Medicare and Social Security.

Many people think that Medicare is necessary to provide health care to seniors who would otherwise have to go without it. This is simply not the case. There was no widespread health crisis for the elderly before the inception of Medicare. Care was much more affordable, seniors were able to pay for it, and charity provided a safety net. Private health insurance was obtainable for seniors, which is no longer true, at least not private insurance that is not secondary to Medicare.

Even if it was true that Medicare was necessary to provide for the elderly, then that would not make it right. To say that something is theft, but that it must be done because it is the only practical way, is wrong. There are certain things that are simply morally wrong, and theft is one of them.

People think that Medicare can never be eliminated, because that would not be fair to the people who have paid in. But how fair is it to keep taking money from people to pay for others, as the system heads toward disaster? With its ever escalating costs, there is no way to keep it afloat. Any taking of money from workers now who will not be getting it back in the future would be just as unfair.

More to the point, nobody receiving Medicare benefits now has ever paid into the system for themselves with their payroll taxes. One generation is robbed to pay for a different generation. Seniors who receive Medicare benefits today have had money taken from them to pay for the previous generation of beneficiaries. They did not put any money away into Medicare for themselves.

If Joe robs Ann, then it does not make things right for Ann to rob Walter. If government robs generation B to pay generation A, then it is still wrong to use government to rob generation C to pay off generation B. This robbery has been continuing, and escalating, for several generations now.

If a corporate pension fund officer employed the methods of Medicare and Social Security, he would be imprisoned. These pension funds are required to keep accounts for the individual pensioners. They cannot just spend that money, and pay the pensions out of money that they expect to collect in the future.

This is not to say that people who are receiving Medicare and Social Security benefits now are committing some great evil, at least not knowingly. Most people actually think that they have paid into these programs for themselves, and are just getting back what is due to them. They do not even realize that their benefits are actually being confiscated from people who have much less, many of whom are struggling to support their families.

The very existence of Medicare makes it very difficult for seniors to refuse to accept Medicare benefits. While the most moral thing may be to reject the payments, the practicality of doing so is very limited now. This is because there is no private health insurance market for people over 65. While a senior may realize that it is wrong to take from younger people who have less, there is no place to turn for primary health insurance. Thus, Medicare has created a problem for which it is the solution, albeit a terrible solution. Seniors are practically forced into Medicare. Most do not know the real workings behind the program, or the damaging effects of it.

While it may be impractical to refuse Medicare and Social Security benefits, I plan to do just that if by some faint chance these programs still exist when I reach the age of eligibility. I do not take Medicare payments as a doctor, and I will not willingly take them, or Social Security payments, as a beneficiary.

Given all these reasons to put a stop to the immensely harmful and inherently immoral program that is Medicare, how should it be done? Obviously, it would be disastrous for millions of people if the spigot of money pouring out of this program was shut off instantly. All those bureaucrats would have to find useful work to do, to make a living, if they could not keep feeding off the citizens. Not all, but many, seniors have depended on the government for so long, with no plans to look after themselves, that they would not be able to get along. They also have been prevented from saving for themselves by having their money confiscated to pay for the previous generation. To some extent, however, that is their fault, for not standing up to put a stop to Social Security and Medicare in their time.

If a person is speeding down the highway in the fast lane, and realizes he is heading the wrong way, he should not immediately slam on the brakes and turn the car around. He should carefully merge over to the right, take an exit, then start in the other direction. Likewise, we should not simply eliminate Medicare tomorrow.

There is no possible future course that we could take which would be completely fair to all involved. Medicare beneficiaries now are receiving money that is being taken from current workers. Today's beneficiaries have had money confiscated from them to pay for people who are now dead. Therefore we cannot reimburse today's beneficiaries from the people who most rightfully owe them. The most unfair thing that we could possibly do would be to continue robbing each successive generation to transfer their money to other people (while the government continues to take its cut).

Phasing Medicare out, as quickly as is reasonably possible, would be best. The first thing could be means testing to receive benefits. Only those who need to do so should live off of the work of others for the time being. Also, any seniors currently entering the program should only receive up to what they have put in, adjusted for inflation. Last of all, there should be no new entries into Medicare after a period of years, perhaps ten or fifteen. This would give people plenty of time to plan for their futures, rather than just waiting to get on the government dole.

There might be different methods of phasing Medicare out, than those briefly outlined above. Whatever way is chosen to eliminate it would be eminently more fair than continuing it. That one generation was robbed to pay for a different generation (and feed the government scavengers) does not make it the least bit fair to continue robbing subsequent generations. Continuing the robbery also continues the harmful effects upon the health care, future security, and economy of Americans.

People say we can never stop Medicare because the benefits have been promised to people. Again, look at the neighborhood scenario. Suppose I promise Ann that I will rob Joe to give her the money, and that I will continue robbing him to support her. That robbery should be stopped, whether it was promised or not.

Some people say that we save money through Medicare and Medicaid, because their administrative costs are much less than that of private insurance. Studies that are used to make this claim do not include many of the administrative costs of Medicare and Medicaid. They only include the budgets of the agencies that directly administer these programs, in their cost calculations. They do not include the cost of legislative sessions to set the rules. This is similar to excluding the cost of the board meetings, and the salaries of those executives in the meetings, where policy is decided for private insurance companies. They do not include the cost of collection of revenue, which is done through the Internal Revenue Service. This is similar to excluding the insurance company departments that collect premiums. They do not include the cost of agencies that oversee Medicare and Medicaid, such as the Government Accountability Office. Most importantly, they do not include the costs that are forced onto the private sector. These are the costs of complying with the rules and regulations, including all the staff that needs to be hired for that compliance. These studies do not include all the work that must be done by private individuals and companies to try to get their taxes paid, without running afoul of the IRS. These costs that are pushed onto the private sector are enormous.

The Council for Affordable Health Care did a study on the true administrative costs of Medicare and Medicaid, including the costs that are incurred by other government departments. They found that "Medicare and Medicaid spend 26.9 cents for every dollar of benefits versus 16.2 cents for private insurance."[9] Even this study did not include costs forced onto the private sector. Medicare costs us much more for its administration than does private insurance. Of course, direct payment by the patient has the least administrative cost of all options. In my office, my collection costs amount to my telling the patient at the end of the visit what the fee is, he or she hands me the money, and it is done.

What would happen if Medicare was abolished? One thing is that private health insurance would once again become available to seniors. There would be a demand, and therefore a supply would be generated. That is what happens in a market economy. Insurance companies would start offering policies to people at rates that would be locked in as they age, as they compete for customers.

Medical care would become much more affordable, as doctors would no longer have all the overhead costs of contending with the bureaucracy of Medicare. The vast majority of seniors would be able to afford their care, just as they seem to be able to afford the necessities of life, and many luxuries as well. Other Americans would also be able to afford their health care. Eliminating the tax incentives, as discussed in the previous chapter, would be an important part of making care affordable as well.

People also might start taking some responsibility for their actions. Without 2.7% of their income being confiscated under threat of deadly force, people could save for their retirements. A phasing out of Social Security as well, for many of the same reasons, would mean that 14.2% of their income would no longer be forcibly taken from people.[10] People might even want to live healthier lifestyles, avoid smoking, and control their weight. When they see higher insurance premiums and out of pocket costs for health care for people with unhealthy lifestyles, those changes would make sense.

If Medicare was gone, with its associated regulations, and we had a free market, then the cost of health care would be much more affordable. The elderly are also, on average, the wealthiest sector of society. They could take advantage of their accumulated wealth, and simply pay their own way, receiving a much higher level of service than they can now find, at reasonable prices. But their wealth is all tied up in property, you may say. Even if somebody did not save any money, and only owns a home, a reverse mortgage can be used to make use of that wealth in the waning years, while still living in the home. Long-term care insurance can also be purchased. Again, which is more moral, to live off of others while retaining a large amount of wealth accumulated over a lifetime, or to use some of that wealth to pay your own way and enable others to accumulate some of their own, or at least to get by?

Above all, the institutionalized theft that is Medicare would no longer be happening. That is a worthy goal in and of itself. If there is a cause worthy of charity, then we should give to it, and try to persuade others to give to it, rather than taking money from other people by force.

Private charity would revive for those cases that need it. Americans are very generous, and when they have money to give, they give it to worthy causes. One example of American generosity was given by Lance Richardson, in whose community a need arose. A young woman was in need of a pancreatic transplant. Lance had a local radio talk show with his brother and dad. They started putting the word out, and it soon spread. They started receiving money from far and wide. "We had a goal to raise $110,000 for the surgery. But when Christmas came, we had raised far more than that. We began telling people to stop sending any more contributions, but still many came into our American Family Institute office pleading to be allowed to just be a small part of the experience and contribute. We were able to use the excess funds to help several other people who were in catastrophic need."[11] There are many similar examples that can be told.

Now, with reports of horrendous waste of taxpayer dollars on natural disasters, and abuse of welfare programs, people develop an attitude that they have already had too much money taken from them by government, and so they are less willing to contribute voluntarily. When the Government Accountability Office reports that between $600 million and $1.4 billion of the Hurricane Katrina federal disaster relief went to fraud,[12] and that report is disseminated in the national media, people get fed up with responding to genuine needs. When people see obvious abuses of welfare they do not want to give. People feel cheated, and rightfully so. However, organizations that carry out charity properly, and these are all non-governmental, still do much good.

With so much money being taken from people, they have less to give. It is difficult to imagine how much money people would voluntarily give, if only the 14% of earnings that go to Medicare and Social Security were not confiscated. There is so much more than that, which the government confiscates for other misguided wealth redistribution programs, but just that 14% increase in people's incomes would be an enormous boon to charitable giving.

It is a wonderful thought, to think of an America without Medicare. Think of health care that is affordable, with good service. Imagine being able to get in to see a doctor quickly, even for routine needs. Imagine house calls, whether you need them, or just for convenience. Think of getting a 14% pay raise, and what you could do with the money.

# Restore Civility to Civil Law

---

*"A judge is a law student who marks his own examination papers."*

*- H.L. MENCKEN*

ALSO IMPORTANT TO THE RECOVERY of American health care is tort reform. If the power of the courts is not restrained to its proper place, then fewer and fewer people will want to become doctors. There is simply no way that American society can survive if people sue for every bad outcome, in medicine, and across the economy as a whole. Anybody who produces and contributes to society is now under threat of lawsuit. If lawsuits were successful only in cases of gross or willful negligence, then productivity would rise, prices would decrease, more useful products would be available, and everybody would benefit (except the tort lawyers, but they could always find something useful to do).

This does not mean that business people would be preying on society. It means that they would be able to provide service without living in constant fear of a lawsuit over a bad outcome that happens in spite of their best efforts to do the right thing.

How then can tort reform be accomplished? Many people advocate for legislating caps on non-economic damages that can be awarded by juries. Many states have passed these caps, and they have resulted in the easing of the malpractice pressures on doctors.[1]

Former President George W. Bush pushed for federal legislation to achieve this across all fifty states. Mitt Romney advocated the same thing. This really is not a federal jurisdiction, however. It is a state matter. Remember, the powers of the federal government are enumerated in Article I, Section 8 of the Constitution. Then the tenth amendment makes clear that powers which are not given to the federal government are reserved to the states, or the people. The only justification for claiming a federal power over medical malpractice suits would be that federal money is paying for health care, through Medicare and Medicaid. However, those programs are unconstitutional abuses of federal power as well.

I was, and still am, in favor of state-level tort jury award limitations, at least temporarily until the system can be repaired. This is just applying pressure to a hemorrhaging major artery, however. We need to repair the damage that has been done to the artery in order to have lasting and meaningful recovery in the system. The pressure is only a temporary solution with partial effect.

The causes for our runaway tort costs need to be addressed. Until the latter part of the twentieth century, litigation was not an enormous problem. Now it represents potential catastrophe for anybody who tries to do anything productive in America. Why did this change occur? It is because of fundamental changes in the way the common law became administered. These changes were the result of a concerted effort to change what common law would do in society. What we have now is totally consistent with the goals of common law reforms that have been instituted over the past several decades.

When the social engineers started wreaking havoc on American society in the twentieth century, tort law became one of their methods. We underwent a transformation from a society of people being held responsible for their actions into a society of blame and wealth redistribution.

Dr. John Hasnas, a legal scholar, described a concerted effort by legal theorists to develop a "theory of torts,"[2] and then to actively change the system to one which provides social justice. "They began to focus on the 'potentialities of tort liability as a means of distributing losses,' or more concisely, as a means of 'social engineering.'"[3]

The changes that have been made in civil law, to achieve the goals of wealth redistribution, have been profound. Not all of these changes apply equally to medical tort as they do to other industries, but they all apply to some extent, and are worthy of consideration.

The basic principles of law that helped to form our constitution have been destroyed in our civil law system. When someone is accused of a crime, certain fundamental rights are granted. These rights were so important to the founders of this country that they were guaranteed in the Constitution. A person has to be tried in the state and district where the crime is alleged to have occurred. He cannot be compelled to be a witness against himself. He cannot be tried more than once for the same crime. He must be told specifically the nature of the charge brought against him. Other rules, not encoded in the Constitution, have also been an important part of criminal law. The prosecuting attorney is salaried, and does not take home an enormous extra amount of money if he is able to get somebody imprisoned. Rules of evidence are enforced, to ensure the reliability of the evidence.

All these protections have been thrown out the window in modern civil law. Plaintiff lawyers are able to choose their court out of many options, as long as there is some vague connection to that jurisdiction. This occurs throughout most industries, but not so much in medicine. For the most part, doctors are still tried in the state and district where the crime is alleged to have occurred. Many are nevertheless pulled in to the big city court from outlying areas where they might be treated more fairly, or even to other states.[4]

Targets of lawsuits are told only vaguely of the nature of the charges against them. What is called "notice pleading," or just a very nonspecific pleading of the charges, has come to be accepted. A list of generalities is often charged to the defendant, making it much more expensive to prepare a defense. The victim does not know the specific points against which to defend. This becomes much more pronounced when the plaintiff attorney really does not have a strong case thought out before trial. Amendment to the original pleading is then allowed, so that the plaintiff can completely change course from even the general nature of what was originally stated, if nothing on the initial list seems to be panning out.

Discovery is then where the plaintiff attorney finds out where his case might lie. No longer are people protected from witnessing against themselves. Through the process of discovery, they are now required to reveal every detail of their lives and businesses that the plaintiff's attorney cares to request, unless the accused can carry a motion to protect certain items from discovery. This can also be enormously expensive and time consuming for the accused. A plaintiff's attorney can quickly make the request for information to be revealed. The victim then needs to spend all the time and money to respond, sometimes with tens of thousands of pages.[5]

With notice pleading, the accuser can state the accusation very generally, without having any supporting evidence, or even knowing what supporting evidence might exist. Then by compelling the accused to testify against himself through discovery, he can hope to find some evidence. Discovery thus is often a fishing expedition, with the accuser hoping something will turn up to support a case.

In a discrimination suit, the United States Supreme Court upheld the forcing of people to offer evidence against themselves when it opined, "under the Second Circuit's heightened pleading standard, a plaintiff without direct evidence of discrimination at the time of his complaint must plead a prima facie case of discrimination, even though discovery might uncover such direct evidence. It thus seems incongruous to require a plaintiff, in order to survive a motion to dismiss, to plead more facts than he may ultimately need to prove to succeed on the merits if direct evidence of discrimination is discovered."[6] In other words, a plaintiff does not need to present evidence in order to get past a motion to dismiss. He only needs to make a claim. Then the fishing expedition of discovery might disclose some evidence that is helpful to the plaintiff. That is perfectly fine with the court, even if the plaintiff had no idea what he was looking for. It is therefore acceptable to force someone to provide evidence against himself, when the plaintiff does not even know what type of evidence might exist. The plaintiff simply needs to request all records that he might find remotely relevant, which drives up defense costs.

This is clearly quite different from the "right of the people to be secure in their persons, houses, papers, and effects, and no warrants shall issue, but upon probable cause, supported by oath or affirmation, and particularly describing the place to be searched, and the persons or things to be seized."[7] A much higher standard of protection is offered the accused in a criminal case. The police cannot just make a general claim without any support, and then expect to be able to search everything belonging to a defendant in hopes of turning up some piece of evidence, the nature of which they could not even guess.

There were rules of evidence which formerly kept out marginal "evidence" that was meant only to distract or play on emotions. Irrelevant displays that were not factually founded were not admissible. Neither was the testimony of an "expert" witness that disagreed substantially with the consensus opinion of experts in the science in question. Those rules have been thrown out the window in modern civil law. Now expert witnesses are allowed even when their professional organizations disagree completely with them. Hired guns, who are willing to testify to just about anything, are brought in by the plaintiff to proclaim whatever expert opinion is desired. These "experts" make a great deal of money, and an internet search turns up scores of websites of companies that arrange these deals. Many individual "experts" even have their own websites, to drum up business. One example of a neurosurgeon who provided expert testimony in malpractice cases, claimed over $220,000 per year in earnings from his testimonies.[8]

Defendants then must recruit, and pay for, their own expert witness to debunk the testimony of the plaintiff's expert. Gone are the days of impartial experts whose role is to help the jury to understand the science behind a case. Now juries simply do not know whom to believe when the experts disagree with each other. It often comes down to charisma and emotion.

There has recently been somewhat of an attempt to have judges filter out expert testimony that is not really expert. This gained steam with the "Daubert rules," and continued with some later modifications. However, the problem still remains, because the fat paychecks for the "experts" continue to be paid. As long as they can make tens of thousands of dollars for a successful testimony, they will continue to work around any rules that are implemented. Professional associations have begun expelling members for flagrant falsehoods in their expert testimony,[9] but it is not common. In the opinion he delivered on the legality of these expulsions, Judge Richard Posner said approvingly, "This kind of personal self-regulation rather furthers than impedes the cause of justice."[10] Most of the civilized world does not allow experts who are paid handsomely by the litigators themselves, because it is such an obvious incentive to bias and perjury.

The prosecuting (plaintiff's) attorney also stands to make a fortune now if the case is successful, by collecting a percentage of the loot. This is called the contingency fee. There does not even need to be a solid case, for the attorney to bank a lot of cash. If he can make it expensive enough just to carry out a defense against a completely false charge, then he can force a settlement and keep his cut. This is one problem that is not a recent change in civil law, however.

Consider the idea of a prosecuting attorney making a larger paycheck if the case is successful in criminal law. That idea is repulsive to most people, including the people who comprise the Supreme Court of the United States. An attorney who was an employee of the Vuitton company was hired as the attorney to prosecute criminal actions in a case involving the Vuitton company. The majority opinion held against that appointment. Allowing a prosecuting attorney in a criminal case, who had allegiance to the aggrieved party, would violate the attorney's "sense of public responsibility for the interests of justice...Such an attorney is required by the very standards of the profession to serve two masters."[11] If this is wrong in criminal law, then the same principle should apply to civil law.

Take the recent prosecution of three Duke LaCrosse players on a charge of rape as another example. It became clear that the district attorney knew they were innocent, yet prosecuted anyway. He ended up being disbarred. Suppose hypothetically that he would have made an extra few hundred thousand dollars from the case if he successfully prosecuted them? People would be outraged at the thought of a D.A. earning a big pile of money if he can get people convicted. This is hypothetical to make the comparison to civil law. I am not suggesting that he stood to make such money from the case. The point is that what would be so clearly a miscarriage of justice in criminal law is equally wrong in civil law.

There is a solution to the problem of a plaintiff driving up the cost of defense to the point where defending parties want to settle in order to avoid those costs. That would be accomplished by "loser pays" laws, also called the "English system." In that scenario, whichever side loses the case has to pay the legal fees of the opposing side.

In civil law in the rest of the developed world, the loser pays the legal costs of the other side, whether the plaintiff or defense wins. Rather than being one sided, loser pays either way. This leads to people being more confident of the soundness of their cases before pursuing them. It also inhibits lawyers from deliberately running up the costs of the other side, or threatening to do so in order to force a settlement. That single reform would probably have the greatest effect of any in reforming our runaway litigation nightmare in the United States.

Reestablishing proper jurisdiction would help bring litigation problems under control. The effects would be felt most strongly in product litigation, but there are also some cases of jurisdictional abuse against doctors and hospitals. If a doctor stays out of a jurisdiction where litigation is dangerous he should not be pulled in to that district to face charges. Jurisdiction would best be enforced by the federal court system, to settle the violations of one state against the citizens of another. The whole idea of indirect contacts with a state as justification for being tried in another state should be rejected.

If civil law was conducted with civility, it could resume its historic function of righting wrong. It is now more of a haphazardly applied wealth redistribution program. One cannot avoid its snare through conscientious behavior. It is simply a matter of luck, somewhat like being forced to play Russian Roulette.

Suppose a state was to enact real civil law reforms, such as described herein. Then suppose that state was to be so bold as to reclaim its own jurisdiction, by not enforcing the judgments of other states when they step outside of their jurisdiction. For example, imagine Idaho refusing to have its police seize the property of its citizens when New Jersey courts entered judgments that were serious violations of Idaho jurisdiction. This would probably attract a tremendous amount of business investment into Idaho, or whatever state pursued this policy, as businesses would love to find a place of refuge from the litigation storm. A company could then avoid the courts of another state if it avoided doing business in that state. Businesses would not need to be afraid to innovate and produce, for fear of being sued. They would need to be cautious, but now no amount of caution seems to be helpful in avoiding a lawsuit.

All these perversions of just law have ensured that there will be an enormous amount of litigation. It was the goal of the "reformers," and they have achieved their goal with smashing success. In the process, they have smashed initiative and productivity. Everybody loses except the attorneys. By deterring industries from producing, we lose their products. By driving doctors away, we lose health care.

There is no justification for ignoring basic principles of law for people being accused in civil cases. The litigators claim that these are not accusations, but are mere assertions of liability. There is no crime being tried, it is simply liability being determined, an attorney would argue.

However, the effect is the same. The defendants are being accused and tried in civil law just as in criminal cases. They lose their livelihoods and reputations. They are put through years of turmoil. They may not be put in prison, but that may be precious little comfort if they are impoverished. They deserve the protections of the accused just as much as criminal defendants do.

Civil law is an essential part of our legal system. It needs to be kept in its proper role, however. Rather than serving the cause of wealth redistribution, it needs to be used to protect people against unjust, injurious, and blameworthy conduct of others. When left to its own self-correcting reforms, one precedent at a time, it will do a reasonable job of accomplishing this. The "reforms" that have been pushed upon the public by the ordained legal "experts," which have corrupted the system in the last several decades, should be undone in order that the system can serve its original purposes.

If we want to get litigation under control, we need to restore the rules of just law to society. Basic principles, such as those firmly ensconced in our Constitution for criminal cases, need to be observed in civil law as well. We need to restore civility to our system of civil law.

# Eliminate the Food and
# Drug Administration

———

*"Democracy is a pathetic belief in the collective*
*wisdom of individual ignorance."*

*- H.L. MENCKEN*

ONE HUGE STEP FORWARD IN the rehabilitation of American health care could be taken by the abolition of the Food and Drug Administration (FDA). There is no constitutional authority for the existence of a federal agency that tells people what they can and cannot eat, for the purposes of nourishment or healing. Nowhere in that binding contract, the United States Constitution, can any jurisdiction be found for the federal government preventing an individual citizen from making his own choice about medication, based on whatever knowledge he is willing to pursue regarding the benefit vs. risk of that medication for himself.

Thomas Jefferson wrote the Declaration of Independence. He also had a very strong influence on the writing of the constitution, although he was not in attendance.[1] He said, "The legitimate powers of government extend to such acts only as are injurious to others." How does this relate to medicine? "It does me no injury for my neighbour to say there are twenty gods, or no god. It neither picks my pocket nor breaks my leg. Was the government to prescribe to us our medicine and diet, our bodies would be in such keeping as our souls are now. Thus in France the emetic was once forbidden as a medicine, and the potatoe as an article of food."[2] Thomas Jefferson clearly chastised the French government for forbidding certain medicines and foods, because government has no jurisdiction over what one individual does to himself. He was right in this.

If someone wants to aggressively research the efficacy and safety profile of any given medication, as regarding his own individual situation, with or without the consultation of an expert, or if he just wants to take the medication for granted with a minimum of research, then that is the moral right of the individual involved. Government should not be driving drug prices clear into the stratosphere, and preventing medicines from being available. Bureaucrats should not be delaying lifesaving medicines from reaching the marketplace, for many years, while people literally die waiting.

But what about safety? What about the "snake oil" salesmen that would be exploiting the ignorance of the people? Who is going to protect us from our own ignorance?

Talk to just about anybody about eliminating the FDA, and they will say they want medications certified for safety. That is precisely the reason that a free market alternative would spring up. With public demand for safety certification, it is obvious that someone would supply that demand. There would probably be competing private agencies. There are examples of free market safety certification in other industries, including Consumer Reports, American National Standards Institute (ANSI) and Underwriters Laboratories (UL). These organizations are much more appropriate in their responsiveness to both consumers and manufacturers than is the FDA. They do not put a disproportionate emphasis on refusal to approve a product, as the FDA does for fear of political repercussions. They are much more prompt in their evaluations. They do not drive prices many times higher than they would otherwise be. For a very thorough discussion of the FDA, in comparison to Underwriters Laboratories, see Noel Campbell's study for the Cato Institute.[3]

These free market solutions also do not have the power of the United States government enforcing their decisions. Men with guns will not arrive on your doorstep if you choose to disregard the recommendations of Consumer Reports or Underwriters Laboratories. This result is, however, the potential outcome for disregarding any mandates of government, including the FDA. It happens in real life, not just in theory.[4]

With a nongovernmental organization performing safety evaluations, people would be able to choose a medicine from the certified list, and be confident in its safety, or they could take their chances with an uncertified medication. It is up to individual choice, augmented if desired by consultation with an expert - a doctor or pharmacist. This is already the case in the expanding market for "herbal" products.

If someone suffers from recurrent sinus infections, and he knows that the old generic doxycycline, some decongestants, and nasal saline spray do the job for him, he could just go and buy some. There would be no need for a visit with a physician in order to get the necessary government permission to do what he already knows he needs to do. In 2012, before it went into shortage due to FDA overzealousness, I could buy a bottle of 500 doxycycline 100 mg capsules for $21. This is enough for almost eighteen courses of treatment, at fourteen days each. Without FDA compulsion, the medicine would simply be available for purchase, most often in single course quantities, for perhaps two or three dollars. It could be purchased the same way someone could purchase a water pump for his car.

If someone does not already know what he needs, then he could consult a doctor or pharmacist, or someone who might be somewhat of a hybrid between the two. He could accept or reject the advice offered, or take some sort of middle course. The decision would ultimately be made by the individual affected by that choice. Similar to the water pump situation, he may decide to rely solely on the skill of an expert, rather than installing the water pump himself.

If someone knows what he needs, but wants to go a little deeper and get at the underlying problem that is causing recurrent sinus infections, he might consult a doctor for that aspect of care. He may find that antihistamines or nasal steroid sprays keep the recurrences down. He may even find that he needs a mechanic to ream his cylinders and clean his ports - an otolaryngologist to perform sinus surgery to open up his sinus passages.

Not only would medications be much more affordable, but many life-saving medications would become available that are currently kept off the market. Many drugs which are available in Europe would be offered in the United States. More drugs which would not otherwise be developed would be produced and sold. The drugs that Dr. Ruwart referred to, half of the potential innovations of her company,[5] could be developed. We could have medications for illnesses which are now untreatable, and remain untreatable as a result of FDA interference.

In the fertile country of Russia, people began starving after their agriculture was taken over by a central economy. Russians had been exporting grain for many years. Then, under Soviet control, they had to start importing food in order to survive. Millions starved to death.[6]

Food is far too important to allow government control to interfere with its production and distribution. Only misery results. Medical research is no different. It is far too important to give the government authority over it. People end up dying who could otherwise be saved. Restore freedom, and our lives will be enriched. One of the most important ways to do this is to allow people to make their own decisions about their own medicines, by eliminating the FDA.

# Eliminate Insurance Mandates

———

*"If most people aren't smart enough to know what's good for them, how do you expect them to be smart enough to know for whom or what to vote?"*

- CHASE LEE

IF STATES STOP MANDATING THAT certain things must be covered by health insurance policies, then insurance policies will become more affordable. Policies would not cost 2.5 times as much in New Jersey as a comparable policy in Pennsylvania,[1] if New Jersey did not mandate that so many more things be covered.

If people were allowed to make their own choices regarding what they want covered, and the employer was not the agent through whom a policy had to be obtained, then a person could get the policy that is best for him. That could be a catastrophic coverage policy. Alternatively, it could be a more costly policy with a lower deductible. There could be more services covered, for a higher premium, or fewer services covered, for a lower premium. It would be a matter of individual choice.

The best policy for someone might be one that does not cover HIV treatment if the person feels that their risk of contracting HIV is limited to the one in 680,000 chance of getting it through transfusion,[2] because he does not engage in fornication, adultery, sodomy, or intravenous drug abuse. The person might want HIV and hepatitis C covered, because he engages in risky behaviors. The person who avoids costly behaviors would thus avoid the costly policy that insures against the consequences of those behaviors.

Someone who has had a tubal ligation, to prevent pregnancy, might not want an insurance policy that covers obstetrics. Someone who is a faithful member of a religion that proscribes alcohol and other recreational drug use, might not want to pay extra for a policy that covers drug treatment. People who have a higher risk of certain conditions could elect to purchase coverage against those conditions, and people without those risks could elect to avoid that cost.

It would be a strictly pro-choice environment in health insurance. The cost of coverage for risky behavior would not be spread over all people. The cost would therefore rise for those who assume the risky behavior. Those people could save cost in other areas that they see as less likely for them, however.

Which is a more moral approach? Should the person who practices risky behaviors have the cost of his policy that covers the costs of those risks spread out over the whole population, to lower it for him? Or should people who avoid behaviors that put them at risk be rewarded for their actions?

Why should we mitigate the consequences of these behaviors, and spread their costs onto people who avoid them? That removes one of the deterrence to risky behaviors, by lowering the insurance costs of those behaviors for the person who engages in them, therefore probably increasing the occurrence rates of those things. If people bear more of the personal consequences of their behaviors, then they would be less likely to engage in reckless behaviors.

People should be free to perform whatever self-destructive activities they choose, so long as they do not bill somebody else for their consequences. Do whatever you want, just don't send me the bill. If you want the laws to allow something as long as it is kept in the privacy of your own bedroom, then don't take it out of your bedroom and into my wallet.

On the other hand, the people getting the bill for your behaviors may very well decide to do something about them someday. We already see society heading away from free choices in matters of what to eat, and smoking. Legislation could well spread to other behaviors.

Sorry, folks, but Michael Bloomberg, former mayor of New York City, has a legitimate point. If society, through government, has to pay your medical costs, then society, through government, has a right to tell you how much soda you can drink. And, for that matter, whether you can have a trampoline, and when you have to wear a helmet, and with whom you can have sex. Like to go four-wheeling, or skydiving, or bullriding, or dirtbiking? Like to eat a bacon double cheeseburger? Then don't bill other people for your health consequences. Otherwise they have every right to say what you can and can't do, and even what you must do. Eat a plateful of brussel sprouts every day, or else, by the precedent set by John Roberts, you can even pay extra tax. Get your exercise every day, or pay extra tax. I call this the Bloomberg effect.

Society has just as much right to outlaw unhealthy behavior, and to mandate healthy behavior, as you do to bill them for the consequences of those behaviors. I do not want the government telling us what we can and cannot do. I want to be free to make my own choices of my own free will, and I want people of other viewpoints to be free to make their own choices, whatever they may be, as long as they do not pick my pocket or break my leg.

If people were allowed to purchase high deductible policies that only cover very costly services, without having to have many routine items covered, then there would probably be fewer uninsured, because the policies would be more affordable. Routine things would be paid for out of pocket. Out of pocket costs and catastrophic coverage health policies would be quite affordable to the vast majority of people. This will be explained in more detail in a later chapter.

The argument against reducing mandates is that the insurance companies would leave many important things uncovered. We therefore need government to mandate that the necessary services are covered. Actually, in a free market, where there is a demand for something, a supply will arise. If it is a very risky situation, however, then the premium will rise. Thus the practicing homosexual would be able to insure against HIV, but he will have to pay a premium which is commensurate with his risk. Someone who wants to pay insurance premiums for expected services, like routine colonoscopy for cancer screening, would be able to buy that more expensive policy in a free market.

Without government mandates on which specific things must be covered, more people would be able to afford insurance. Freedom would increase.

People would be free to pursue whatever lifestyles they choose, without being forced to pay for the lifestyles of other people. Choices have consequences. In a truly free society, people bear the consequences of their own choices, rather than forcing those consequences on others.

# Remove Controls Over Price and Supply

---

*"Government 'help' to business is just as disastrous as*
*government persecution ... the only way a government*
*can be of service to national prosperity*
*is by keeping its hands off."*

- AYN RAND

WE MUST REMOVE PRICE CONTROLS if we are to alleviate the shortages that chronically plague us. We will have to prevent Congress from modifying Medicare Part D to impose pharmaceutical price controls, or pharmaceutical innovation will die in America. The threat of price controls on medicines is very real. It has already been discussed as a likely point of attack from the Democrats following recent electoral success.[1] If price controls are instituted on medicines, then we will need to be satisfied with the medicines that we have now, as there will not be a motivation to develop new drugs. Without the profit motive, there is no great engine of innovation. There may be some new findings, funded with tax money. The pace will be slow, and the emphasis will be on conditions that receive the greatest lobbying. Politically motivated, taxpayer funded research will dominate, and the myriad advances from which we have benefited will become past history.

Price controls on doctors are an essential part of Medicare and Medicaid. These systems are virtually made for fraud, and their costs must be controlled somehow. When doctors lose money on Medicaid patients, they must increase their fees for other patients. As discussed in a previous chapter, these programs would be best left in the dust bin of history.

We also need to remove the control of the federal government on physician supply. If we are to eliminate the waiting times of specialist appointments, then we must allow market forces to dictate the training of specialists. It can take months to get in to see a rheumatologist, for example, in many states. Waiting times are much worse in the more socialist nations. In a market situation without government interference, shortages lead to quickly increased production. The same applies to labor markets. More people would train to be rheumatologists when they realize the great demand for them, if the residency positions were available.

Before Medicare took over the funding of residencies, they were administered privately. Private hospitals paid residents a meager salary, taken out of patient revenues. In return, the hospitals received work. They also retained a fair number of their residents to continue working in the area, bringing patients to the hospital. It was thus a mutually beneficial arrangement. A doctor with whom I spent some time in medical school discussed this situation with me. He was paid $300 - 400 per month, to the best of his memory, during the late 1950s. $350 per month adjusts for inflation to about $25,000 per year in 2000, when I did my residency. I was paid about $42,000 per year in my residency. He was paid less, but it was livable.

There are still some residencies that are privately funded, generally part of the larger HMO plans. Group Health Cooperative of Seattle trains family practice physicians. The Southern California Kaiser-Permanente Medical Group trains family practice physicians as well as some subspecialists.[2] These organizations then derive the benefit of having a steady stream of freshly trained doctors, trained to suit them. More private funding of residencies through hospitals, like other types of apprenticeships, could go a long way toward reducing waiting times for specialty care.

If we remove price controls, then America will retain its place as the center for innovations. Medicines will continue to be developed, to combat the illnesses that we have not yet been able to overcome. New antibiotics will be developed, to keep ahead of emerging resistance to our existing antibiotics. New fields of endeavor, such as genetic engineering, and adult stem cell research, while starting to show promise, could become fully developed. This will only happen if the free market, with its profit motive, is allowed to flourish. It is the reason for the amazing pace of technological development that we have enjoyed in the past, and it will be the factor on which future development will depend.

A leftist friend of mine reviewed this book, and told me that while it was very informative, it did not offer any solutions. The past eight chapters have all been about solutions. He did not see them as solutions, however, because I am not advocating any new government programs. I am not arguing for a more efficient, smarter government system to handle health care.

After removing a skin cancer, I do not replace it with anything. The skin heals, and the body takes care of itself, after the cancer is removed. The solution is the removal of the cancer. Likewise, the myriad of government programs that interfere with efficient delivery of healthcare is a malignancy that is threatening the life of our country. It needs to be excised. That cancer does not need to be, and should not be, replaced with any other government program. Millions of people making their own decisions in a free market will heal the health care system just like the body heals itself once a cancer is excised.

# Applications of These Solutions

# Free Market Practices at Work Today

---

*"The only way that has ever been discovered to have a lot of*
*people cooperate together voluntarily is through the free market.*
*And that's why it's so essential to preserving individual freedom."*

*- MILTON FRIEDMAN*

IN ORDER TO ESCAPE THE high prices that result from American socialism, some people go overseas for major surgeries. No, they do not go to the more socialist nations; they go to places like India, Taiwan, or Costa Rica. There they can find physicians who have been trained very well, often in the United States, and are board certified in their specialties. They do fine work for a fraction of the cost. The difference is in the regulatory environment, the lawsuits, and all those other things that were discussed previously in this book.

The Wall Street Journal reports that cardiac surgery costs about $4,000 (US dollars) in India, compared to at least $30,000 in America.[1] The Canadian Broadcasting Corporation reports that dental work through medical tourism costs about 10% of U.S. prices, gall bladder surgery costs about 12%, cardiac surgery costs about 16%, and hip replacements cost about 10%.[2]

Somebody might say that these cost differences are due to lower physician salaries. American doctors would not be satisfied to make that kind of money, and so the cost comparison is irrelevant. This argument does not hold up to the facts. The percentage of U.S. health spending that is physician compensation is only 22.7%.[3] Even if the salary of the physician treating the medical tourist was only one third of the American physician salary, this would only result in a 15% reduction in cost. Differences in surgeon salary are not a very major part of the cost differences, if any. The third party payment system, with all its attendant costs, as previously described, is the reason for the vast majority of the cost difference between American and medical tourist facilities.

Some people worry about the quality of the care that might be delivered overseas. They worry that the decreased amount of regulation would lead to slipshod care. The opposite is actually true. It is much easier to get around government regulation than it is to escape a bad reputation. The hospitals in places like India and Argentina are thriving because the news of their top notch care spreads. If they skimped and left patients hanging then that news would quickly spread and they would lose their business. The reports coming back from these patients are generally quite positive.

Media outlets such as National Public Radio have broadcast glowing patient reports from medical tourists they have interviewed.[4] A patient of mine related a similar experience to my wife. She was very pleased with the service and skill that were provided. Every report I have heard from these patients has been enthusiastic.

The more heavily regulated a system is, the less people consider the reputations of its hospitals and doctors. They simply go where they are assigned. The places with the worst reputations are only able to survive in more heavily socialized systems. The Veterans Affairs (VA) system is the quintessential example of that in America.

As a side note, regarding veterans, I certainly do believe that the promises that we made to them in exchange for their service should be honored. The VA system is not a welfare system. It is payment for service. The problem is that our veterans are shunted off into a separate system. They are not offered the same care that other Americans can receive. The bureaucratic inefficiencies of that system are terrible. Our veterans deserve better than that. They deserve to be able to partake of the bounty of American medicine, and have it paid in fulfillment of their contracts. They should be able to get their care wherever they want it, without having to stay within a separate system.

The technology in medical tourist destinations is at least as advanced, and often more so, than is commonly found in America outside of the large teaching hospitals. Apollo Hospitals in India lists among its resources a 64 slice CT - PET scanner. This is available in some places in the United States, but it is not typical. A manager at a radiology facility with which I am familiar proudly told me of the 16 slice CT - PET scanner that they had just purchased.[5] This was after I had read of the more advanced equipment already at Apollo Hospitals.

Veterinary care provides another good example of free market based medicine. I once did a call to a baseball field for a patient with a knee injury. I assessed her as having a torn anterior cruciate ligament (ACL), with severe instability, and referred her to an orthopedic surgeon for repair. Her surgery cost $12,000, and she actually quit her job in order to get onto Medicaid for the surgery to be done. My dog suffered from a torn ACL, and the price tag for that surgery was $1,000. The initial assessment of the dog cost $33, including other issues that were attended to at the time. The primary reason for veterinary care costing just a fraction of human care, is the same reason it can be offered so much cheaper in many other countries. It is paid directly.

Although we do not have a free market for health care generally in the United States, there are some oases of free market activity. There are many examples of free market based medical practices that exist now, even in America. There is a small but growing movement to escape the controls of Medicare and preferred provider networks, advocated by the Association of American Physicians and Surgeons. AAPS describes themselves as "a voice for private physicians."[6]

I recently learned of a surgical center in the United States that only takes direct payment. It is called the Surgery Center of Oklahoma, and can be found at www.surgerycenterok.com. They have a very low complication rate. They post prices online, including the hospital fee, surgeon's fee, and anesthesiologist's fee. The price listed for an inguinal hernia repair is $3,060, as of March 2014. This is not as low as going overseas, but they do not have the same competition yet in the United States. Expect fees to decrease if multiple competitors were to spring up.

I had an arthroscopic knee surgery there myself in 2013. After calling the doctors and hospitals in my city of Idaho Falls, and negotiating them down with cash up front, the best cost I could get was about $12,000. The all-inclusive fee at the Surgery Center of Oklahoma was $3,740. The quality was excellent. I did not need a single pain pill afterward. I was riding my bicycle hard on day 12 post-op.

My practice is an example of what can be done when a free market approach is taken. Care is affordable. Service is of a high level, and timely. Adequate time is spent with the patient. My logo is "Modern Medical Care with Old Time Service," and I believe that I live up to that lofty goal. I do not have a whole crew of clerical staff, because I do not need them to contend with insurance companies or government clerks for payment. I do not have to convince some flunky that a medical decision was appropriate, in order to get paid. The patient pays me directly.

Fees are low. As of this writing, I charge $2.62 per minute, plus what I have to pay for medications and labs. My average fee is $55 when patients come to my office, including medications dispensed, and lab fees. I spend an average of 19 minutes per patient. My average fee for a housecall is $168. There is no financial incentive to gloss over an issue quickly, or to have to reschedule a separate issue for a separate appointment. Just like a plumber or mechanic, I am paid by time, plus any supplies that need replacement such as $5 worth of laceration repair supplies, at my cost. Because I do not have the $272,000 overhead of the average family practice doctor, and I collect all my charges instead of only 58%, my fees are typically near one third of customary fees. Actually, I have even collected a little more than my charges, because patients often leave me a tip.

Because I am not dependent on staff, I am able to offer house calls and flexible hours of service. I only need my wife to be present for female visits, and help with the phone. I can make as much money as the average family practice doctor by seeing a reasonable workload of patients. I believe that charging by time is the most fair and reasonable way to quantify my work. I have gone to jobsites to see patients there, with a minimum of lost work time for the employee. I have not only gone to a ballfield, but welding shops and pharmacies to attend to their employees. I have stitched children up in their homes several times.

I offer service usually on the same day as the call, and intend to continue doing so. This is also possible because I do not depend on staff.

In order to offer this type of care, I needed to "opt out" of Medicare, and cancel all insurance contracts. Otherwise, I would have had to charge the same high insurance prices for everybody. I would have had to hire all the staff that would be required to deal with the third party payers. I would have had to raise fees to compensate for frequent payment denials from Medicare, Medicaid, and insurance companies. I would not be able to get paid for housecalls.

These increased fees would have to be charged to my uninsured patients as well, if I played the insurance game. This is one way that the uninsured subsidize the health care of the insured. It does not happen in my practice. Several patients have told me that my fees end up being about the same or lower than their co-pays. When labs are done, it is usually quite a bit less expensive to pay directly through me than to work through insurance. For example, $9 is what I charge for a thyroid stimulating hormone (TSH) level, $4 for a complete blood count, and $8 for a lipid profile (a breakdown of the different types of cholesterol). These are the lab fees that are added to my time. For comparison, a patient told me that she worked in one of the big labs, and she had to pay $130 for a TSH (just the lab fee).

As it turns out, lack of health insurance does not equate with lack of care. Most of my patients do not have health insurance. Some of my patients are insured, and prefer to come to me because of their deductibles and co-pays. Some prefer my service over what they can find from an "insurance doctor," and submit their claims for reimbursement for an out of network doctor, or do not bother submitting claims. Some people on Medicare even sign up for my care, knowing that the fee is out of pocket with no possibility of reimbursement. Some of my elderly patients are homebound, and prior to finding out about me, had not been able to see a doctor for years because of what Medicare did to housecalls.

Dr. Todd Coulter, of Ocean Springs, Mississippi, was charging $40 for all his patient visits. He has changed his fee schedule, but still charges patients directly, and his fees are still low. He has also opted out of Medicare and insurance company contracts.[7]

Dr. Charles Steuart was recently charging a mere $10 per patient visit. He was an oncologist, and changed to general medicine, seeing patients four days per week, four hours per day, in the tiny high desert town of Arco Idaho, near Craters of the Moon National Monument.[8]

Dr. Michael Harris, of Traverse City Michigan, is a urologist who opted out of Medicare and opened a free market based practice. There are several Medicare urologists within a few miles of him, but he is doing fine. He offers value and expertise, and patients come to him and pay.[9]

The major news media are constantly whining about people who have "no access to health care." Most people who come to these free market types of practices fall into the category to which they are referring. Somehow the journalists miss the point that health insurance is not health care. In Canada, everybody has health insurance. Health care is an entirely different matter for them. These patients of mine, and of Drs. Coulter, Steuart, Harris, etc. are mostly uninsured middle class workers. Many own their own small businesses. They appreciate value, and do not mind paying for it.

No matter how good a doctor is, he can always be better if he can spend more time. No doctor can remember everything. I frequently refer to a book while a patient is in front of me. I look up medication interactions far more frequently than anybody else I know. A urologist in my town told me he thought I was "brilliant," because any referrals already have a very thorough workup done. I am not so much brilliant as I am simply willing to work at my knowledge frontier, by looking things up. I see what labs should be done for something like a testicular cancer, and get them done quickly so that the urologist has the results with the initial referral. I do not know these things, but I know where to find them. I frequently need to clean up after a doctor that botches the job because he does not take the time needed to be thorough.

Once a patient came to me because he had terrible muscle weakness. A high antinuclear antibody level was found by another doctor, and that triggered an automatic referral to a rheumatologist. Have I mentioned how long it takes to get in to a rheumatologist? Months. In the meantime, this patient was unable to work. He decided to see me. I looked at his labs, and I noticed a severe V-shaped rash on the front of his neck and chest. I thought, hmmm, this is ringing a bell somewhere from my training, and I was thinking about myositis, a muscle disease. I hit the books, while the patient waited, and found what I was looking for under dermatomyositis. I ran a muscle enzyme test and found it quite high. It was a classic case of a rare disease that most doctors do not see. I was able to start treatment, fine tune it as much as I could with my training and reference materials, and get him recovering his strength. When he got to the rheumatologist he was greatly improved. I have found things that specialists have even missed because they did not take the time to be thorough.

In my residency, when I was in my first year, I started the hospital internal medicine rotation and one of my first patients to see was unconscious in the intensive care unit, with overwhelming sepsis (infection) that her body was simple unable to tackle even with heavy antibiotics. It stemmed from a urinary tract infection. She was rapidly approaching death. She was on meds to keep her blood pressure up to a life-sustaining level. The second year resident and the full doctor that was supervising could not make any headway. They thought they were doing all they could. I took the initiative to go to our family practice clinic and look through her chart. It turned out that she was on long-term prednisone and therefore in any severe infection she needed a steroid boost, because the ability of her adrenal glands to respond to infection with increased steroid production was blunted. Every doctor should know this. It was missed by the very resident who took care of her in the clinic, who was now on the hospital rotation taking care of her. I ordered a steroid boost, and she came back from the brink of death. She would have been dead within two days if somebody did not go read her clinic chart.

I saw a 93 year old patient in 2007 on a housecall, after she was discharged from the hospital. She was failing. She was weak, dizzy, hardly eating or talking. Family was gathering, possibly for her death. They wanted me to see what I could do to help her. I simply tuned up some medication doses, allowing her blood pressure to run a bit higher as was appropriate for her age, adjusted thyroid treatment, and restarted vitamin B12 which was forgotten in the hospital. These were things to make her more comfortable; to help her feel better. She ended up coming around and is still alive and reasonably healthy as of late 2015. She is over 100 years old now. All she needed was somebody to be thorough in adjusting her medications.

Whatever the skill level and intelligence of a doctor, he can be ever so much better if he takes the time to be thorough. It does not take real brilliance to appear brilliant, but it does take effort. That effort takes time. Proper time cannot be spent if a doctor has to see so many patients just to pay his staff, that he is rushed. Mistakes then get made.

Some of my patients are illegal aliens. That does not matter, and I do not bother to find out, because they are not using any tax dollars for their medical care. Once a woman called me for her homebound frail mother. I told her that I had opted out of Medicare, so it would be out of pocket. She said that it did not matter, because her mother was "illegal." I restrained a chuckle. I arrived, treated her and another family member, and told her the fee. She paid in cash and gave me a $22 tip besides. People worry about illegal aliens sucking up our health care dollars. It would not matter if they were simply charged reasonable fees and they paid themselves. Like others, they do not mind paying for value. Free markets would thus be the solution to the problem of health care as it relates to illegal aliens, just as it is the solution to our other health care woes.

If a doctor is out there somewhere reading this, and wants to set up a free market practice, please contact me. You can send me an email at drjbrook@ brookharbor.com. I have a website at www.drjimbrook.com. I will spend time on the phone with you if you call my office, or you can come to my house/office combination, have dinner with my wife and I, and even shadow me in my practice for a time. I will explain everything I can. Neils Bohr, the brilliant physicist, once said that "an expert is someone who has made every mistake possible in a very narrow field" [but he has learned from them]. I am therefore an expert in free market medicine.

While we have not had free markets overall in American health care in many decades, we do have these islands of free market activity. These isolated practices give us an insight into the practicality of free market health care.

# Why Free Markets Are
# the Moral Choice

———

*"'Need' now means wanting someone else's money. 'Greed' means wanting*
*to keep your own. 'Compassion' is when a politician arranges the transfer."*

*- JOSEPH SOBRAN*

THE NEXT TOPIC IN THIS discussion is morality. Which choice is more moral,
free markets or socialism?

Free markets allow people to choose whether to purchase goods or services, in exchange for money they have earned by supplying goods or services
to others. Socialism has money forcibly confiscated from people in order to
pay for other people.

A free market is a true pro-choice system. All individuals who are involved in a transaction get to choose what they are willing to transact, at what
price, and under what conditions. Those most closely affected can make informed choices based on their knowledge of the immediate situation, without
coercion by distant governmental forces. People are rewarded for work, and
are motivated by the prospect of success.

Socialism denies all choice; it is pro-force. If the government leaders decide that people should support some cause, then they confiscate money from
the people to support that cause, of course keeping a cut for themselves. If

someone does not want to support some governmental cause, and withholds his money, then ultimately, men with guns will be sent to enforce compliance. If he resists them, he will be imprisoned; if he resists strongly enough, he will be shot. "Government is not reason; it is not eloquence; it is force. Like fire, it is a dangerous servant and a fearful master."[1]

As so many of our founding fathers have said, it is not the place of government to take the money of their constituents to provide for objects of benevolence. That is the proper place of voluntary charity. This is a principle that is anathema to a socialist. A socialist simply does not believe in the capacity of human beings to do good, and therefore does not believe that we can depend on voluntary giving to meet the needs of the less fortunate.

People argue about what constitutes a "conservative" and a "liberal" in the modern day misuse of the word.[2] I would say that a conservative is one who voluntarily gives his own time and money to a cause in which he believes, and a liberal is one who votes other people's money to a cause in which he believes.

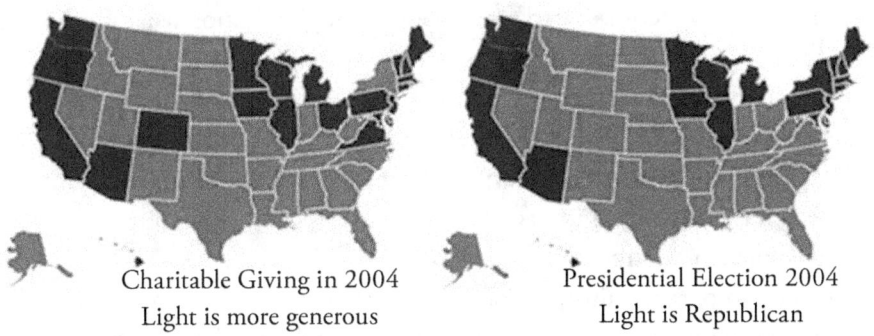

Charitable Giving in 2004
Light is more generous

Presidential Election 2004
Light is Republican

The above maps are of the average generosity in charitable giving by state on the left,[3] and the electoral vote in the 2004 presidential election on the right.[4] The two maps look almost identical. The lowest 10 states in charitable giving all voted Democrat, and the highest 26 states all voted Republican. It would appear that the level of charitable giving in a state is probably the best predictor of voting tendencies, at least at the presidential level.

Keep in mind, that this pattern reflects the attitudes of the people who vote Republican, not necessarily of those in leadership of the Republican Party.

Most people who identify themselves as "conservative" vote Republican in the general presidential elections. This discussion in no way implies that I support the top leaders of the Republican Party. How could I, if I believe in limited constitutional government? The politicians who are served up to the people under the Republican banner often behave far differently than the people voting for them would want. I think that is the main reason that the Republicans lost power in the 2008 election.

The simple fact of the matter, as proven by history, is that Americans are a very generous people. They always have been. When there is a need, they rise up to meet it. In 2004, the American average of itemized charitable contributions per taxpayer was $4,012.[5] Over the past ten years, the average adjusted gross income increased by 44%, while the average itemized giving rose 64%.[6] This does not include all charitable giving, just the gifts that have been itemized on tax returns. It also does not include time donated.

For a disaster that did not hit America, the tsunami of December 2004, Americans voluntarily gave approximately $1.8 billion.[7] This does not count the money that was confiscated from them through taxation, that our government then sent to the relief effort.

Americans can be depended upon to give to those in need. If they have money to give, they will give it to those who truly need it. A website has been created in 2010 called gofundme.com, through which they claim over $1 billion has been raised in just the past year (2015).[8] Anybody can list any personal cause for voluntary fundraising.

Socialist programs diminish our voluntary giving. They take our money, leaving us with much less to give. They give us a feeling of being cheated. They give us a jaded view of people in need, because we have seen so much fraud.

We have all seen cases like the woman using a government welfare check, through the WIC program, to pay for baby food, while wearing a diamond ring and then getting into a new $20,000 car.[9] We feel robbed when we realize that our paychecks have been looted to provide that money. This makes us not want to give to people in need, because we have the "I already gave at the office" mentality. We also wonder if the need is real, or if we are being defrauded again.

The vast majority of government spending is in the form of welfare payments. Medicare, Medicaid, Social Security, agricultural subsidies, much of our foreign aid, Women Infants and Children (WIC), food stamps, Aid to Families with Dependent Children (AFDC), housing subsidies, student loan subsidies and grants, the list goes on and on. Our national debt is entirely due to these misguided programs. Government serving its true purposes - national defense, police, and other ways of maintaining law and order, amount to at most one fourth of our government expenditures, probably much less.

The federal government spends $30,500 per year per family,[10] and state and local governments spend roughly another $9,500,[11] totaling roughly $40,000 per family. If, instead of taking the money of their constituents to provide for objects of benevolence, our governments were securing us in our rights to life, liberty, and the pursuit of happiness, this bill would be reduced to maybe about $10,000 per family. This is assuming the high end of one fourth of spending being proper for government.

Imagine the extent of voluntary charitable giving if we had an extra $30,000 per family per year. Actually, prosperity would increase even more than the simple math would indicate. We would not have the drag on our productivity that all the regulation and taxation causes. If government simply governed, instead of trying to provide for people, and protect them from themselves, then people would have so much money that it would be easy to handle the needs of the less able or less fortunate. The American people have shown that they have the character and generosity to do that. If they did not have their money taken, they would give to whoever needed it.

It is probably a mistake to use the word "generous" when discussing government programs, such as saying that a politician "generously" funded such and such a program. If that politician gave his own money, then the word "generous" would apply. When having other people's money forcibly confiscated for a program, the term "greedy" would be more applicable. The more money confiscated, the greedier are the legislators who pass the act. It is being used as a surrogate for personal giving.

If a cause should be supported, but it is funded by money confiscated from others, then that reduces the need for voluntary giving, and stifles the guilt that a person might have for withholding voluntary contributions. A person can feel good about having supported a cause, without actually having to give to it, if he supports a government program funded with money confiscated from other people. These programs are also a way to buy votes, from the people who are receiving the funding, and from people who are assuaging their guilt for not giving. Some people support these programs because they honestly think that socialism is the way to cure societal ills. So a politician is being greedy by using socialist programs in order to remain in power, by buying votes, with money confiscated from other people. An election is therefore an advance auction on stolen goods.[12]

How can these things be called stolen goods? Take a neighborhood example. If Bob thought that Mary should be given some money, for whatever reason, and took money by force from his neighbor Joe to give to her, that would rightly be called theft. It would not matter how worthy a cause it was, it would still be theft. Bob can morally give Mary his own money, and could try to persuade Joe to give, but he cannot forcibly take it from Joe. What if the neighborhood got together, and declared by majority vote that Joe must have money taken from him to give to Mary? It would still be theft.

Yet that is precisely what we do with government. We elect people, who forcibly take money from some people, to give to others. That is theft. There are certain things that a government needs to fund through taxation, such as police, and an army, to protect us in our rights, which is the purpose of government in the first place. Going beyond those functions into the non-governmental areas of wealth redistribution through confiscation is simply theft.

Individuals band together to form governments. Individuals give government the authority to do certain things that they would themselves be morally able to do, but for which a collective strength is needed. An individual cannot morally do through his agent, the government, that which would be immoral for that individual to do himself. Thus, government can act for protection against crime, because an individual has the right to protect himself against criminals. Likewise for protection against an aggressive nation, with an army. An individual cannot forcibly take money from his neighbor to transfer to another, no matter how worthy the cause. Nor can he properly send a government agent to do the same.

Ezra Taft Benson described a test that he would apply to see whether he should support a governmental act, as being within the proper role of government. He asks, "Do I as an individual have a right to use force upon my neighbor to accomplish this goal? If I do have such a right, then I may delegate that power to my government to exercise on my behalf. If I do not have that right as an individual, then I cannot delegate it to government, and I cannot ask my government to perform the act for me."[13]

With free markets, if a person wants to obtain the service of another, he has to pay for that service. The way that he is able to pay, is by serving yet other people, and being paid for it. On the other hand, under socialism, someone can receive service while doing nothing to help others. He just has to take the money that other people are forced to cough up.

So, which is the more moral system, capitalism or socialism? The answer seems obvious to this writer, that capitalism is not only the better way to prosperity, but also the more ethical approach.

Wait a minute! Doesn't everybody have a right to health care? If you look carefully through the United States Constitution, you will see nothing resembling a right to health care. You will see many rights listed specifically, and health care is not among them. This means that the federal government cannot take away those rights that are listed. Don't worry, this does not mean that you do not have a "right" to health care, because those rights not reserved to the federal government are reserved to the states or the people. Something does not have to be specified in the constitution for it to be a right.

In the constitution, however, one of the rights of the people which is explicitly guaranteed is the right to keep and bear arms. Does my right to keep and bear a gun compel others to have to pay for it? If so, let me just place my order now. I have been thinking about a Glock Model 29 in 10 mm. No, hold on a minute! If somebody else is paying for it, that $3185 50 GI by Guncrafter Industries in .50 caliber sounds just about right. After all, money is no object for something that is my right, if somebody else is paying for it.

I also have the right to free speech. Does this mean that somebody else has to buy me radio air time to voice my opinions, with their taxes? Should taxes be taken to pay the publishing and marketing costs of this book? No, my right to free speech, or my right to keep and bear arms, do not compel somebody else to pay for them. It simply means that government cannot prevent me from exercising those rights. Likewise, a "right" to health care does not obligate somebody else to pay for it. It just means that others cannot stand in the way. What is a right for one person cannot require the involuntary servitude of another.

For government to grant an individual a "right" to health care, or free education, a job, etc., another individual must have his rights taken away as he is forced to provide it. Nothing gives a person a right to somebody else's money; nobody has a right to the fruits of somebody else's labor.

People prosper when they have individual freedom and protection of property. The purpose of government is to protect people in their rights. People organized governments in order to protect their lives and property from the assaults of others who may be stronger. A collective strength was needed, hence government with laws, police, and armies. When government violates property rights it becomes destructive of the very ends that it was established to protect.

I can sleep better at night knowing that nobody has money confiscated from their paychecks, to pay my fees, for somebody else's health care. I have taken the moral approach.

Under free market conditions, as we have already explored in detail, health care becomes affordable. Even the big ticket items would no longer have big tickets. Major surgeries, other costly procedures, and hospitalizations would be in the neighborhood of 20% of their current cost.[14]

Catastrophic coverage, or true insurance, could be purchased very affordably. In 2003, I purchased a health insurance policy with a $20,000 deductible for a family of five for $1350 in annual premiums. With the vastly lower fees of a free market, the premium would be correspondingly lower. Imagine health insurance for a family being purchased for a few hundred dollars per year.

The thing that is most worrisome regarding health care costs is the big ill-ness that costs $300,000. That financially destroys a family or an individual, if they do physically survive the illness. If costs of the large services are in the neighborhood of 20%, as we have seen they are, then that $300,000 is reduced to something approximating $60,000.

Catastrophic, high deductible insurance coverage would be very afford-able. This is because the rare big outlay from the insurance company becomes not such a big outlay. Insurance would not often kick in because it would not be often that an expense exceeds the deductible. Insurance would become affordable for virtually everybody, to cover catastrophic events. It should cost just a fraction of what many people, government classified as poor, spend on cigarettes. If I was able to pay $1350 for a $20,000 deductible policy for a family of five in our current environment, then it would seem reasonable for even a $10,000 deductible policy to be had for a few hundred dollars annually if we had a free country.

What about paying out of pocket, up to the deductible? Suppose you have to pay up to $20,000. This would be unusual - remember that would cost $100,000 in our current system of third party payment. Over time, $20,000 could be handled. After all, almost half of people classified as poor own their own homes, 31% own 2 or more cars, and 62% have cable or satel-lite TV.[15] We are a wealthy nation. Remember that the average American family has $7,340 confiscated from them each year just to pay for Medicare and Medicaid. Then there is the tax shifting from non-health items which amounts to $2,100 per family per year. That is a total of $9,140 that the average American family is now having extracted from them.[16] In just 2.2 years, that would pay up to your $20,000 deductible. A lower deductible could be chosen, based on whatever the individual chose. The principle remains the same.

People would be able to obtain a CT scan for less than they now pay for a brake job. When it is needed, as determined by the patient in consultation with a physician, it would be quickly obtained. There would be no hassles with pre-authorization, and no $1800 price tag. Just cash on the barrel head. Hospitalizations would become affordable.

The economics are not a matter of the fundamental morality of the issue. However, these factors are relevant to the discussion, as they bear upon the following.

With the economics that have been discussed, who would be "left behind" in a free market of health care? With the majority of our "poor" having computers, VCRs, and satellite TV, just who is it that would not be able to afford a catastrophic coverage policy, and out of pocket medical costs for the remainder?

With heart surgeries costing one fifth as much as an average domestic new car,[17] and with "poor" people owning as many cars as they do, what would be the problem? Again, this is what heart surgeries cost in the free market health economy of India.[18]

There would be two classes of people who might be left behind. The first is comprised of people who have severe illnesses, genetic or otherwise, that disable them from working and fending for themselves in any way. In the past, family helped those individuals, with private charity making up the difference if the family is not willing or able to do it by themselves. Insurance could be purchased against the risk of having to support a child with this type of illness. They would not be left behind for these reasons.

The second class of people who could be left behind is those who simply could not be bothered with taking care of themselves. Some people simply want a free ride. They do not want to work. They will not expend any effort to learn skills for which somebody would be willing to pay them. Those people make up the vast majority of those who depend on the government for their ride today. They demand that ride, thinking it is their right.

Americans are very willing to help others who are needy and cannot care for themselves. It is part of our Christian heritage and faith. We generally do not want to help those who simply refuse to care for themselves. There are plenty of less obvious people in that second class that we do not see for what they are. These are the people who fritter away their lives, somehow managing to avoid learning any skills or work ethic, and still doing entry level jobs later in life.

I have met some of these people, who want to take advantage of my hard-earned skills without paying anything for them, because they claim not to be able to afford even my low fees. One man, in his fifties, told me he only made about $500 per month, and could not afford anything. He appeared quite physically able. The question, then, is not why he could not even make minimum wage for 40 hours per week. The question is why he has not advanced well beyond that in over thirty years of work. Some people move from one skilled career to the next, picking up many marketable talents on the way. Others advance simply through their work ethic, becoming valuable to a company, or else moving to another company which will recognize and reward their value. People who are willing to work will eventually become valued and rewarded for that work. They will also pick up skills. It must be difficult to avoid learning any marketable skills over a lifetime. For an able bodied person of sound mind to remain at entry level for thirty years takes a special kind of laziness.

For anybody in this second class of people, those who will not provide for themselves even though they can, why should others be forced to provide for them? People can voluntarily provide help, which they so often do. However, why should gunmen from our government be sent to take money from people who are willing to work, to pay for those who will not work? Why should a willing worker expend more effort on someone than that person is willing to expend on himself, and be forced to do so? That would be, and is, highly immoral.

There is the rare person in the first class of people who cannot care for themselves. Family should take care of them. If they cannot or will not, then society does voluntarily step up when they are able. Society is not terribly able when such vast amounts are being confiscated by government as happens in our current situation. Under free market conditions, with the abundance that people enjoy, there would be plenty, and more to spare, for providing for these people.

Which is the better society, then? One in which tens of millions of people suffer hardship, and often go without, in order to provide the regulatory safety net for the very few? Where standards are lower for all? Or one in which all but the very few have an abundance, and those few are helped by private charity? A society of coercion or of freedom? Is it better to provide an unequal distribution of blessings or an equal distribution of misery? The choice is clear. I hope Americans will see it clearly.

# Feasibility of These Solutions

———

*"A democracy cannot exist as a permanent form of government. It can only exist until the voters discover that they can vote themselves largesse out of the public treasury. From that moment on, the majority always votes for the candidates promising the most benefits from the public treasury with the result that a democracy always collapses over loose fiscal policy, always followed by a dictatorship. The average age of the world's greatest civilizations has been 200 years."*

*- Alexander Tytler (attribution disputed by some)*

It seems clear that restoring a free market would do wonders for the affordability of health care. It would also result in better service and more satisfied patients. It would restore fiscal soundness to the American economy. It is morally superior to socialism. Are these reforms actually feasible, though?

The perpetrators of our current system would say that the solutions that I have put forth would not work for health care, because it is far too complicated. A free market would not work in health care because there are far too many factors involved. They use terminology like "stop loss arrangement," "case-mix index," "prospective payment system," "quality improvement organization," and other words in a way to confuse people, so they will leave the fixes to the "experts."

True, there are a great many programs, systems, and laws in health care that are very complicated. This complexity, however, only exists because health care is not a free market in the United States. The experts do not want common people to be able to understand the system, because the common people would realize that the complexity is unnecessary. If you hear some so-called health system expert bandying about words in a way that seems to be deliberately confusing, you should immediately suspect that person's motives. Is it somebody that benefits from perpetuating a complex system? Is he hired by people who work that system? Economics are really not that complicated. It is mostly just common sense. We do not have any of this complexity in the purchasing of plasma TVs or automobiles. Why should we need it in the purchasing of a CT scan?[1]

As it turns out, there is a large support base for many of the reforms that I have proposed. It is only a matter of educating the public to increase that support, and developing the political will to make the necessary changes. People need to understand that not only is a free market the best way to prosperity, but it is by far the more moral approach.

As far as elimination of employer based health insurance goes, Health Savings Accounts are already showing that a consumer oriented approach is not only practical, but better. They are restoring some of the connection between consumer and cost, and therefore influencing people to be more efficient consumers of health care.

The elimination of tax incentives may seem like only a fantasy, but some type of overhaul of the federal income tax is spoken of by a large number of politicians. More specifically, the Fair Tax Act of 2009 had 39 cosponsors in the U.S. House of Representatives.[2] Neil Boortz has written a book on the subject, The FairTax Book, which spent several weeks as number one on the New York Times bestseller list. This act would create a consumption based tax to replace other federal taxes, including the income tax. It would eliminate deductions for all those things that the social engineers are now subsidizing, including health care. If enacted, it would probably give a tremendous boost to the American economy, by making America a more attractive place to have a business. Even the Washington Post ran a commentary criticizing the fact that health care is connected to employment and is tax deductible, because, among other reasons, it "separates the decision to spend money from the responsibility for paying."[3]

Concerning elimination of the FDA, we already have a burgeoning market for unregulated herbal products. 60 million Americans report using herbal products frequently.[4] People are avoiding prescription medications just for the sake of avoiding them. They do not seem to be dying in droves. These herbal medications are obviously drugs, as they are chemical entities intended to treat disease, although their manufacturers claim they are not. The differences are that the active ingredient is often not isolated from the plant, they usually do not have scientifically sound studies to prove their usefulness and safety, although they sometimes do, and they lack FDA regulation. Many of them work very well.

Regarding the reduction of regulations, there has already been a recommendation by a task force of the Department of Health and Human Services that the Evaluation & Management codes of the CPT coding scheme be scrapped.[5] These are codes that are used to describe most doctor visits. The American public are realizing that regulations are out of control. Politicians are continually talking about reducing overly burdensome regulations. If we would just elect some that actually do what they campaign on, then we would see a reduction in regulations.

Concerning phasing out Medicare, many doctors are already doing just that. Increasingly, doctors are not taking new Medicare patients. I have had patients come to me because they tell me that, of the dozens of family practice and internal medicine physicians in Idaho Falls, they could not find a single one who was willing to take a new Medicare patient. Since I had opted out of Medicare, I could see those patients without Medicare involvement.

As far as tort reform is concerned, there is a huge public outcry against the abuse of lawsuits, more states are passing tort reform legislation all the time, and it has been a campaign issue in George W. Bush's second presidential campaign. Some elements were part of the Republican Contract With America, which helped the Republicans win a sweeping victory in the 1994 congressional elections.

People just need to understand the root causes of our litigation crisis. Then we might get real reforms. There has already been some trifling around at the edges of the problem. For example, Rule 11 of the Federal Rules of Civil Procedure is an attempt to punish lawyers for filing lawsuits that have no merit or are intended to harass or drive up defense costs.[6] However, the civil procedure system was remade in recent decades to encourage that very behavior by attorneys. Rule 11 only sanctions lawyers for exploiting that system while leaving intact the incentives for their behavior. Daubert rules attempt to restore some scientific integrity to expert testimony by disallowing some testimony, while leaving intact the system of adversarial hired experts which is the root of the problem.[7]

Regarding the reform that I believe would be the most important of all in our civil system, loser-pays rules, Alaska has had that in place since its purchase from Russia in 1867. "Tort lawsuits comprise only 5% of Alaska's litigation docket, while they make up nearly 10 percent in the rest of the U.S."[8] In 2011, Texas passed loser-pays legislation for their civil law system.

As explained in the chapter on lawsuits, the reason many diagnoses are missed is because the testing is too expensive. At our current prices, we cannot afford to test as frequently as we need to, in order to pick up on the relatively rare but serious illness. In a free market, with CT scans, MRI scans, etc. costing just a fraction of what they cost now, these tests could be done much more frequently when appropriate. What is now punished as "malpractice" could therefore occur much less often. Restoring a free market should lead to better quality care, as people could more easily afford diagnostic testing.

There are many free market medical practices already at work. Medical tourism is receiving a great deal of media attention. Stories have appeared in the Wall Street Journal[9] and the New York Times,[10] and have been heard on National Public Radio,[11] among many others. There is a free market surgery center in the U.S., the Surgery Center of Oklahoma. That has been replicated recently in Torrance California and even in New York City.

Regarding state health insurance mandates, people in heavily mandated states are already getting angry at having to pay much more for insurance premiums than their neighbors from other states are paying. Federal legislation was introduced to allow individuals to purchase health insurance across state lines, to bypass this problem. It was the Health Care Choice Act of 2005, and it had 71 cosposnsors.[12] The problem here, however, comes from the state level. It is found in state insurance law and boards of insurance. States could change this, and then compete with each other on the matter of mandates, in order to attract insurance business from people in other states.

Concerning Obamacare, there is strong voter opposition. A nationwide poll of 840 registered voters conducted after the 2008 elections asked if they would support federal legislation mandating that individuals purchase health insurance. Only 15% of respondents favored, and 53% opposed the idea. The pollsters said, "There is no base of support among any major demographic subgroup. Indeed, opposition is in the high double-digits in every major region of the country."[13] Opposition is continuing and getting more vocal now.

While elimination of licensure does not have a groundswell of support yet, licensure in general has been the subject of much anger in some places. In Idaho, for example, recent contractor licensure legislation, and the increased costs that result, has drawn the heated wrath of conservatives across the state. These types of debates start to focus attention on the principles of choice vs. government force in plying one's trade.

Concerning HIPAA, doctors generally recognize the high costs and difficulties of compliance with it, and the patient care problems that sometimes result. There are also patient advocacy groups, such as the Institute for Health Freedom,[14] that are drawing attention to the serious privacy breaches that HIPAA causes. 92% of people are opposed to government agencies having access to their health records without the individual's prior consent.[15] 88% of people are opposed to a national health information database when they are forced to have their records in it.[16] Opposition is already strong in principle, but most people are unaware of HIPAA and the drive toward a mandatory internet-based health information database. Making people aware of the reality behind these privacy breaching programs will bring about a public outcry.

If the reforms described above are not carried out, and we continue to become more socialist in our approach to medicine in the United States, the results will be inevitable. Canadians often flee their country to obtain the care that they cannot otherwise get in a timely manner. We will also have to travel more often for health care. We will come to recognize the severe shortages and high costs with which socialism hobbles us. Our taxes will become even more painfully high. The problems that have become common knowledge concerning VA care will become obvious throughout American health care.

Eventually, socialism will collapse under its own weight. We simply cannot continue to grow government indefinitely. The Greek economy provides a good example of that. Americans can only have so much of their money seized from them, before the economy completely collapses. A governmental collapse will leave anarchy, chaos, and misery in its wake. We are seeing the economies of Europe grind to a halt already. Many of the socialized medicine countries are even now being forced to look at restoring elements of the free market in order to save their collapsing systems. Some, like Sweden, have already done that.[17]

Establishing free markets in health care in America, for the first time in at least 60 years, is a matter of educating the people. Once people understand the underlying causes of our problems, then they can begin to exert pressure on government to stop interfering with the delivery of health care. As explained above, there are many efforts underway to deal with the causes of our problems. Those efforts will become stronger as more people come to a realization that government is the cause, not the solution, to our health care problems.

I do not expect a critical mass of people to immediately start petitioning government to remove our shackles concerning health care. If we could at least start to effectively resist further encroachments of socialism for now, that would be a good start. The idea of phasing out Medicare and Medicaid is completely unthinkable to far too many people now. Hopefully a movement can be started to get such people thinking of it, however. Once people look clearly at the facts of history and start to think logically, rather than emotionally, the conclusions are obvious. Simply tinkering around with the tax incentives and the Medicare program, while leaving them intact, can only delay economic catastrophe a little longer. It is like changing the formulation of intravenous fluid in a severely fluid overloaded patient, rather than shutting it off and working to remove excess fluid. If we just fritter around at the edges of the problem, rather than directly addressing the causes, then our problems will only get worse, but at a somewhat different rate of decline. Only the most hardened opponent of true free market reform will be able to deny the need for it eventually. These systems of government intervention are truly unsustainable. They will end one way or another. The earlier we restore free markets, the less the damage that will be done in the meantime. We should begin the fight now, and stay with it as long as it takes.

America has got to stand fast against the onslaught of socialism. We represent the founding of freedom in the world, and we are the last bastion of freedom remaining. If freedom dies fully here, it likely dies everywhere in the world. If we do restore free markets, we will be that light on the hill, the example that the rest of the world will envy. Our light will shine out over the world. America will once again be the place to go for the best medical care that can be found, with prompt and high levels of service, at affordable costs, as it was before socialism started here. Our example can then inspire others to emulate us, and help to restore freedom and prosperity in the rest of the world. This will only happen if we restore free markets here, before it is too late.

It is clear that the solutions I put forth in this book are completely workable if they are instituted. The drawback is political. Too many Americans, including their political masters, are addicted to OPM (other people's money). We run into the roadblock that Alexander Tytler described, quoted at the beginning of this chapter. Ultimately, it is inevitable that our current health care system will be dismantled. Unfortunately, it will probably happen only when the American economy collapses over deficit spending. When that happens, Medicare and Medicaid will stop functioning. So will all our other government programs. I would rather see government interference in health care phased out starting now, so that our society can continue to operate.

# Conclusion

———

THE MAJOR DEVELOPMENTS IN THE history of our current health care problems are now summarized. Health care was affordable, with good service, and lifespans were increasing by leaps and bounds. Then wages were controlled during World War II which led to employer-purchased, tax preferred health insurance. Costs began to increase. Then the government instituted Medicare and Medicaid. Regulations multiplied, and costs skyrocketed. In an effort to contain cost, Congress passed the HMO Act of 1973. Costs continued to rise, and service got worse. The Emergency Medical Treatment and Active Labor Act, Stark laws, FDA interference with medications, and other layers of bureaucracy were all put in place along the way. These layers upon layers of government regulation have led us to where we are now.

We cannot indefinitely continue to increase our debt through the Medicare system. Increasing government controls to the point of full socialism will only accelerate our worsening problems. Only by restoring free markets to American health care can we achieve better results. It is the only way to avoid economic disaster for America.

History is replete with examples of failed socialist systems. The Soviet Union only continued as long as they did because of the steady infusion of western capital. For the entire time of their existence, people lived in the most dismal conditions. The same is true everywhere complete socialism, or in other words, communism, has been tried.

Nations with fully socialized medicine are all in crisis. They have terrible shortages and waiting lists. Some of those countries have been forced to reintroduce market competition in order to get the problems under control.

Free market capitalism has brought more goods and services to more people than any other system on earth. Capitalism has blessed every level of society with abundance. It lifts the lower classes, the middle classes, and the wealthier classes. This happens in every area of the economy where capitalism is allowed to operate.

Our problems in health care are many, but they are basically reduced to high costs and low levels of service. These problems are the inevitable result of government interventions into free markets. The solution, then, is not more government intervention, but less.

If I have a patient suffering from fluid overload, in congestive heart failure, the last thing I want to do is give more fluid. A diuretic medicine to reduce excess fluid is needed. Likewise, if our patient is the American health care system, we need to treat the cause rather than exacerbate it. Our system suffers from government overload. We need to diurese, or drain, the system of excess government interventions. The worst thing we could do is to increase government control.

We have a system of third party payment for even the most minor and routine issues. We need a system of true insurance, where the smaller services are paid out of pocket. Insurance should be for costs that would otherwise be financially devastating. That is the reason that insurance was developed in the first place.

We need to separate health insurance from employment. That way, the customer of the insurance company will once again be the patient, whom the insurance company will therefore have to satisfy if they want to keep their business. Employers have no logical obligation to provide health care to their employees, any more than they are obliged to provide automotive care.

We need to restore choice. People have a right to choose what to do with their own bodies. The government has no place denying somebody the right to choose a particular medicine. They have no place prohibiting two mutually consenting adults from committing health care in exchange for money.

They have no place setting prices or controlling the supply of doctors. If the government simply got out of the way of the free market providing medicines and doctors, shortages would vanish.

America is the last best hope for freedom in the world. We do not live in a free country with respect to health care, however. We are a better country than that. We should not allow ourselves to sink to the level of the Europeans in our health care system. Our founding fathers established a land of freedom and opportunity. It is time we let freedom bring prosperity to us in our health care, just as it has done in every other avenue of pursuit where it has been tried.

We will have prosperity, or we will have devastation. This is about more than health care. It is important enough to affect our entire economy and future. The experiments have been run, and the results are there for everyone to see. Freedom brings prosperity, and socialism brings misery. We only have to look to see. We have a clear choice to make. I hope Americans will be able to see clearly. Either way, as a nation we will get what we deserve.

# References

---

## CRISIS? WHAT CRISIS? CONDITIONS BEFORE GOVERNMENT INTERFERENCE

1.  Health care expenditures per capita 1929 - 1970 from:

    U.S. Bureau of the Census, *Historical Statistics of the United States: Colonial Times to 1970,* (Washington, DC, United States Government Printing Office, 1975), p. 73. These were the first years for which data were available.

2.  Health care expenditures per capita 1971 - 2005 from:

    U.S. Bureau of the Census, *Statistical Abstract of the United States, 2008,* (Washington, DC, United States Government Printing Office, 2008), p. 96.

3.  Consumer price index to adjust for inflation from: "Consumer Price Index, 1913-," Federal Reserve Bank of Minneapolis, accessed June 14, 2013. <http://www.minneapolisfed.org/community_education/teacher/calc/hist1913.cfm>

4.  Longevity increased from 47.3 years in the year 1900 to 68.2 years in 1950, then increased to 77 years by 2000. Longevity from 1900 - 1970 from:

    U.S. Bureau of the Census, *Historical Statistics of the United States: Colonial Times to 1970,* (Washington, DC, United States Government Printing Office), 1975, p. 55.

5.  Longevity from 1971 - 2004 from:
    U.S. Bureau of the Census, *Statistical Abstract of the United States, 2008,* (Washington, DC, United States Government Printing Office), 2008, p. 74.

6.  "Salving With Science," *American Chemical Society,* accessed November 10, 2008. <http://pubs.acs.org/journals/pharmcent/Ch2.html>

7.  Alan J. Wright, M.D., "The Penicillins," *Mayo Clinic Proceedings,* March 1999, p. 290.

8.  Gerald L. Mandell, M.D., John E. Bennett, M.D., and Raphael Dolin, M.D., *Mandell, Douglass, and Bennett's: Principles and Practice of Infectious Diseases, Sixth Edition,* (Philadelphia, PA, Chruchill Livingstone), 2005, p. 356.

9.  Randall S. Edson, M.D., and Christine L. Terrell, M.D., "The Aminoglycosides," *Mayo Clinic Proceedings,* May 1999, p. 519.

10. Mary Jo Kasten, M.D., "Clindamycin, Metronidazole, and Chloramphenicol," *Mayo Clinic Proceedings,* August 1999, p. 830.

11. Courtney M. Townsend Jr., M.D., R. Daniel Beauchamp, M.D., B. Mark Evers, M.D., and Kenneth L. Mattox, M.D., *Townsend: Sabiston Textbook of Surgery, Eighteenth Edition,* (Philadelphia, PA, Saunders Elsevier), 2008, p. 8.

12. Ibid., p. 13.

13. Ibid., p. 13.

14. There were many separate advances which led to the electrocardiogram (EKG). The one I chose to define its date was Einthoven's publishing of the first ekg using a string galvanometer, which gave it the sensitivity to be useful. He won the Nobel Prize for it in 1924. See <http://www.ecglibrary.com/ecghist.html>

15. "Blood Bank," *Encyclopedia Brittanica,* accessed November 10, 2008. <http://www.britannica.com/EBchecked/topic/69739/blood-bank>

16. David G. Gardner, M.D., and Delores Shoback, M.D., editors, *Greenspan's Basic and Clinical Endocrinology, Eighth Edition,* (New York, NY, McGraw-Hill Medical, 2004), pp. 422-423.

17. "Paying for Medical Care," *AAPS News*, Volume 61, No. 10, October 2005, Association of American Physicians and Surgeons, accessed October 7 2008. <http://www.aapsonline.org/newsletters/oct05.php>

## AMERICA IS THE WORLD LEADER IN INNOVATIONS

1. "All Nobel Laureates in Medicine," *Nobel Foundation*, accessed October 8, 2008. <http://www.nobelprize.org/nobel_prizes/medicine/laureates/>

   Places of birth, residences, and university affiliations from: "Nobel Prize in Physiology or Medicine Winners 2008-1901," *The Nobel Prize Internet Archive*, accessed October 8, 2008. <http://www.almaz.com/nobel/>

2. Kenneth Rogoff, Ph.D., former Chief Economist and Director of Research of the International Monetary Fund, "A Prescription for Marxism," January/February 2005, *Foreign Policy*, accessed November 11, 2008. <http://www.foreignpolicy.com/story/cms.php?story_id=2739>

3. *2006 World Almanac and Book of Facts*, (New York, NY, World Amanac Books, 2006), pp. 316-318.

4. Ibid, pp. 316-318.

5. Susan Raymond, Ph.D, "Healthcare Philanthropy and the Future: Engine or Caboose?," April 30, 2004, *On Philanthropy*, accessed October 17, 2008. <http://www.onphilanthropy.com/site/News2?page=NewsArticle&id=5278&security=1&news_iv_ctrl=1163>

## THE REASON FOR OUR PROSPERITY IS FREEDOM

1. Marianne Ward and John Devereux, "Relative British and American Income Levels During the First Industrial Revolution," July 30 2004,

*International Institute of Social* History, p. 16, accessed October 21, 2008. <http://www.iisg.nl/hpw/papers/ward-devereux.pdf>

2.  Ibid., p. 7
3.  Ibid., Figure 1, p. 17
4.  Ibid., p. 18
5.  Jeffrey Madrick, *The End of Affluence*, (New York, NY, Random House, 1995), pp. 19-20. Figures are in 1985 U.S. dollars. Also accessible at:

    Frontline, "Does America Still Work?," Public Broadcasting Service, accessed October 21, 2008. <http://www.pbs.org/wgbh/pages/frontline/america/madrickbookexcerpt.html>
6.  Ibid., pp. 19-20.
7.  Mark Trumbull, "Better living ... as measured by PCs, VCRs," December 30, 2005, *Christian Science Monitor*, acessed October 21, 2008. <http://www.csmonitor.com/2005/1230/p01s02-usec.html?s=hns>
8.  Robert E. Rector, "How Poor Are America's Poor? Examining the 'Plague' of Poverty in America," Backgrounder #2064, August 27, 2007, *The Heritage Foundation*, accessed October 21, 2008. <http://www.heritage.org/Research/Welfare/bg2064.cfm>
9.  "Income Mobility in the U.S. from 1996 to 2005," November 13, 2007, *U.S. Treasury Department*, p. 7, accessed October 28, 2015. <www.treasury.gov/resource-center/tax-policy/Documents/incomemobilitystudy03-08revise.pdf>
10. "The World Factbook," 2008, *Central Intelligence Agency*, accessed October 21, 2008. <https://www.cia.gov/library/publications/the-world-factbook/geos/us.html>
11. Ibid. < https://www.cia.gov/library/publications/the-world-factbook/geos/mx.html>
12. Ibid. < https://www.cia.gov/library/publications/the-world-factbook/geos/ni.html>
13. < https://www.cia.gov/library/publications/the-world-factbook/geos/zi.html>

14. Ibid. < https://www.cia.gov/library/publications/the-world-factbook/geos/cg.html>

16. Ibid. < https://www.cia.gov/library/publications/the-world-factbook/geos/sa.html>

17. Ibid. < https://www.cia.gov/library/publications/the-world-factbook/geos/sa.html>

18. "2008 Index of Economic Freedom," Executive Summary, *The Heritage Foundation*, p. 6, accessed November 11, 2008. <http://www.heritage.org/research/features/index/chapters/pdf/index2008_execsum.pdf>

19. I use the term "federal" throughout this book for simplicity, as it is the term still in common use. In reality, we no longer have a federal government. Federalism, a system in which powers that are not interstate in nature are retained by the states, has long been dead in the United States. We now have a central government, which our founders tried to avoid in the writing of the constitution. States are mere field offices of our current central government.

20. Declaration of Independence of the United States of America, preamble.

21. Alexander H. Stephens, *History of the United States*, 1872, (republished Bridgewater, Virginia, American Foundation Publications, 1999), pp. 250-251.

22. Constitution of the United States of America, Article VI.

23. U.S. Supreme Court in Ex parte Siebold, 100 U.S. 376 (1879), accessed January 30, 2014. <https://supreme.justia.com/cases/federal/us/100/371/case.html. The same principle was also expressed in the famous case, Marbury v. Madison.

## What Is Money?

1. Walter Williams developed this idea, calling dollars "certificates of performance." See "Understanding Liberals," May 18, 2001,

*Townhall.com*, accessed January 30, 2014. <http://townhall.com/columnists/walterewilliams/2011/05/18/understanding_liberals>

2. "The Golden Constant," 2011, accessed September 24, 2013. <http://ekishek.com/index.php?option=com_content&view=article&id=12:the-golden-constant&catid=4:gold&Itemid=11>

   Also see www.pricedingold.com for the gold value of common items like oil and food for the past two decades.

3. "Historic Gold Prices - 1833 to Present", *National Mining Association*, accessed September 24, 2013. <nma.org/pdf/gold/his_gold_prices.pdf>

4. Gold on September 24, 2013 was posted on http://goldprice.com as selling for $1325 per troy ounce. 1 troy ounce is 31.1 grams.

5. Laurence M. Vance, "The U.S. Global Empire," March 16, 2004, *LewRockwell.com*, accessed September 24, 2013. <http://www.lewrockwell.com/2004/03/laurence-m-vance/the-us-has-troops-in-135-countries/>

6. For a more in-depth discussion, read the chapter "Of Property," in *The Second Treatise of Civil Government*, by John Locke, 1690.

7. This idea is explored in depth by Walter Williams in "Are Americans Pro-Slavery?, June 11, 2008, *TownHall.com*, accessed September 24, 2013. <http://townhall.com/columnists/walterwilliams/2008/06/11/are_americans_pro-slavery>

# Socialism - The Equal Sharing of Misery

1. Gary North, "Ron Sider Has Moved in the Right Direction," October/November 1997, *Biblical Economics Today*, accessed May 22, 2013. <http://reformed-theology.org/ice/newslet/bet/bet97.10.htm>

2. This quote is commonly attributed to Sir Winston Leonard Spencer Churchill, but the particular speech or occasion remains elusive. Either way, the quote is spot on. I believe it to be accurate, as it does seem to reflect his beliefs concerning socialism and capitalism.

For example, see Harry V. Jaffa, president of the Winston Churchill Association, speech entitled "Churchill's Relevance to the Challenges of the Present," November 30, 1990, *The Churchill Centre*, accessed 10/22/08. <http://www.winstonchurchill.org/i4a/pages/index.cfm?pageid=823>

3.  Olaf Gersemann, "Europe's Not Working," *The American Enterprise*, November 2005.

4.  Peter Wallison, "Hey, Barney Frank: The Government Did Cause the Housing Crisis," December 31, 2011, *The Atlantic*, accessed May 22, 2013. <http://www.theatlantic.com/business/archive/2011/12/hey-barney-frank-the-government-did-cause-the-housing-crisis/249903/>

5.  Robert E. Rector, "How Poor Are America's Poor? Examining the 'Plague' of Poverty in America," Backgrounder #2064, August 27, 2007, *The Heritage Foundation*, accessed October 21, 2008. <http://www.heritage.org/Research/Welfare/bg2064.cfm >

6.  Robert E. Rector, "How "Poor" are America's Poor?," Backgrounder #791, September 21, 1990, *The Heritage Foundation*, accessed October 22, 2008. <http://www.heritage.org/Research/PoliticalPhilosophy/BG791.cfm>

7.  W. Cleon Skousen, *The Naked Communist*, (Salt Lake City Utah, The Ensign Publishing Company), 1958, p. 118.

8.  Jishnu Das and Jeffrey Hammer, "Money for Nothing: The Dire Straits of Medical Practice in Delhi, India," World Bank Policy Research Working Paper 3669, July 2005, *The World Bank*, accessed November 11, 2008.
    <http://papers.ssrn.com/sol3/papers.cfm?abstract_id=770977>
    Italics in original.

9.  Personal communication of the author with the director of King's Academy, Idaho Falls, ID, in 2006.

10. Idaho total expenditures in 2011-2012 were $2,243,262,037. From "Statewide Summary, Combined Statement of Revenues & Expenditures With Changes In Fund Balances," *Idaho State Department of Education*, accessed October 31, 2013. <http://www.

sde.idaho.gov/site/statistics/docs/financial_summaries/11_12/Statewide%20Summary.pdf>

Idaho public school enrollment 2011-2012 was 281,854, from "Public School Membership, 2011-2012 School Year," accessed February 14, 2014. <http://www.sde.idaho.gov/site/statistics/fall_enrollment.htm>

This equals $7,959 per pupil in 2011-2012.

11. "D.C.'s Distinction: $16,334 Per Student, But Only 12% Read Proficiently," May 23, 2006, *Human Events*, accessed October 22, 2008. <www.humaneventsonline.com/article.php?id=13458>

12. Denis P. Doyle, Brian Diepold, and David A. DeSchryver, "Where Do Public School Teachers Send *Their* Kids to School?,", *Thomas B. Fordham Institute*, September 7, 2004, Table 1, accessed October 22, 2008. <http://www.edexcellence.net/doc/Fwd-1.1.pdf>

13. "D.C.'s Distinction: $16,334 Per Student, But Only 12% Read Proficiently," May 23, 2006, *Human Events*, accessed October 22, 2008. <www.humaneventsonline.com/article.php?id=13458>

14. Jay P. Greene, *Education Myths*, (Lanham, Maryland, Rowman & Littlefield Publishers, 2005), p. 161. This entire book is recommended to anyone interested in the study of education.

15. Ibid., pp. 179-190.

# THE DISASTERS OF FULLY SOCIALIZED MEDICINE

1. Commonly attributed to Benjamin Franklin, but with no specific speech or other source cited. It is unknown whether Dr. Franklin actually said this, but whoever originally said it was very wise indeed.

2. "Obese Patients Denied Hip Replacements," November 23, 2005, *London Daily Mail*, accessed November 12, 2008.

<http://www.dailymail.co.uk/pages/live/articles/health/dietfitness.html?in_article_id=369464&in_page_id=1774&ito=1490>

3. Matt Chorley and Daniel Martin, "Care Pathway Scrapped After Damning Report Reveals How Relatives Were Shouted At By Nurses For Giving Loved Ones A Drink," July 15, 2013, *London Daily Mail*, accessed October 29, 2015. <www.dailymail.co.uk/news/article-2364029/How-Liverpool-Care-Pathway-used-excuse-appalling-care.html>

4. Dr. Ian Bogle, CBE, former British Medical Association, Chairman of Council, retirement speech, June 30, 2003. This speech is no longer available on the website of the British Medical Association. Portions of it, and an analysis of it, are available at <http://news.heartland.org/newspaper-article/2008/06/20/consumer-power-report-132>, accessed August 20, 2014.

5. Sarah Lyall, "For British Health System, Grim Prognosis," New York Times, January 30, 1997, p. A1.

6. "Summary Report, 2004 Survey of Physician Appointment Wait Times," *Merrit, Hawkins & Associates*, p. 5, accessed October 23, 2008. <http://www.merritthawkins.com/pdf/mha2004waitsurv.pdf>

7. "'Four Year Wait' for Outpatient Appointment," November 11, 1999, *BBC News*, accessed October 23, 2008. <http://news.bbc.co.uk/1/hi/health/515365.stm>

8. Rebecca Smith, "NHS Waiting Times Rise For First Time in a Year: Official Figures," August 17, 2012, *The Telegraph*, accessed May 22, 2013. <http://www.telegraph.co.uk/health/healthnews/9479664/NHS-waiting-times-rise-for-first-time-in-a-year-official-figures.html>

9. Nic Fleming, "Where Britons Go, And What They Pay," *Daily Telegraph* (London), May 17, 2006, accessed October 24, 2008. <http://www.telegraph.co.uk/global/main.jhtml?xml=/global/2006/05/17/nhs117.xml>

10. Sarah Lyall, "In a Dentist Shortage, British (Ouch) Do It Themselves," May 7, 2006, *NY Times*, accessed October 24, 2008. <http://www.nytimes.com/2006/05/07/world/europe/07teeth.html?_r=1&scp=1&sq=in%20a%20dentist%20shortage,%20british%20(ouch)%20do%20it%20themselves&st=cse&oref=slogin>

11. Lisa Priest, "U.S. Clinic Lures Canadians," *The Globe and Mail of Canada*, Friday, November 25, 2005, p. A1.

12. Ibid.

13. Nadeem Esmail, "Leaving Canada for Medical Care 2011," July/August 2012, *Fraser Forum, The Fraser Institute*, p. 18, accessed January 16, 2014. <http://www.fraserinstitute.org/uploadedFiles/fraser-ca/Content/research-news/research/articles/leaving-canada-for-medical-care-2011-ff0712.pdf>

14. Ronald Bailey, "2005 Medical Care Forever: What Universal Health Care Would Really Bring," June 15, 2005, *Reason Online*, accessed October 31, 2013. <http://www.reason.com/news/show/34979.html>

15. Clifford Krauss, "Canada's Private Clinics Surge as Public System Falters," February 28, 2006, *New York Times*, accessed January 16, 2014. <http://www.nytimes.com/2006/02/28/international/americas/28canada.html?pagewanted=all&_r=0>

16. Arthur Weinreb, "Dr. Brian Day - the Left's Worst Nightmare," August 28, 2006, *Canada Free Press*, accessed January 16, 2014. <http://www.canadafreepress.com/2006/weinreb082806.htm>

17. "Marsh Canada Introduces a Private Health Care Treatment Program," October 22, 2008, *Marsh Canada Limited*, accessed October 22, 2008. <http://www.marsh.ca/news/newsItem.cfm?cms_news_id=119>

18. Beth Duff-Brown, "Canada Proud of Healthcare, Not Wait," April 10, 2005, *Los Angeles Times*, accessed November 20, 2008. <http://articles.latimes.com/2005/apr/10/news/adfg-wait10>

    For Canada, the CIA lists their expenditures/gdp as 42%. "The World Factbook," *Central Intelligence Agency*, accessed May 30, 2013. <https://www.cia.gov/library/publications/the-world-factbook/geos/ca.html>

19. David Hogberg, Ph.D., "Sweden's Single-Payer Health System Provides a Warning to Other Nations," May 2007, National Policy Analysis, *The National Center for Public Policy Research*, accessed December 1, 2008. <http://www.nationalcenter.org/NPA555_Sweden_Health_Care.html>

20. Tommie Ullman, "Shorter Waiting Lists for Surgery in Sweden," October 12, 2013, *Stockholm News*, accessed October 11, 2013. <http://www.stockholmnews.com/more.aspx?NID=3389>

21. "Swedes Buy Health Insurance to Skip Long Health Queues," January 17, 2014, *The Local - Sweden's Newspaper in English*, accessed January 22, 2014. <http://www.thelocal.se/20140117/hospital-queues-tied-to-insurance-trend>

22. Gerald F. Anderson, Ph.D., Varduhi Petrosyan, and Peter S. Hussey, of Johns Hopkins University, "Multinational Comparisons of Health Systems Data, 2002," October 2002, *The Commonwealth Fund*, pp. 57-58, accessed December 1, 2008. <http://www.cmwf.org/usr_doc/Anderson_healthpop_multi99_354.pdf>

23. Ibid., pp. 59-60.

24. "CBO Staff Memorandum: Factors Contributing to the Infant Mortality Ranking of the United States," February 1992, *Congressional Budget Office*, p. 41, accessed December 1, 2008. <http://www.cbo.gov/ftpdocs/62xx/doc6219/doc05b.pdf>

25. Ibid., p. 38.

26. Nicholas Eberstadt, "America's Infant Mortality Problem: Parents," *Wall Street Journal*, January 20, 1992.

27. Donald J. Hernandez, ed., *Children of Immigrants: Health, Adjustment, and Public Assistance*, (Washington, DC, The National Academies Press), 1999, p. 253. Also available online, accessed December 1, 2008. <http://books.nap.edu/openbook.php?chapselect=yo&page=253&record_id=9592>

28. David M. Cutler, Ph.D., Allison B. Rosen, M.D., M.P.H., Sc.D., and Sandeep Vijan, M.D., "The Value of Medical Spending in the United States, 1996-2000" *New England Journal of Medicine*, December 7, 2006, pp. 2491-2492.

29. Even though the medical literature refers to these countries as "developing nations," we cannot honestly call them that just because they are now undeveloped. This makes the assumption that they are progressing forward, which many are not.

30. Anderson, p. 65.

31. Robert L. Ohsfeldt and John E. Schneider, *The Business of Health*, (Washington, D.C., American Enterprise Institute for Public Policy Research, 2006), p. 22.

32. Peter J. Pitts, "Japan's Cancer Refugees," February 23, 2007, *Washington Times*, accessed December 1, 2008. <http://www.washingtontimes.com/commentary/20070222-084946-2121r.htm>

33. Anderson, pp. 57-58.

34. Ibid., p. 65.

35. Chaoulli v Quebec, Supreme Court of Canada, June 9, 2005, paragraph 124, accessed March 22, 2012. <http://scc.lexum.org/en/2005/2005scc35/2005scc35.pdf>

36. Ibid., paragraph 191.

37. Ibid., paragraph 241.

# What Turned Dr. Brook from a Socialist into A Pro-freedom Radical?

1. Gordon Moore, M.D., "Going Solo: Making the Leap," February 2002, *Family Practice Management*, accessed January 15, 2009. <http://www.aafp.org/fpm/20020200/29goin.html>

# Costs Are Skyrocketing

1. "Appendectomy Costs," February 11, 2004, *Ehealthforum*, accessed December 4, 2008. <http://ehealthforum.com/health/topic8529.html>

# What Happened to the Housecall?

1. Sign in Jimmy John's sub restaurant in Rexburg, Idaho, seen last by the author in May 2013.
2. Liz Kowalczyk, "Long waits for doctors targeted: Hospitals urge faster response," December 12, 2005, *Boston Globe*, accessed December 19, 2008. <http://www.boston.com/business/healthcare/articles/2005/12/12/long_waits_for_doctors_targeted/?page=2>
3. Ibid.
4. "Summary Report, 2004 Survey of Physician Appointment Wait Times," *Merrit, Hawkins & Associates*, p. 1, accessed December 19, 2008. <http://www.merritthawkins.com/pdf/mha2004waitsurv.pdf>
5. Ibid, p. 5.

# Health Care Is Driving Our Economy Toward Collapse

1. "National Health Expenditure Data, Historical," last modified January 11, 2012, *Centers for Medicare and Medicaid Services*, accessed March 29, 2012.
   <http://www.cms.gov/NationalHealthExpendData/02_NationalHealthAccountsHistorical.asp>
2. David M. Walker, former Comptroller General of the United States, "True State of our Federal Finances," September 30, 2012, *Comeback America Initiative*, accessed June 4, 2013. <http://keepingamericagreat.org/assets/2012/03/020613-CAI-Trifold-Final-TEST.pdf>
3. U.S. Representative Ron Paul, "Government Debt - The Greatest Threat to National Security," October 25, 2004, in his weekly column *Texas Straight Talk*, accessed December 19, 2008. <http://www.house.gov/paul/tst/tst2004/tst102504.htm>
4. Dennis Cauchon and John Waggoner, The Looming National Benefit Crisis," October 3, 2004, *USA Today*, accessed December 19, 2008.

<http://www.usatoday.com/news/nation/2004-10-03-debt-cover_x.htm>

5.  Heather Timmons, "Greenspan Points to Danger of Rising Budget Deficits," *New York Times*, December 3, 2005.

6.  David M. Walker, "Saving Our Future Requires Tough Choices Today," *United States Government Accountability Office*, February 21, 2007, p. 9, accessed December 19, 2008. <http://www.gao.gov/cghome/d07527cg.pdf>

7.  A provocative, hypothetical look at this type of future was described by Aaron Zelman and Claire Wolfe, "Can the Second Amendment and Social Security Coexist?," 2002, *Jews for the Preservation of Firearms Ownership*, accessed December 19, 2008. <http://www.jpfo.org/filegen-n-z/ssandguns.htm>

8.  Christian Hagist and Laurence J. Kotlikoff, "Health Care Spending: What the Future will Look Like," Executive Summary, NCPA Study #286, June 28, 2006, National *Center for Policy Analysis*, accessed December 19, 2008. <http://www.ncpa.org/pub/st/st286/>

9.  "Summary: NASBO State Expenditure Report," December 20, 2012, National Association of State Budget Officers, accessed June 14, 2013. <http://www.nasbo.org/sites/default/files/Summary%20-%20State%20Expenditure%20Report_0.pdf>

10. Ibid.

11. "New Zimbabwe $10B Note Buys Bread," December 19, 2008, *CNN.com,* accessed December 19, 2008. <http://edition.cnn.com/2008/WORLD/africa/12/19/zimbawe.currency/index.html?iref=24hours>

12. "Cholera Zimbabwe's 'Worst Crisis'," November 26, 2008, *BBC News,* accessed December 19, 2008. <http://news.bbc.co.uk/1/hi/world/africa/7750824.stm>

13. David Vachon, "Doctor John Snow Blames Water Pollution for Cholera Epidemic," May & June 2005, *UCLA Department of Epidemiology*, accessed December 19, 2008.
    <http://www.ph.ucla.edu/epi/snow/fatherofepidemiology_part2.html#TWO>

# EVER INCREASING TAXES

1.  "Fiscal Year 2013, Historical Tables, Budget of the U.S. Government," 2013, *United States Government Printing Office*, Table 3.1, pp. 50 - 55, accessed June 14, 2013.
    <http://www.whitehouse.gov/sites/default/files/omb/budget/fy2013/assets/hist.pdf>
2.  "State Expenditure Report Examining Fiscal 2010 - 2012 State Spending," 2012, *National Association of State Budget Officers*, p. 44, accessed June 14, 2013.
    <http://www.nasbo.org/sites/default/files/State%20Expenditure%20Report_1.pdf>
3.  Statistical Abstract of the United States, 2012, Table 59, U.S. Census Bureau, accessed April 12, 2012. <http://www.census.gov/compendia/statab/2012/tables/12s0059.pdf>
4.  One billion dollars divided by 120 million families equals $8.33, or roughly rounded to $10 per family. $8 would be more accurate, but $10 as a rough figure makes for quick and easy math that is pretty close.
5.  "Fiscal Year 2013, Historical Tables, Budget of the U.S. Government," 2013, *United States Government Printing Office*, Table 3.1, pp. 50 - 55, accessed June 14, 2013.
    <http://www.whitehouse.gov/sites/default/files/omb/budget/fy2013/assets/hist.pdf>
6.  "2010 State Expenditure Report Examining Fiscal 2009 - 2011 State Spending," 2011, *National Association of State Budget Officers*, Figure 14, p. 45, accessed June 14, 2013.
    <http://www.nasbo.org/sites/default/files/2010%20State%20Expenditure%20Report.pdf>   and
    "State Expenditure Report Examining Fiscal 2010 - 2012 State Spending," 2012, *National Association of State Budget Officers*, p. 44, accessed June 14, 2013.
    <http://www.nasbo.org/sites/default/files/State%20Expenditure%20Report_1.pdf>

7. "Key Issues in Analyzing Major Health Insurance Proposals," December 2008, Congressional Budget Office, p. 31, accessed March 12, 2014. <http://www.cbo.gov/sites/default/files/ftpdocs/99xx/doc9924/12-18-keyissues.pdf>

8. "Historical Payroll Tax Rates," January 2, 2008, *Tax Policy Center*, accessed December 22, 2008.
   <http://www.taxpolicycenter.org/taxfacts/Content/PDF/ssrate_historical.pdf>

## SHORTAGES OF DOCTORS AND MEDICINES

1. Robert Davis, "Shortage of Surgeons Pinches U.S. Hospitals," February 26, 2008, *USA Today*, accessed April 18, 2012. <http://www.usatoday.com/news/health/2008-02-26-doctor-shortage_N.htm>

2. "The Medicus Firm Physician Survey: Health Reform May Lead to Significant Reduction in Physician Workforce," January 2010, The Medicus Firm, accessed April 18, 2012. <http://www.themedicusfirm.com/pages/medicus-media-survey-reveals-impact-health-reform>

3. Summary Report, 2004 Survey of Physician Appointment Wait Times, 2004, *Merrit, Hawkins & Associates*, pp. 3-5, accessed December 22, 2008. <http://www.merritthawkins.com/pdf/mha2004waitsurv.pdf>

4. Amy Snow Landa, "North Carolina Project Aims to Shorten Wait Times for Pediatric Subspecialists," September 11, 2006, *American Medical News, American Medical Association*, accessed December 22, 2008. <http://www.ama-assn.org/amednews/2006/09/11/gvsa0911.htm>

5. Nadia Kounang, "Is the FDA to Blame for Drug Shortages?," July 25, 2012, *CNNHealth*, accessed October 17, 2013. <http://www.cnn.com/2012/07/25/health/fda-drug-shortages/index.html>

6. Ibid.

7. George Santayana, *The Life of Reason*, 1905.

Further recommended reading: Thomas Sowell, *Basic Economics: A Citizen's Guide to the Economy.* This is a very enjoyable read, despite the topic which at first glance seems a bit dry. Every person in congress should read it, before they are given the power they have to destroy our economy.

## Don't Worry about the Cost - It's Covered

1. "Fact #219: June 3, 2002: Average Price of a New Car: 1970-2001," January 12, 2006, *United States Department of Energy,* accessed December 24, 2008.
   <http://www1.eere.energy.gov/vehiclesandfuels/facts/favorites/fcvt_fotw219.html>
2. Damon Darlin, "Falling Costs of Big-Screen TV's to Keep Falling," August 20, 2005, *New York Times,* accessed November 29, 2013. <http://www.nytimes.com/2005/08/20/technology/20tvprices.html?_r=0>
3. Samsung PN51F4500 51-inch plasma TV on www.amazon.com, selling for $569 on November 29, 2013.
4. "Quality of Life Improved Through Lasik Eye Surgery," October 16, 2003, *Eye Surgery Education Council,* accessed December 24, 2008. <http://www.lasikinstitute.org/Newsroom_qualityoflifeimproved.htm>
5. "Laser Eye Surgery: More Popular, Less Unprofitable," March 17, 2003, *Business Week,* accessed December 24, 2008. <http://www.businessweek.com/bwdaily/dnflash/oct2000/nf20001018_576.htm?chan=search>
6. Liz Segre, "Cost of LASIK and Other Corrective Eye Surgery," *All About Vision,* accessed December 24, 2008. <http://www.allaboutvision.com/visionsurgery/cost.htm>
7. Noel Blisard and Hayden Stewart, "Food Spending in American Households, 2003-2004," March 2007, *US Department of Agriculture,*

accessed December 25, 2008. <http://www.ers.usda.gov/publications/
eib23fm.pdf>

8.  Franklin D. Roosevelt, Executive Order 9017 Establishing the
National War Labor Board, January 12, 1942, *The American
Presidency Project*, accessed December 25, 2008.
    <http://www.presidency.ucsb.edu/ws/print.php?pid=16264>

9.  Ibid.

10. Richard E. Schumann, "Compensation from World War II through
the Great Society," originally printed in the Fall 2001 issue of
*Compensation and Working Conditions, U.S. Department of Labor
Bureau of Labor Statistics*, accessed December 25, 2008. <http://www.
bls.gov/opub/cwc/cm20030124ar04p1.htm>

11. "History of Health Insurance Benefits," March 2002, *Employee
Benefit Research Institute*, accessed December 25, 2008. <http://www.
ebri.org/publications/facts/index.cfm?fa=0302fact>

12. Dorothy L. Pennachio, "Expense Survey: What to Spend, What
to Cut," Chart 3, January 21, 2005, *Medical Economics*, accessed February 14, 2014. <http://medicaleconomics.modern-
medicine.com/medical-economics/news/clinical/personal-finance/
expense-survey-what-spend-what-cut>

13. Michael J. Wiley, "Practice Pointers: Is Your Practice Staffed
Correctly?," *Medical Economics*, June 21, 2002.

    The figure cited is total receipts divided by charges. Many refer-
ences can be found to a collection ratio that is much higher than this,
by dividing "adjusted" charges by receipts. Adjusted charges means
what a doctor expects to collect, not what he actually charges. The
uninsured patient is charged the full fee, without adjustment.

14. 30 per day, 5 days per week, 50 weeks per year equals 7,500 patient
visits, which would be a fairly typical number for most family practice
doctors.

15. Gary Claxton, Bianca DiJulio, Benjamin Finder, Eric Becker,
"Employer Health Benefits 2007 Annual Survey," September 11, 2007,

*The Henry J. Kaiser Family Foundation*, p. 20, accessed December 25, 2008. <http://www.kff.org/insurance/7672/upload/76723.pdf>

16. National Center for Health Statistics, *Health, United States, 2005, With Chartbook on Trends in the Health of Americans*, (Hyattsville, Maryland, US Department of Health and Human Services, 2005), Table 127, also available online, accessed December 25, 2008. <http://www.ncbi.nlm.nih.gov/books/bv.fcgi?rid=healthus05.table.475>

17. Michael F. Cannon and Michael D. Tanner, *Healthy Competition: What's Holding Back Health Care and How to Free It*, (Washington D.C., Cato Institute, 2005), p. 47, quoting OECD Health Data 2004.

18. Jay P. Greene, *Education Myths*, (Lanham, Maryland, Rowman & Littlefield Publishers, 2005), p. 10.

19. Lisa Girion, "Blue Cross Cancellations Called Illegal," March 23, 2007, *Los Angeles Times*, accessed May 3, 2012. <http://www.latimes.com/business/la-fi-insure23mar23,0,2655938.story>

20. Lisa Girion, "State Fines 2 Health Plans Over Cancelled Coverage," July 18, 2008, *Los Angeles Times*, accessed May 3, 2012. <http://articles.latimes.com/2008/jul/18/business/fi-blue18>

21. Milt Freudenheim, "Late Payment of Medical Claims Adds to the Cost of Health Care," *New York Times*, May 25, 2006.

## MEDICARE AND MEDICAID

1. Health care expenditures per capita 1929 - 1970 from:
   U.S. Bureau of the Census, *Historical Statistics of the United States: Colonial Times to 1970*, (Washington, DC, United States Government Printing Office, 1975), p. 73.

2. Health care expenditures per capita 1971 - 2005 from:
   U.S. Bureau of the Census, *Statistical Abstract of the United States, 2008*, (Washington, DC, United States Government Printing Office, 2008), p. 96.

3. Longevity increased from 47.3 years in the year 1900 to 68.2 years in 1950, then increased to 77 years by 2000. Longevity from 1900 - 1970 from:

  U.S. Bureau of the Census, *Historical Statistics of the United States: Colonial Times to 1970,* (Washington, DC, United States Government Printing Office), 1975, p. 55.

4. Longevity from 1971 - 2004 from:

  U.S. Bureau of the Census, *Statistical Abstract of the United States, 2008,* (Washington, DC, United States Government Printing Office), 2008, p. 74.

5. Lawrence R. Huntoon, M.D., Ph.D., "Medicare Myths and Facts: What the Government Doesn't Want You to Know," August 2002, *Association of American Physicians and Surgeons,* accessed October 31, 2013. <http://www.aapsonline.org/brochures/myths.htm>

6. Gary Mecklenburg, President and Chief Executive Officer, Northwestern Memorial Healthcare, Chicago, Illinois, Testimony Before the Subcommittee on Health of the House Committee on Ways and Means, March 15, 2001, *U.S. House of Representatives Committee on Ways and Means,* accessed December 27, 2008. <http://waysand-means.house.gov/Legacy/health/107cong/3-15-01/3-15meck.htm>

7. "Trends in Physician Productivity," *US Department of Health and Human Services, Health Resources and Services Administration,* accessed December 27, 2008. <http://bhpr.hrsa.gov/healthworkforce/reports/physiciansupplydemand/trendsinphysicianproductivity.htm>

8. Tony Fay, Vice President, Government Affairs, Province Healthcare Company, Brentwood, Tennessee, on behalf of the American Hospital Association, Testimony Before the Subcommittee on Health of the House Committee on Ways and Means, February 13, 2003, *U.S. House of Representatives Committee on Ways and Means,* accessed December 27, 2008. <http://waysandmeans.house.gov/hearings.asp?formmode=view&id=76>

9. "Patients or Paperwork : The Regulatory Burden Facing America's Hospitals," 2001, *American Hospital Association,* p. 3, accessed

December 27, 2008. <http://www.aha.org/aha/content/2001/pdf/FinalPaperworkReport.pdf>

10. David Bernd, Chief Executive Officer, Sentara Healthcare, Norfolk, Virginia, on behalf of the American Hospital Association, Testimony Before the Subcommittee on Labor, Health, and Human Services of the Senate Committee on Appropriations Regulatory Relief and Reform Efforts, June 11, 2003, *American Hospital Association*, accessed December 27, 2008.

    <http://www.aha.org/aha/testimony/2003/030611-tes-bernd-senate.html>

11. Robert G. Schwartz, M.D., Medicare Opt Out: Why Doctor Opted Out of Medicare, June 12, 1998, at http://www.piedmontpmr.homestead.com/home.html, icon under "Challenge and Choice."

12. John A. Bennett, D.O., A Declaration of Independence from the Medicare Program, at http://www.aapsonline.org/medicare/bennett.htm

13. Richard Wolf, "Doctors Limit New Medicare Patients," June 21, 2010, *USA Today*, accessed September 3, 2013. <http://usatoday30.usatoday.com/news/washington/2010-06-20-medicare_N.htm>

14. Crisis Builds: More FPs Stop Taking New Medicare Patients, FPReport, September 2002, at http://www.aafp.org/fpr/20020900/1.html.

15. Richard Franki, "One-Fourth of Doctors Not Taking New Medicare Patients," *Family Practice News*, accessed September 3, 2013. <http://www.familypracticenews.com/news/practice-trends/single-article/one-fourth-of-doctors-not-taking-new-medicare-patients/b27f1f1ec84327ad44e42e81972f08>

16. "Group Practices Forced to Limit Access for Medicare Patients in '08; More Hard Times to Come," March 6, 2008, *Medical Group Management Association*, accessed December 27, 2008. <http://www.mgma.com/press/article.aspx?id=17338>

17. Railroad Retirement Board v. Alton Railroad Company, 295 U.S. 350 (1935), accessed December 27, 2008. <http://supreme.justia.com/us/295/330/case.html>

18. Helvering v. Davis, 301 U.S. 640 (1937), accessed December 27, 2008. <http://supreme.justia.com/us/301/619/case.html>

# WE ARE REGULATING OURSELVES TO DEATH

1. See www.eicd9.com, click on "alphabetical index" at left, click on "M," then "Mo," scroll down to "Moron," and it lists "moron" with code 317.

2. Senator Trent Lott, Letter to Tommy Thompson, Secretary of the Department of Health and Human Services, July 27, 2001, accessed December 27, 2008. <http://www.aapsonline.org/medicare/lottcptletter.htm>

3. MGT America and the United States/Mexico Border Counties Coalition, "Medical Emergency: Costs of Uncompensated Care in Southwest Border Counties," September 2002, *Border Counties Coalition*, p. 26, accessed December 27, 2008.
    <http://www.bordercounties.org/vertical/Sites/%7BB4A0F1FF-7823-4C95-8D7A-F5E400063C73%7D/uploads/%7BFAC57FA3-B310-4418-B2E7-B68A89976DC1%7D.PDF>

4. Madeleine Pelner Cosman, Ph.D., Esq., "Illegal Aliens and American Medicine," Spring 2005, *Journal of American Physicians and Surgeons*, p. 6, accessed December 27, 2008. <http://www.jpands.org/vol10no1/cosman.pdf>

5. I will not disclose which hospital this was. All hospitals and all doctors have had both satisfied and dissatisfied patients. I have worked as a doctor in several different cities, so the hospital may have been in or near any of those cities.

7. Catherine Hanssens, Esq., "One (Very) Small Step for Health Care Reform: What Does the Kennedy-Kassebaum Act Mean for You?," Spring/Summer 1997, *Lambda Legal*, accessed December 27, 2008. <http://www.thebody.com/hanssens/reform.html>

8. For a discussion of the greatly decreased lifespan of people who practice homosexual behavior, see:

    Paul Cameron, Ph.D., and Kirk Cameron, Ph.D., "Federal Distortion of Homosexual Footprint (Ignoring Early Gay Death)?," March 23, 2007, *Family Research Institute*, accessed December 27, 2008. <http://www.lifesitenews.com/ldn/2007_docs/CameronHomosexualFootprint.pdf>

    Also see Hogg Robert S, Strathdee Steffanie A, Craib Kevin J P, O'Shaugnessy Michael V, Montaner Julio S G, Schechter Martin T, "Modelling the Impact of HIV Disease on Mortality in Gay and Bisexual Men," June 1997, *International Journal of Epidemiology*, accessed December 27, 2008. <http://ije.oxfordjournals.org/cgi/reprint/26/3/657>

9. Christopher J. Conover, "Health Care Regulation: A $169 Billion Hidden Tax," October 4, 2004, *Cato Institute*, accessed December 27, 2008. <http://www.cato.org/pub_display.php?pub_id=2466>

## CONTROLS ON PRICE AND PHYSICIAN SUPPLY

1. Hugh Rockoff, "The Concise Encyclopedia of Economics: Price Controls," *The Library of Economics and Liberty*, accessed December 29, 2008. <http://www.econlib.org/LIBRARY/Enc/PriceControls.html>

    Also see Joe Benton, "Gasoline Prices Spur Talk of Regulation and Price Controls," August 29, 2005, *ConsumerAffairs.Com*, , accessed December 29, 2008. <http://www.consumeraffairs.com/news04/2005/gas_prices_regulation.html>

2. Jerry Taylor and Peter VanDoren, "California's Electricity Crisis: What's Going On, Who's to Blame, and What to Do," July 3, 2001, *Cato Institute*, accessed December 29, 2008. <https://www.cato.org/pubs/pas/pa406.pdf>

Also see P.J. O'Rourke, "California's Dim Bulbs," June 7, 2001, *Cato Institute*, accessed December 29, 2008. <http://www.cato.org/pub_display.php?pub_id=4277>

3. Dow Jones & Company, Inc., "Hillary's Vaccine Shortage," *Wall Street Journal*, August 15, 2003.

4. Vaccines for Children home page, Centers for Disease Control and Prevention, US Department of Health and Human Services, at <http://www.cdc.gov/vaccines/programs/vfc/default.htm>

5. Committee on the Evaluation of Vaccine Purchase Financing in the United States, Financing Vaccines in the 21st Century: Assuring Access and Availability, Institute of Medicine, National Institutes of Health, The National Academies Press, Washington D.C., 2003, p. 1, at http://www.nap.edu/catalog.php?record_id=10782.

6. Ibid., pp. 1-2.

7. Ibid., p. 1.

8. Alexandra Minna Stearn and Howard Markel, "The History of Vaccines and Immunization: Familiar Patterns, New Challenges," May/June 2005, *Health Affairs*, p. 615, accessed December 29, 2008. <http://content.healthaffairs.org/cgi/reprint/24/3/611>

9. Kenneth Rogoff, Ph.D., "A Prescription for Marxism," January/February 2005, *Foreign Policy*, accessed November 11, 2008. <http://www.foreignpolicy.com/story/cms.php?story_id=2739>

10. Frank A. Sloan and Chee-Ruey Hsieh, "Effects of Incentives on Pharmaceutical Innovation," July 27, 2006, *Oberlin College Economics* Department, p. 26, accessed December 29, 2008. <http://www.oberlin.edu/economic/Papers/HealthConf/Sloan.pdf>

11. Thomas A. Abbott and John A Vernon, "The Cost of US Pharmaceutical Price Regulation: A Financial Simulation Model of R&D Decisions," 2007, *Managerial and Decision Economics*, accessed December 29, 2008. <http://econpapers.repec.org/article/wlymgtdec/v_3A28_3Ay_3A2007_3Ai_3A4-5_3Ap_3A293-306.htm>

12. Rod Cavin, "Forecasting Medicare: Price Controls in the Years Ahead," December 1, 2006, *Pharmaceutical Executive*, accessed

December 29, 2008. <http://pharmexec.findpharma.com/pharmex-ec/article/articleDetail.jsp?id=389275&pageID=1&sk=&date=>

13. David Hogberg, Ph.D., "Letting Medicare "Negotiate" Drug Prices: Myths vs. Reality," January 2007, *National Center for Public Policy Research*, accessed December 29, 2008. <http://www.nationalcenter.org/NPA550MedicareDrugPrices.html>

14. "Medicare Price Negotiation Should Get Senate, White House Approval so Seniors Get Chance for Lower Drug Costs," January 12, 2007, *ConsumersUnion.org*, accessed December 29, 2008. <http://www.consumersunion.org/pub/campaignprescriptionfor-change/004144.html>

15. H.R. 4, "Medicare Prescription Drug Price Negotiation Act of 2007," see "Organizations that Support H.R. 4," *U.S. House Committee on Energy and Commerce*, accessed December 29, 2008. <http://energy-commerce.house.gov/index.php?option=com_content&task=view&id=961&Itemid=65>

16. H.R. 4, Medicare Prescription Drug Price Negotiation Act of 2007, available through http://thomas.loc.gov/. See also H.R. 1102 and S. 117 which were introduced in 2013, and are in committee as of October 31, 2013.

17. U.S. Code, Title 42, Chapter 7, Section 1395, accessed October 31, 2013. <http://uscode.house.gov/browse/prelim@title42/chapter7/subchapter18&edition=prelim>

18. Alan Enthoven and Kyna Fong, "Medicare: Negotiated Drug Prices May Not Lower Costs," December 18, 2006, *National Center for Poicy Analysis*, accessed December 29, 2008. < http://www.ncpa.org/pub/ba/ba575/ba575.pdf>

19. Mark Duggan and Fiona Scott Morton, "The Distortionary Effects of Government Procurement: Evidence from Medicaid Prescription Drug Purchasing," November 2004, *National Bureau of Economic Research*, accessed December 29, 2008. <http://www.nber.org/papers/10930>

20. "Physician Workforce Policy Guidelines for the United States, 2000-2020," January 2005, *Council on Graduate Medical Education*, Figure 1, accessed December 29, 2008. http://www.cogme.gov/report16.htm#f1.

21. Functions and Structure of a Medical School: Standards for Accreditation of Medical Education Programs Leading to the M.D. Degree," last updated February 2007, *Liaison Committee on Medical Education*, p. 8, accessed December 29, 2008. <http://www.lcme.org/functions2007feb.pdf>

22. "Combined BS Premedical and Health Studies BS/Doctor of Medicine With Ross University (Professional Pathway)," *Massachusetts College of Pharmacy and Health Sciences*, accessed December 29, 2008. <http://www.mcphs.edu/academics/programs/pre-med_and_health_studies/phd_medicine/>

23. Elisabeth A. Wright, "Why Can't Wyoming Get It's Own Med School?," June 10, 1999, *Salon.com*, accessed December 29, 2008. <http://www.salon.com/health/log/1999/06/10/wyoming/>

24. Anup Malani and Albert Choi, "Are Non-Profit Firms Simply For-Profits in Disguise?" Evidence from Executive Compensation in the Nursing Home Industry," January 27, 2005, *Columbia Law School*, p. 3, accessed December 29, 2008. <http://www.law.columbia.edu/null/Malani+&+Choi+-+Spring+05+WS?exclusive=filemgr.download&file_id=94469&showthumb=0>

25. "AAMC Calls for 30% Increase in Medical School Enrollment," June 19, 2006, *Association of American Medical Colleges*, accessed December 30, 2008. <http://www.aamc.org/newsroom/pressrel/2006/060619.htm>

26. Rebecca E. Bruccoleri and Braden J. Hexom, "Graduate Medical Education Funding," *American Medical Student Association*, accessed December 30, 2008. <http://www.amsa.org/pdf/Medicare_GME.pdf>

27. Alex Wayne, "A Looming U.S. Doctor Shortage," September 27, 2012, *Bloomberg Businessweek*, accessed September 3, 2013. <http://www.businessweek.com/articles/2012-09-27/a-looming-u-dot-s-dot-doctor-shortage>

# Uncivil Law

1. Amitai Etzioni, "There Are Too Few Lawsuits, Not Too Many," *Los Angeles Times*, October 5, 2004.

2. Mimi Marchev, "The Medical Malpractice Insurance Crisis: Opportunity for State Action," July 2002, *National Academy for State Health Policy*, pp. 5-6, accessed December 30, 2008. <http://www. nashp.org/Files/gnl48_medical_malpractice.PDF>

3. "Malpractice Awards Reach Record High," AAPS News of the Day April 15, 2004, *Association of American Physicians and Surgeons*, quoting from Jury Verdict Research, accessed December 30, 2008. <http://www.aapsonline.org/nod/newsofday61.htm>

4. "The Factors Fueling Rising Healthcare Costs 2006," January 2006, *PricewaterhouseCoopers*, p. 7, accessed December 30, 2008. <http://www.pwc.com/extweb/pwcpublications.nsf/docid/ BB82984D3A7DF2A485257267003C98BC>

5. Lawrence J. McQuillan, Hovannes Abramyan, and Anthony P. Archie, "Jackpot Justice: The True Cost of America's Tort System, *Pacific Research Institute*, p. xii accessed December 31, 2008.

    <http://www.pacificresearch.org/pub/sab/entrep/2007/Jackpot_ Justice/Jackpot_Justice.pdf>

    This web page could not be accessed directly. Go to <http:// www.pacificresearch.org> then search on "Jackpot Justice," scroll down to Publications, and select Jackpot Justice.

6. Chad C. Karls, FACS, MAAA and Kevin J. Atinsky, ACAS, MAAA, "Medical Malpractice Insurance: A Market in Transition," 2003, *Milliman USA*, p. 3, accessed December 31, 2008.

    <http://www.milliman.com/expertise/property-casualty/pub- lications/published/pdfs/Med-Mal-Ins-Market-in-Transition- MM-09-01-03.pdf>

7. Robert T. Hartwig, Ph.D., and Claire Wilkinson, "Medical Malpractice Insurance," June 2003, *Insurance Information Institute*, p.

12, accessed December 31, 2008. <http://server.iii.org/yy_obj_data/binary/729103_1_0/Medmal.pdf>

8.  Kristen A. Walsh, "AEDs: Do They Belong in Your Facility?," March 2005, *Recreation Management*, accessed December 31, 2008. <http://www.recmanagement.com/200503gc01.php>

9.  "Cesarean Section Rates in the United States," last updated January 8, 2008, *American College of Obstetricians and Gynecologists*, accessed December 31, 2008. <http://www.acog.org/departments/dept_notice.cfm?recno=20&bulletin=264>

10. Newsmakers: John Edwards, *Findlaw.com*, accessed December 31, 2008. <http://news.findlaw.com/newsmakers/john.edwards.html>

11. Charles Hurt, "Edwards' Malpractice Suits Leave Bitter Taste," August 16, 2004, *Washington Times*, accessed December 31, 2008. <http://washingtontimes.com/national/20040816-011234-1949r.htm>

12. Karin B. Nelson, M.D., and Jonas H. Ellenberg, Ph. D., "Antecedents of Cerebral Palsy: Multivariate Analysis of Risk," *New England Journal of Medicine*, July 10, 1986.

13. Ibid.

14. "Edwards, Wife Made $39 Million in Past Decade," September 6, 2004, *CNN.com*, at <http://www.cnn.com/2004/ALLPOLITICS/09/03/edwards.tax.returns/>

15. Charles Hurt, "Edwards' Malpractice Suits Leave Bitter Taste," August 16, 2004, *Washington Times*, accessed December 31, 2008. <http://washingtontimes.com/national/20040816-011234-1949r.htm>

16. "ACOG News Release: Medical Liability Survey Reaffirms More Ob-Gyns Are Quitting Obstetrics," July 16, 2004, *American College of Obstetricians and Gynecologists*, accessed December 31, 2008. <http://www.acog.org/from_home/publications/press_releases/nr07-16-04.cfm>

17. Ibid.

18. Stewart B. Dunsker, MD, "The Campaign Starts Here: NPHCA Charts Course for Federal Medical Liability Reform," Fall 2003, *American Association of Neurological Surgeons Bulletin*, accessed December 31, 2008. <http://www.aans.org/library/Article.aspx?ArticleId=18632>

19. Richard E. Anderson, MD, "One in Two Neurosurgeons Is Sued Annually, Dr. Richard E. Anderson Tells American Association of Neurological Surgeons," May 1, 2003, *The Doctors Company*, accessed December 31, 2008. <http://www.thedoctors.com/newsroom/press/2003/2003may1aaonsameeting.asp>

20. "Statement to the Press," September 20, 2004, *New York State Neurosurgical Society Medical Tort Symposium*, accessed December 31, 2008. <http://www.nysns.org/resources/Statement%20to%20Press.pdf>

21. Bob LaMendola, "Stroke Victim's Family Sues W. Boca Hospital," *Sun Sentinel*, December 22, 2004, accessed March 18, 2014. <http://articles.sun-sentinel.com/2004-12-22/news/0412220106_1_stroke-patients-emergency-room-hospital>

22. Jan Michelson, 4/20/07, *Mickelson in the Morning*, WHO Radio, Des Moines, Iowa, podcast at <http://www.mickelson.libsyn.com>

# FOOD AND DRUG ADMINISTRATION

1. "Tufts Center for the Study of Drug Development Pegs Cost of a New Prescription Medicine at $802 Million," November 30, 2001, *Tufts Center for the Study of Drug Development, Tufts University*, accessed December 31, 2008. <http://csdd.tufts.edu/NewsEvents/RecentNews.asp?newsid=6>

2. "Has The Pharmaceutical Blockbuster Model Gone Bust? A New Bain & Company Study Reveals New Drug Commercialization Costs Have Now Reached $1.7 Billion While ROI Has Plummeted To Just

5%," December 8, 2003, *Bain & Company*, accessed December 31, 2008. <http://www.bain.com/bainweb/About/press_release_detail. asp?id=14243&menu_url=for_the_media.asp>

3. Ibid.

4. Ibid.

5. Dale E. Wierenga, Ph.D. and C. Robert Eaton, "Phases of Product Development," *Office of Research and Development, Pharmaceutical Manufacturers Association.*

6. Ibid.

7. "Theories, Evidence, and Examples of FDA Harm," *FDAreview.org, A Project of The Independence Institute,* accessed January 3, 2009. <http://www.fdareview.org/harm.shtml>

8. Walter E. Williams, Ph.D., "Unpleasant Economists," September 2008, *George Mason University Department of Economics,* accessed January 3, 2009. <http://gmu.edu/departments/economics/wew/articles/fee/Unpleasant%20Economists.htm>

9. Sam Kazman, "Red Tape for the Dying: The Food and Drug Administration and AIDS," April 8, 1988, *The Heritage Foundation,* accessed January 3, 2009. <http://www.heritage.org/Research/Religion/bg644.cfm>

10. Mary Ruwart, Ph.D., "The Law Most Likely to Kill You," October 11, 2005, *LewRockwell.com,* accessed January 3, 2009. <http://www.lewrockwell.com/orig3/ruwart2.html>

    Arthur Allen, "A Giant Pain in the Wallet," March 29, 2011, accessed June 18, 2011. <http://www.slate.com/articles/health_and_science/medical_examiner/2011/03/a_giant_pain_in_the_wallet.html>

11. On June 18, 2013, the price listed from the author's medication wholesaler was $148.41 for 30 colchicine pills, or $4.95 per pill.

12. MDConsult drug monograph on colchicine, revised August 9, 2011, accessed June 18, 2013. Available by subscription at <http://www.mdconsult.com>

13. "FDA Raid on Raw Milk: Rawsome Food Club," August 2, 2010, *Youtube*, accessed September 27, 2013. <https://www.youtube.com/watch?v=X2jgpGyyQW8>

14. For an interview with Dr. Streeter, see "A FDA Raid Sent This Doctor to Prison," July 11, 2012, *Youtube*, accessed September 27, 2013. <https://www.youtube.com/watch?v=Gzs9rhaSItM>

15. U.S. Representative Ron Paul, M.D., in floor speech to U.S. House of Representatives November 10, 2005, accessed January 3, 2009. <http://www.house.gov/paul/congrec/congrec2005/cr111005.htm>

16. "A National Survey of Oncologists Regarding the Food and Drug Administration," April 30, 2002, *Competitive Enterprise Institute*, accessed January 3, 2009. <http://www.cei.org/pdf/2987.pdf>

17. U.S. House of Representatives Committee on Oversight and Government Reform, "FDA's Contribution to the Drug Shortage Crisis," June 15, 2012, p. 3, accessed October 17, 2013. <http://oversight.house/gov/wp-content/uploads/2012/06/6-15-2012-Report-FDAs-Contribution-to-the-Drug-Shortage-Crisis.pdf>

18. Ibid, p. 3.

19. Gardiner Harris, "Medicines Made in India Set Off Safety Worries," February 14, 2014, *New York Times*. <http://www.nytimes.com/2014/02/15/world/asia/medicines-made-in-india-set-off-safety-worries.html?ref=health&_r=3>

# LICENSURE - PROTECTING OURSELVES FROM OUR OWN DECISIONS

1. Rebecca E. Bruccoleri and Braden J. Hexom, "Graduate Medical Education Funding," *American Medical Student Association*, accessed December 30, 2008. <http://www.amsa.org/pdf/Medicare_GME.pdf>

2. Idaho Statutes Title 54, Chapters 5,8, and 11, accessed January 3, 2009. <http://www.legislature.idaho.gov/idstat/Title54/T54.htm>

3. Louisiana Revised Statutes 3:3804, accessed January 3, 2009. < http://www.legis.state.la.us/lss/lss.asp?doc=86356>

4. Stanley J. Gross, "Professional Licensure and Quality: The Evidence," December 9, 1986, *The Cato Institute*, accessed January 3, 2009. http://www.cato.org/pub_display.php?pub_id=945&full=1

## STATE INSURANCE MANDATES

1. Victoria Craig Bunce and J.P. Wieske, "Health Insurance Mandates in the States 2008," 2008, *Council for Affordable Health Insurance*, p. 4, accessed January 16, 2009. <http://www.cahi.org/cahi_contents/resources/pdf/HealthInsuranceMandates2008.pdf>

2. Ibid, p. 4.

3. Gail A. Jensen, Ph.D., and Michael A. Morrisey, Ph.D., "Mandated Benefit Laws and Employer-Sponsored Health Insurance," January 1999, *Health Insurance Association of America*, p. ii, accessed January 3, 2009. <http://membership.hiaa.org/pdfs/jensenrpt.pdf>

4. Bunce and Wieske, pp. 4-6.

5. Jensen and Morrisey, p. i.

6. Jesse Helms, former United States Senator, *Here's Where I Stand: A Memoir*, (New York, NY, Random House), 2005, P. 188.

7. Paul Zane Pilzer, *The New Health Insurance Solution: How to Get Cheaper, Better Coverage Without a Traditional Employer Plan*, (Hoboken, NJ, John Wiley & Sons, Inc.), 2005, p. 27, quoting data from eHealthInsurance.

## "PRIVACY" REGULATIONS THAT WILL DISCLOSE YOUR HEALTH INFORMATION

1. U.S. Code of Federal Regulations, 45CFR160.310(c), accessed January 7, 2009.

&lt;http://edocket.access.gpo.gov/cfr_2007/octqtr/pdf/45cfr160.310.pdf&gt;

2. Code of Federal Regulations, 45CFR164.528, accessed January 7, 2009.

&lt;http://edocket.access.gpo.gov/cfr_2007/octqtr/pdf/45cfr164.528.pdf&gt;

For further information on HIPAA, read "The Truth About the Modified, Final Federal Medical Privacy Rule," October 21, 2002, *Institute for Health Freedom*, accessed January 7, 2009. &lt;http://www.forhealthfreedom.org/Publications/Privacy/Rule.html&gt;

3. "Memorandum of Points and Authorities in Support of Defendants' Motion to Dismiss, Association of American Physicians and Surgeons v. US Department of Health and Human Services," in US District Court for the Southern District of Texas, Houston Division, last paragraph of Section II under heading "Argument," p. 39, accessed January 7, 2009. &lt;http://www.aapsonline.org/judicial/hipaadismiss.doc&gt;

Also see "Escape HIPAA 'Administrative Simplification,'" *Association of American Physicians and Surgeons*, accessed January 7, 2009. &lt;http://www.aapsonline.org/confiden/escape.htm&gt;

4. United States Code, Title 42, Chapter 7, Section 1320d-6(b)(3), accessed January 7, 2009. &lt;http://uscode.house.gov/&gt;

5. American Medical News, December 13, 2004.

6. Peter Kilbridge, M.D, "The Cost of HIPAA Compliance," *New England Journal of Medicine*, April 10, 2003, P. 1424.

7. Maria Blackburn, "HIPAA, Heal Thyself," November 2004, *Johns Hopkins Magazine*, accessed January 8, 2009. &lt;http://www.jhu.edu/~jhumag/1104web/hipaa.html&gt;

8. David Armstrong, Eva Kline-Rogers, Sandeep M. Jani, Edward B. Goldman, Jianming Fang, Debabrata Mukherjee, Brahmajee Nallamothu, and Kim Eagle, "Potential Impact of the HIPAA Privacy Rule on Data Collection in a Registry of Patients With Acute Coronary Syndrome," *Archives of Internal Medicine*, May 23, 2005, p. 1127.

9. Ibid., p. 1129.

10. Kim A. Eagle, M.D., quoted by Kara Gavin, University of Michigan Health System Public Relations, in "HIPAA Rule Hikes Cost of Research," June 23, 2005, *The University Record Online*, at http://www.umich.edu/~urecord/0405/Jun13_05/11.shtml.

11. Ibid.

12. American Recovery and Reinvestment Act of 2009, Subtitle A, Title XXX, Sec. 3002 (b)(2)(B)(ii, iii), p. 234, accessed May 3, 2012. <http://www.gpo.gov/fdsys/pkg/PLAW-111publ5/pdf/PLAW-111publ5.pdf> Also found in 42 US Code 300jj-12.

13. United States Constitution, Fourth Amendment.

14. "A Statement from the Department of Veterans Affairs," 22, 2006, *United States Department of Veterans Affairs*, May accessed January 8, 2009. <http://www1.va.gov/opa/pressrel/pressrelease.cfm?id=1123>

15. Sgt. 1st Class Doug Sample, "Triwest Answers Questions on Stolen Computer Info, Increased Security," February 3, 2003, *United States Department of Defense, USA American Forces Press Service*, at <http://www.defenselink.mil/news/newsarticle.aspx?id=29491>

## Fraud - Inevitable when Somebody Else Pays the Bill

1. "Financial Management:  Increased Attention Needed to Prevent Billions in Improper Payments," October 1999, *United States General Accounting Office*, p. 6, accessed January 8, 2009.  <http://www.gao.gov/archive/2000/ai00010.pdf>

2. Clifford J. Levy and Michael Luo, "New York Medicaid Fraud May Reach into Billions," *New York Times,* July 18, 2005.

3. Ibid.

4. Ibid.

5. Nancy E. Roman, "Medicare Scam Veterans Tell Panel How Easy It Was to Cheat," *Washington Times*, November 3, 1995.

6. Stuart Wright, Deputy Inspector General for Evaluation and Inspections, US Department of Health and Human Services, "Testimony before the US Senate Subcommittee on Health, Hearing on Medicare Program Efficiency and Integrity," April 18, 2007, *U.S. House of Representatives Committee on Energy and Commerce*, accessed January 8, 2009. <http://energycommerce.house.gov/cmte_mtgs/110-he-hrg.041807.Wright-testimony.pdf>

7. "AAPS Report on Medical Fraud," *Association of American Physicians and Surgeons*, accessed January 8, 2009. <http://www.aapsonline.org/fraud/medfraud.htm>

8. Frank York, "Doctor Seeks Justice After DEA's Clinic Assault," February 21, 2000, *WorldNetDaily.com*, accessed January 8, 2009. <http://www.worldnetdaily.com/news/article.asp?ARTICLE_ID=17428>

Also see AAPS News, July 1997, at <http://www.aapsonline.org/newsletters/july97.htm> for an account written by Dr. Westmoreland himself.

# HMOs - Washington's Attempt to Rein in the Cost of Medicare and Medicaid

1. Gregory R. Kaufman, M.D., J.D., and Cherie L. LaCour, J.D., "HMO Liability: Avoiding ERISA Preemption in Light of Pacificare: Precedent Setting Tenth Circuit Case Opens Door for HMO Negligence Suits," accessed January 8, 2009. <http://www.mydoctor-lawyer.com/L-HMO-Liability.cfm>

Also see "HMOs and Medical Insurance," *Brayton and Purcell, LLP*, accessed January 8, 2009. <http://www.braytonlaw.com/practiceareas/hmoliability.htm>

2. "Kaiser Permanente Founding and History," *Kaiser Permanente Santa Rosa Medical Center*, accessed January 8, 2009. <http://www.kaiser-santarosa.org/about/kaiser/history>

3.  Senator Edward (Teddy) Kennedy was the author and sponsor of the Health Maintenance Organization Act of 1973. To verify this, go to <http://thomas.loc.gov>, click on "Try the Advanced Search" (in small writing) in the middle of the page, then following "Select Congress," choose "View 100-93," then click on "93," under "Enter Search," select "Bill Number," and in the field to the right, enter "S 14" then hit enter. The only sponsor listed is Edward Kennedy. Accessed January 9, 2009.

    Also see Twila Brase, "Blame Congress for HMOs," *Citizens' Council on Health Care* accessed January 9, 2009. <http://www.cchc-mn.org/privacy/hmoart.php3> Originally published in *Ideas on Liberty* by the Foundation for Economic Education, February 2001.

4.  Peter R. Kongstvedt, *The Managed Health Care Handbook*, (Boston, Jones & Bartlett Publishers), 2001, p. 6.

5.  Twila Brase, "Blame Congress for HMOs."

    Also see Janet Firshein and Lewis G. Sandy, "The Changing Approach to Managed Care," chapter 4 in *To Improve Health and Health Care, Volume 4*, 2001, *Robert Woods Johnson Foundation*, accessed January 9, 2009.

    <http://www.rwjf.org/files/publications/books/2001/chapter_04.html>

6.  Twila Brase, "Blame Congress for HMOs."

    Also see Firshein and Sandy, "The Changing Approach to Managed Care."

7.  Twila Brase, "Blame Congress for HMOs."

8.  "Ted Kennedy on HMOs: Then and Now," June 22, 2001, *Institute for Health Freedom*, accessed January 9, 2009. <http://www.forhealthfreedom.org/Publications/Choice/ThenAndNow.html>

9.  Ibid.

10. "Report: HMO Enrollment Stabilizing, HMO Medicaid Continues to Grow," *Health Care Strategic Management*, September 2002.

11. Anne E. Hall, Federal Reserve Board of Governors, "The Value of Medicare Managed Care Plans and Their Prescription Drug Benefits,"

March 2007, *The Federal Reserve Board*, Table 2, accessed January 10, 2009. <https://www.federalreserve.gov/pubs/feds/2007/200719/index.html>

12. David Blumenthal and Roger Herdman, editors, *Description and Analysis of the VA National Formulary*, VA Pharmacy Formulary Analysis Committee, Institute of Medicine, (Washington DC, National Academy Press), 2000, p. 175, accessed January 10, 2009. <http://books.nap.edu/openbook.php?record_id=9879&page=175>

## STATE ATTEMPTS AT PROVIDING HEALTH INSURANCE

1.  Mark Niesse, "Hawaii Ending Universal Child Health Care," October 17, 2008, *Associated Press, USA Today*, accessed January 19, 2009. <http://www.usatoday.com/news/health/2008-10-17-3270593205_x.htm>
2.  Legislature of the Commonwealth of Massachusetts, Chapter 58 of the Acts of 2006, SECTION 47, Section 188 (c) (10), accessed January 19, 2009. <http://www.mass.gov/legis/laws/seslaw06/sl060058.htm>
3.  Ibid., Section 44 (b).
4.  Kay Lazar, "Firms Cancel Health Coverage," July 18, 2010, *The Boston Globe*, accessed May 3, 2012. <http://www.boston.com/news/health/articles/2010/07/18/firms_cancel_health_coverage/>
5.  Jeffrey Krassner, "Penalties to Rise for Shunning Insurance," January 1, 2008, *The Boston Globe*, accessed January 19, 2009. <http://www.boston.com/business/articles/2008/01/01/penalties_to_rise_for_shunning_insurance/>
6.  "2011 Penalty Table," *Massachusetts Department of Revenue*, accessed May 3, 2012. <http://www.mass.gov/dor/>, click "Individuals," click "Filing and Payment Information," click "Guide to Personal Income Tax," click "Assessment, Interest and Penalties," click "Assessment of Penalties," scroll down to "Health Insurance, Penalty for Failure to Purchase."

7.  Legislature of the Commonwealth of Massachusetts, Chapter 58 of the Acts of 2006, SECTION 30, Section 57 (a), accessed January 19, 2009. <http://www.mass.gov/legis/laws/seslaw06/sl060058.htm>

8.  Victoria Craig Bunce and J.P. Wieske, "Health Insurance Mandates in the States 2008," 2008, *Council for Affordable Health Insurance*, pp. 4-6, accessed January 16, 2009. <http://www.cahi.org/cahi_contents/resources/pdf/HealthInsuranceMandates2008.pdf>

9.  "Benefits Required Under MCC," *Commonwealth Connector*, accessed January 19, 2009. <http://www.mahealthconnector.org>, click "2009 minimum coverage rules" at upper right of screen.

10. Debra A. Draper, Laurie E. Felland, Allison Liebhaber, and Johanna Lauer, " Massachusetts Health Reform: High Costs and Expanding Expectations May Weaken Employer Support," October 2008, *Center for Studying Health System Change*, accessed January 19, 2009. <http://www.hschange.org/CONTENT/1021/>

11. Karen Brown, "Mass. Health Care Reform Reveals Doctor Shortage," November 30, 2008, *National Public Radio*, accessed January 19, 2009. <http://www.npr.org/templates/story/story.php?storyId=97620520>

12. Liz Kowalczyk, "The Doctor Will See All of You Now," November 30, 2008, *The Boston Globe*, accessed January 19, 2009. <http://www.boston.com/news/local/massachusetts/articles/2008/11/30/the_doctor_will_see_all_of_you_now/?p1=Well_MostPop_Emailed1>

13. "Physician Workforce Study, Executive Summary-2008," 2008, *Massachusetts Medical Society*, pp. 7-8, accessed January 19, 2009. <http://www.massmed.org/AM/Template.cfm?Section=Home&CONTENTID=23165&TEMPLATE=/CM/ContentDisplay.cfm>

14. Ibid, p. 5.

15. Ibid, p. 6.

16. Jeremy Smerd, "Future of Nation's Health Care May Take It's Cue from Massachusetts," November 11, 2008, *Workforce Management*, accessed January 19, 2009. <http://www.workforce.com/section/00/article/25/94/47.php>

17. Alice Dembner, "Subsidized Care Plan's Cost to Double," February 3, 2008, *The Boston Globe*, accessed January 19, 2009. <http://www.boston.com/news/health/articles/2008/02/03/subsidized_care_plans_cost_to_double/>
18. Massachusetts had 2,443,580 households in 2000. $1.35 billion divided by 2,443,580 equals $553. Number of households from "State and County Quick Facts, Massachusetts," *U.S. Census Bureau*, accessed January 19, 2009. <http://quickfacts.census.gov/qfd/states/25000.html e>

# OBAMACARE - IT MUST BE AFFORDABLE, IT SAYS SO IN THE TITLE

1. "Health Care," *BarackObama.com*, accessed January 19, 2009. <http://www.barackobama.com/issues/healthcare/>
2. "McCain and Obama Health Care Policies: Cost and Coverage Compared," October 8, 2008, *The Lewin Group*, p. ES-1, accessed January 19, 2009. <http://www.lewin.com/content/Files/The_Lewin_Group_McCain-Obama_Health_Reform_Report_and_Appendix.pdf>
3. Ibid, p. ES-4.
4. "The Budget and Economic Outlook: 2014 to 2024," February 4, 2014, *Congressional Budget Office*, p. 105, accessed March 1, 2014. <http://www.cbo.gov/sites/default/files/cbofiles/attachments/45010-Outlook2014_Feb.pdf>
5. Sue A. Blevins, *Medicare's Midlife Crisis*, (Washington, DC, Cato Institute), 2001, p. 55.
6. "The Budget and Economic Outlook: 2014 to 2024," February 4, 2014, *Congressional Budget Office*, p. 111, accessed March 1, 2014. <http://www.cbo.gov/sites/default/files/cbofiles/attachments/45010-Outlook2014_Feb.pdf>

7. Ibid., p. 107.

8. Tracy Seipel, "Obamacare's Winners and Losers in Bay Area," October 5, 2013, *San Jose Mercury News*, accessed October 11, 2013. <http://www.mercurynews.com/nation-world/ci_24248486/obamacares-winners-and-losers-bay-area>

9. Karen Garloch, "Insurance Premium Increases Shock Charlotte Consumers," October 6, 2013, *Charlotte Observer*, accessed October 11, 2013. <http://www.charlotteobserver.com/2013/10/06/4365331/insurance-premium-increases-shock.html>

10. John Goodman, "Death Spirals," October 21, 2013, *National Center for Policy Analysis*, accessed October 24, 2013. <http://healthblog.ncpa.org/death-spirals/>

11. Society of Actuaries, "Cost of the Future Newly Insured under the Affordable Care Act (ACA)", March 2013, p. 21, accessed July 25, 2013. <http://cdn-files.soa.org/web/research-cost-aca-report.pdf>

12. Robert Pear, "Health Insurance Companies Seek Big Rate Increases for 2016," July 3, 2015, *New York Times*, accessed October 28, 2015. <www.nytimes.com/2015/07/04/us/health-insurance-companies-seek-big-rate-increases-for-2016.html?_r=0>

13. Terence P. Jeffrey, "HHS: 5.6M of 6M Who Signed Up on Exchanges Will Get Federal Funding," January 13, 2014, *CNSNews*, accessed January 16, 2014. <http://cnsnews.com/news/article/terence-p-jeffrey/hhs-56m-6m-who-signed-exchanges-will-get-federal-funding>

14. Frederic Bastiat, as quoted on <http://www.goodreads.com/author/quotes/89275.Fr_d_ric_Bastiat>

15. *Brief of Amicus Curiae Blue Cross and Blue Shield of Massachusetts, Inc. in Support of Petitioners*, DHHS v. State of Florida, U.S. Court of Appeals for the Eleventh Circuit, January 2012, accessed December 11, 2013. <http://aca-litigation.wikispaces.com/file/view/Blues+of+Massachusetts+amicus+%2811-398%29.pdf>

16. *Brief Amici Curiae of the American Hospital Association et al. in Support of Defendants-Apellants/Cross-Appellees*, State of Florida v. DHHS, U.S. Court of Appeals for the Eleventh Circuit, April 8,

2011, accessed December 11, 2013. <http://digitalcommons.law.scu.edu/cgi/viewcontent.cgi?article=1128&context=aca>

17. Matthias Gafni, "Concord: Half of Affordable Care Act call center jobs will be part-time," July 25, 2013, *Contra Costa Times*, accessed July 30, 2013. <http://www.contracostatimes.com/rss/ci_23733819>

18. *Washington Post*, 2012 Presidential Election Results, accessed July 30, 2013. <http://washingtonpost.com/wp-srv/special/politics/election-map-2012/president/> Click on "county results," then click on Contra Costa County, which is just east of the San Francisco Bay.

19. "The Budget and Economic Outlook: 2014 to 2024," February 4, 2014, *Congressional Budget Office*, p. 117, accessed March 1, 2014. <http://www.cbo.gov/sites/default/files/cbofiles/attachments/45010-Outlook2014_Feb.pdf>

20. "Physicians' Point of View on Election 2008 and Healthcare Reform," 2008, *LocumTenens.com*, accessed January 19, 2009. <http://www.locumtenens.com/lt/media/gallery/pdf/2008ElectionSurveyHighlights.pdf>

21. Chaoulli v Quebec, Supreme Court of Canada, June 9, 2005, paragraph 124, accessed December 1, 2008. <http://scc.lexum.umontreal.ca/en/2005/2005scc35/2005scc35.html>

22. National Federation of Independent Business, et. al. v. Sebelius, Secretary of Health and Human Services, et. al., p. 3, accessed October 12, 2013. <http://www.supremecort.gov/opinions/11pdf/11-393c3a2.pdf>

23. Ibid., p. 31.

24. Ibid., pp. 31-32.

25. Manya F. Newton, M.D., et. al., "Uninsured Adults Presenting to U.S. Emergency Departments: Assumptions vs. Data," October 22/29, 2008, *Journal of the American Medical Association*, 1920.

26. Jan Crawford, "Medicaid Enrollment Spike a Threat to Obamacare Structure?," October 25, 2013, *CBS This Morning*, accessed October 29, 2013. <http://www.cbsnews.com/8301-505267_162-57609254/medicaid-enrollment-spike-a-threat-to-obamacare-structure/>

27. Amanda Peterson Beadle, "Study: Many Doctors Not Accepting Medicaid Patients," August 7, 2012, *ThinkProgress*, accessed October 29, 2013. <http://thinkprogress.org/health/2012/08/07/651591/doctors-not-accepting-medicaid-patients/>

28. Carl Campanile, "Docs Resisting Obamacare," October 29, 2013, *New York Post*, accessed October 29, 2013. <http://nypost.com/2013/10/29/docs-resisting-obamacare/>

29. "Fixing Our Broken Health Care System," *California Office of the Governor*, accessed January 19, 2009. <http://www.fixourhealthcare.ca.gov/>

30. "2014 Survey: Physician Appointment Wait Times and Medicaid and Medicare Acceptance Rates," *Merrit, Hawkins & Associates*, p. 6, accessed November 4, 2015. <www.merritthawkins.com/uploaded-Files/MerrittHawkings/Surveys/mha2014waitsurvPDF.pdf>

31. "Key Issues in Analyzing Major Health Insurance Proposals," December 2008, Congressional Budget Office, p. 31, accessed March 12, 2014. <http://www.cbo.gov/sites/default/files/ftpdocs/99xx/doc9924/12-18-keyissues.pdf>

    $246 billion divided by 116 million families in America equals approximately $2,100 per family.

32. For Medicare expenditures, see "Historical Tables, Budget of the U.S. Government, Fiscal Year 2011," 2010, *United States Government Printing Office*, Table 3.1, p. 55, accessed April 12, 2012.

    <http://www.whitehouse.gov/sites/default/files/omb/budget/fy2011/assets/hist.pdf> For Medicaid expenditures, see "2010 State Expenditure Report Examining Fiscal 2009 - 2011 State Spending," 2011, *National Association of State Budget Officers*, Figure 14, p. 45, accessed April 12, 2012.

    <http://www.nasbo.org/sites/default/files/2010%20State%20Expenditure%20Report.pdf > For number of households, see Statistical Abstract of the United States, 2012, Table 59, U.S. Census Bureau, accessed April 12, 2012. <http://www.census.gov/compendia/statab/2012/tables/12s0059.pdf>

33. See the chapter in this book entitled "Don't Worry about the Cost - It's Covered."

34. U.S. Code, Title 42, Section 1396p, accessed January 2, 2014. <http://uscode.house.gov/browse/prelim@title42/chapter7/subchapter19&edition=prelim>

35. Stephanie Condon, "WH Defends DNI Director Clapper After Congressional Testimony Draws Fire," June 12, 2013, *CBS News*, accessed January 9, 2014. <http://www.cbsnews.com/news/wh-defends-dni-director-clapper-after-congressional-testimony-draws-fire/>

36. Leigh Ann Caldwell, "Christie Drops Swagger Amid Heat of Scandal," January 9, 2014, *CNN Politics*, accessed January 9, 2014. <http://www.cnn.com/2014/01/09/politics/christie-bridge/index.html>

37. "51% Favor Government Shutdown Until Congress Cuts Health Care Funding," September 17, 2013, *Rasmussen Reports*, accessed September 20, 2013. <http://www.rasmussenreports.com/public_content/politics/general_politics/september_2013/51_favor_government_shutdown_until_congress_cuts_healthcare_funding>

38. "Union Letter: Obamacare Will 'Destroy the Very Health and Wellbeing' of Workers," July 15, 2013, *Teamsters Local Union 988*, citing letter signed by James P. Hoffa, General President of the International Brotherhood of Teamsters as well as two other union presidents, accessed September 20, 2013. <http://www.teamsterslocal988.org/index.cfm?zone=/unionactive/view_article.cfm&homeID=296954>

39. Drew Zahn, "Oh, The Irony! IRS Agents Beg Out of Obamacare," July 26, 2013, *World Net Daily*, accessed September 20, 2013. This article links to the website of the National Treasury Employees Union, to an action alert that is requesting their members to send the letter. <http://www.wnd.com/2013/07/oh-the-irony-irs-agents-beg-out-of-obamacare/>

40. Kenric Ward, "Volunteer Firefighters Battle IRS, Obamacare on Capitol Hill," December 17, 2013, *Watchdog.org*, accessed December 21, 2013. <http://watchdog.org/120523/firefighters-irs-obamacare/>

41. Stella Paul, "Obamacare May Devastate the Real Estate and Travel Industries," December 19, 2013, *American Thinker*, accessed December 21, 2013. <http://www.americanthinker.com/2013/12/more_obamacare_devastatin.html>

42. Gerry R. Partido, "Guam and the 'Obamacare" Dilemma," July 6, 2013, Marianas Variety (Guam Edition), accessed December 21, 2013. <http://mvguam.com/island-stir/24517-guam-and-the-obamacare-dilemma.html>

43. A patient of mine told me the analogy of the stool sample, which I thought was right on the mark. I do not know who originally thought of it, as this analogy can be found all over the internet.

# HEALTH SAVINGS ACCOUNTS - ONE STEP FORWARD AND ONE STEP BACK

1. "News Release: AAPPO Survey Finds 95 Percent of Health Savings Account (HSA) Enrolles Recieve Health Care Through Preferred Provider Organizations (PPOs)," March 13, 2007, *Association of Preferred Provider Organizations*, accessed January 14, 2009. <http://www.aappo.org/index.cfm?pageid=31&newsid=112>

2. Sally Pipes, "How High Deductible Plans Lead to Low Healthcare Spending," May 28, 2012, Forbes, accessed April 3, 2013. <http://www.forbes.com/sites/sallypipes/2012/how-high-deductible-plans-lead-to-low-healthcare-spending/>

3. "HAS Enrollment Grows Amid Cost Cuts," May 23, 2010, *Business Insurance*, accessed May 3, 2012. <http://www.businessinsurance.com/article/20100523/ISSUE01/305239994>

4. "January 2007 Census Shows 4.5 Million People Covered By HSA/High Deductible Health Plans," April 2007, *America's Health Insurance Plans*, p. 1, accessed January 14, 2009. <http://www.ahipresearch.org/PDFs/FINAL%20AHIP_HSAReport.pdf>

5.  John C. Goodman and Devon M. Herrick, "Health Savings Accounts: Answering the Critics, Part II," National Center for Policy Analysis, March 21, 2006, accessed January 14, 2009. <http://www.ncpa.org/pub/ba/ba545/>

## Restore Free Markets

1.  Burton W. Folsom, Jr, *The Myth of the Robber Barrons: A New Look at the Rise of Big Business in America, 4th edition*, (Hendon, Virginia, Young America's Foundation), 2003.

## Restrict Government to Governing

1.  Declaration of Independence of the United States of America, preamble.
2.  James Madison, 4 Annals of Congress 179 (1794), *George Mason University Department of Economics*, accessed January 14, 2009. <http://www.gmu.edu/departments/economics/wew/quotes/govt.html>
3.  Thomas Jefferson, First Inaugural Address, March 4, 1801, *George Mason University Department of Economics*, accessed January 14, 2009. <http://www.gmu.edu/departments/economics/wew/quotes/govt.html>
4.  Grover Cleveland, 18 Congressional Record 1875 [1877], *George Mason University Department of Economics*, accessed January 14, 2009. <http://www.gmu.edu/departments/economics/wew/quotes/govt.html>
5.  Franklin Pierce, *George Mason University Department of Economics*, accessed January 14, 2009. <http://www.gmu.edu/departments/economics/wew/quotes/govt.html>

6. James Madison, Speech at the Virginia Convention, December 2, 1829, *George Mason University Department of Economics*, accessed January 14, 2009. <http://www.gmu.edu/departments/economics/wew/quotes/govt.html>

7. Vanhornes Lessee v. Dorrance, 2 U.S. 304, 310 (Pa. 1795), accessed January 14, 2009. <http://supreme.justia.com/us/2/304/case.html>

8. Walter Williams, "Modern Day Lunacy," 2009, accessed May 3, 2012. <http://econfaculty.gmu.edu/wew/articles/09/ModernDayLunacy>

## Eliminate Tax Incentives

1. "Paying for Medical Care," *AAPS News*, Volume 61, No. 10, October 2005, Association of American Physicians and Surgeons, accessed October 7 2008. <http://www.aapsonline.org/newsletters/oct05.php>

## Reduce Regulations - Phase Out Medicare

1. Markian Hawryluk, "E&M Guidelines Still Don't Work; Panel Says Dump 'Em," *American Medical News*, June 10, 2002.

2. Thomas Sowell, *Basic Economics: A Citizen's Guide to the Economy*, (New York, NY, Basic Books), 2000, pp. 69-70.

3. David M. Walker, former Comptroller General of the United States, "True State of our Federal Finances," September 30, 2012, *Comeback America Initiative*, accessed June 4, 2013. <http://keepingamericagreat.org/assets/2012/03/020613-CAI-Trifold-Final-TEST.pdf>

4. Scott Burns, "Revising Our Ideas of 'Rich,'" September 7, 2003, *The Dallas Morning News*, citing data from the VIP Forum, accessed January 14, 2009.

<http://www.dallasnews.com/sharedcontent/dws/bus/scottburns/alsoonline/wealth_scoreboard.html>

5.  Howard N. Fullerton, Jr., "Labor Force Participation: 75 Years of Change, 1950-98 and 1998-2025," December 1999, *U.S. Department of Labor, Bureau of Labor Statistics*, p. 4, accessed January 14, 2009. <http://www.bls.gov/opub/mlr/1999/12/art1full.pdf>

6.  David M. Walker, "Saving Our Future Requires Tough Choices Today," p. 9.

7.  David M. Walker, on *Michelson in the Morning*, WHO Newsradio 1040 AM, Des Moines Iowa, host Jan Michelson, February 1, 2007, 22:20 into podcast, available at <http://www.mickelson.libsyn.com/>

8.  "Medicare Trustees Report to Force Reform Debate," April 23, 2007, *National Center for Policy Analysis*, accessed January 14, 2009. <http://www.ncpa.org/prs/rel/2007/20070423.html>

9.  Mark Litow and the Technical Committee, "Rhetoric vs. Reality: Comparing Public and Private Health Care Administrative Costs," *The Council for Affordable Health Insurance*, March 1994.

10. For every $100 that is called "gross pay", $7.65 more has to be paid by the employer to the federal government for Social Security and Medicare taxes. An equal amount is sent to the government as a "deduction" from the paycheck. Thus, for every $107.65 that the employer must pay, $15.30, or 14.2%, goes to Medicare and Social Security. The Medicare portion of that is $2.90, or 2.7%.

11. Lance Richardson, *The Message*, (Idaho Falls, ID, American Family Publishing), 2000, pp. 150-152.

12. "Hurricanes Katrina and Rita Disaster Relief: Improper and Potentially Fraudulent Individual Assistance Payments Estimated to be Between $600 Million and $1.4 Billion," 6/14/06, *US Government Accountability Office*, accessed January 15, 2009. <www.gao.gov/new.items/d06844t.pdf>

# Restore Civility to Civil Law

1. "Update on the Medical Litigation Crisis: Not the Result of the 'Insurance Cycle,'" September 25, 2002, *U.S. Department of Health and Human Services, Office of the Assistant Secretary for Planning and Evaluation*, accessed January 14, 2009. <http://aspe.hhs.gov/daltcp/reports/mlupd2.htm>

2. John Hasnas, J.D., Ph.D., "What's Wrong With a Little Tort Reform?," 1996, *Georgetown University, McDonough School of Business*, accessed January 14, 2009. <http://faculty.msb.edu/hasnasj/GTWebSite/TortWeb.html> Originally published in 32 Idaho Law Review 557 (1996).

3. Ibid., quoting Harry Shulman & Fleming James, Jr., Cases and Materials on the Law of Torts viii (1942).

4. Walter K. Olson, *The Litigation Explosion: What Happened When America Unleashed the Lawsuit*, (New York, NY, Penguin Books), 1991, pp. 178-179.

5. Ibid., pp. 117-118.

6. Swierkiewicz v. Sorema N.A., 534 U.S. 506 (2002), accessed January 14, 2009. <http://supreme.justia.com/us/534/506/case.html>

7. United States Constitution, Fourth Amendment.

8. Austin v American Association of Neurological Surgeons, 253 F 3d 967 (2001), accessed January 14, 2009. <http://www.projectposner.org/case/2001/253F3d967>

9. Russell M. Pelton, J.D., "Professing Professional Conduct: AANS Raises the Bar for Expert Testimony," Spring 2002, *Bulletin of the American Association of Neurological Surgeons*, accessed January 14, 2009. http://www.aans.org/library/article.aspx?ShowMenu=false&ShowPrint=false&articleid=9916

10. U.S. Court of Appeals, 7th Circuit, *Austin v American Association of Neurological Surgeons*, 2001, accessed October 31, 2013. <http://caselaw.findlaw/us-7th-circuit/1429913.html>

11. Olson, p. 278, quoting Justice William Brennan in Young v. U.S. e. rel. Vuitton, 481 U.S. 787 (1987).

## ELIMINATE THE FOOD AND DRUG ADMINISTRATION

1.  Thomas Jefferson, in a letter to James Madison, suggested a "Federal Head," dividing powers into the three branches of Legislative, Executive, and Judicial, and retain distinct divisions of power between national and state levels. This idea was incorporated into the Pinckney plan, put forth by Charles Pinckney of South Carolina. This idea found its way into the constitution, and is central to the organization of the federal government. See

    Alexander H. Stephens, *History of the United States*, 1872, reprinted by American Foundation Publications, Bridgewater Virginia, 1999, pp. 244-245.

2.  Thomas Jefferson, *Notes on the State of Virginia*, Chapter XVII, accessed January 15, 2009. <http://classicliberal.tripod.com/jefferson/vnotes.html>

3.  Noel D. Campbell, "Replace FDA Regulation of Medical Devices with Third-Party Certification," Nov 12, 1997, *Cato Institute*, accessed January 15, 2009.

    <http://www.cato.org/pubs/pas/pa-288.pdf>

4.  Ethan A. Huff, "Armed Agents Invade Maxam Nutraceutics and Steal Natural Health Products in Shocking FDA Raid," April 27, 2011, *Natural News*, accessed May 4, 2012. <http://www.naturalnews.com/032203_Maxam_Nutraceutics_FDA_raid.html> Also see "FDA Raid on Raw Milk: Rawsome Food Club" on www.youtube.com to watch a surveillance camera video of agents with drawn guns raiding Rawsome Foods for the heinous crime against humanity of selling unpasteurized milk. July 30, 2010, accessed May 4, 2012. <http://www.youtube.com/watch?v=X2jgpGyyQW8&feature=related>

5.  Mary Ruwart, Ph.D., "The Law Most Likely to Kill You," October 11, 2005, *LewRockwell.com*, accessed January 3, 2009. <http://www. lewrockwell.com/orig3/ruwart2.html>

6.  Thomas Sowell, *Basic Economics: A Citizen's Guide to the Economy*, (New York, NY, Basic Books), 2000), pp. 249-250. Also see W. Cleon Skousen, *The Naked Communist*, (Salt Lake City UT, The Ensign Publishing Company), 1958, pp. 119-120.

## Eliminate Insurance Mandates

1.  Paul Zane Pilzer, *The New Health Insurance Solution: How to Get Cheaper, Better Coverage Without a Traditional Employer Plan*, (Hoboken, NJ, John Wiley & Sons, Inc.), 2005, p. 27, quoting data from eHealthInsurance.

2.  "Blood Transfusion / Knowing Your Options: Frequently Asked Questions," Pall Corporation, accessed January 15, 2009. <http:// www.bloodtransfusion.com/faq.asp>

## Remove Controls over Price and Supply

1.  Bruce Jaspen, "With Dems in Power, Part D Could Get a Makeover," November 12, 2006, *Chicago Tribune*, accessed January 15, 2009. <http://www.post-gazette.com/pg/06316/737432-321.stm>

2.  "Models of Private-Sector GME Financing," *Council on Graduate Medical Education*, accessed January 15, 2009. <http://www.cogme. gov/ManagedCare/9.htm>

## Free Market Practices at Work Today

1.  Jay Solomon, "Traveling Cure: India's New Coup In Outsourcing," April 26, 2004, Wall Street Journal.

2. "Medical Tourism: Need Surgery, Will Travel," June 18, 2004, *Canadian Broadcasting Corporation, CBC News Online,* at <http://www.cbc.ca/news/background/healthcare/medicaltourism.html>

3. Uwe E. Reinhardt, Peter S. Hussey, Gerard F. Anderson, "Cross-National Comparisons of Health Systems Using OECD Data, 1999," *Health Affairs,* May/June 2002.

4. "Insurance Industry Watches 'Medical Tourism,'" February 27, 2007, National Public Radio, podcast accessed January 15, 2009. <http://www.npr.org/templates/story/story.php?storyId=7615619>

5. Information about Apollo Hospitals from <http://www.apollohospitals.com/> Information about American radiology facility via personal communication with manager.

6. Association of American Physicians and Surgeons, at <http://www.aapsonline.org/>

7. "Boutique Docs Set Up Shops," November 22, 2002, *CBS Evening News,* accessed January 15, 2009. <http://www.cbsnews.com/stories/2002/11/22/eveningnews/main530550.shtml>

8. Personal communication.

9. Mac Overmeyer, "Urologist Who Opted Out: No Regrets After 5 Years," Urology Times, April 1, 2006, also available online, accessed January 15, 2009. <http://www.northernurology.com/articles/healthcarereform/optout.html>

   Taking the icon for Articles on this website leads to several good articles on health care and free markets.

# WHY FREE MARKETS ARE THE MORAL CHOICE

1. George Washington, unknown when or where he said this.

2. When someone was called a "liberal," it used to mean someone who supported freedom. Thomas Jefferson is an example of a classical liberal. Now he would not even be able to get 5% of the vote in a Republican presidential primary, as he would be viewed as a right-wing radical. The root "liber" means free. The word has been

hijacked and misused by socialists in modern days to mean somebody who favors government welfare programs and government controls over the people.

3. "U.S. President/Electoral Vote Count," 2004, *CNN.com*, accessed January 15, 2009. <http://www.cnn.com/ELECTION/2004/pages/results/electoral.college/>

4. Adapted from "National Generosity Index 2006," *Catalogue for Philanthropy*, accessed January 15, 2009. <http://www.catalogueforphilanthropy.org/cfp/generosity_index/2006/data/> For each state, the average itemized charitable contributions (ICC) were divided by the average adjusted gross income (AGI), yielding a percentage. 7.45% was chosen as the dividing line between more generous and less generous states.

5. "National Generosity Index 2006," *Catalogue for Philanthropy*, accessed January 15, 2009. <http://www.catalogueforphilanthropy.org/cfp/generosity_index/2006/data/United%20States.xls>

6. Ibid.

7. Emma Batha, "Reuters Tsunami Aidwatch," December 19, 2005, *Thompson Reuters Foundation*, click on "Government vs Private Aid," accessed January 15, 2009. <http://www.alertnet.org/thefacts/aidtracker/>

8. www.gofundme.com/about-us/

9. This was an experience of the author, at a supermarket whose location I do not remember.

10. Total federal expenditures in 2012 were $3.54 trillion dollars. "Historical Tables," *Office of Management and Budget*, Table 1.1, accessed October 22, 2013. <http://www.whitehouse.gov/omb/budget/Historicals/>

 There are 116 million families in the United States. This divides to $30,500 per family.

11. I take Idaho as a typical state for expenditures. Expenditures by the state of Idaho were $6.46 billion in 2013. 36% of the state budget,

or $2.32 billion, comes from the federal government. Deducting that amount to avoid duplication leaves $4.14 billion. There are 518,488 households in Idaho. This equals $8,000 per Idaho family. There are perhaps another $1,500 in county and municipal expenditures per family, I merely guessed at that, but even if it is off by a factor of 2, it would only change the total by 3%. I did not do this calculation for every state; Idaho is similar enough to the others to make the point.

Expenditures from: "Idaho Fiscal Facts," April 19, 2006, *Idaho Legislative Services Office*, pp. 10-11, accessed October 22, 2013. <http://www.legislature.idaho.gov/budget/publications/FiscalFacts/current?FF.pdf>

Number of households from "State and County Quick Facts, Idaho," *U.S. Census Bureau*, accessed January 15, 2009. <http://quickfacts.census.gov/qfd/states/16000.html>

12. This is adapted from a quote attributed to H.L. Mencken, "Every election is a sort of advance auction sale of stolen goods."

13. Ezra Taft Benson, *An Enemy Hath Done This*, (Salt Lake City, Utah, Parliament Publishers), 1969, p. 135.

14. See the chapter in this book entitled "Free Market Practices at Work Today."

15. Robert E. Rector, "How Poor Are America's Poor? Examining the 'Plague' of Poverty in America," Backgrounder #2064, August 27, 2007, *The Heritage Foundation*, accessed October 21, 2008. <http://www.heritage.org/Research/Welfare/bg2064.cfm>

16. See the chapter in this book entitled "Ever Increasing Taxes."

17. The average price of a domestic new car in 2001 was $19,654. "Fact #219: June 3, 2002: Average Price of a New Car: 1970-2001," *United States Department of Energy*, accessed January 15, 2009.
    <http://www1.eere.energy.gov/vehiclesandfuels/facts/favorites/fcvt_fotw219.html>

18. Jay Solomon, "Traveling Cure: India's New Coup In Outsourcing," *Wall Street Journal*, April 26, 2004.

# Feasibility of These Solutions

1. Dr. Keith Smith, owner of the Surgery Center of Oklahoma, wrote a thoughtful piece on this topic in his blog. See "Eschew Obfuscation" at http://surgerycenterofoklahoma.tumblr.com/post/67635334216/eschew-obfuscation.

2. H.R. 25, "Fair Tax Act of 2009," <http://thomas.loc.gov/> 39 co-sponsors as of January 15, 2009.

3. Sebastian Mallaby, "Ownership Society Still Needs Rules," *The Washington Post*, November 22, 2004.

4. David M. Eisenberg, M.D., Roger B. Davis, Sc.D., Susan L. Ettner, Ph.D., Scott Appel, M.S., Sonja Wilkey, Maria Van Rompay, Ronald C. Kessler, Ph.D., "Trends in Alternative Medicine Use in the United States, 1990-97: Results of a Follow-up Survey," *Journal of the American Medical Association*, 1998, 280:1569-1575.

5. Markian Hawryluk, "E&M Guidelines Still Don't Work; Panel Says Dump 'Em," *American Medical News*, June 10, 2002.

6. "Federal Rules of Civil Procedure, Pleadings and Motions: Rule 11," *Legal Information Institute, Cornell Law School*, accessed January 15, 2009. <http://www.law.cornell.edu/rules/frcp/Rule11.htm>

7. Professor David E. Bernstein, "Expert Witness, Adversarial Bias, and the (Partial) Failure of the Daubert Revolution," *George Mason University School of Law*, accessed January 15, 2009. <http://www.law.gmu.edu/faculty/papers/docs/07-11.pdf>

8. Marie Gryphon, "Common-Sense Justice in Alaska," October 28, 2008, *National Review Online*, accessed March 25, 2014. <http://nationalreview.com/articles/226102/common-sense-justice-alaska/marie-gryphon>

9. Jay Solomon, "Traveling Cure: India's New Coup In Outsourcing," *Wall Street Journal*, April 26, 2004.

10. Joshua Kurlantzick, "Sometimes, Sightseeing is a Look at Your X-Rays," *New York Times*, May 20, 2007.

11. "Insurance Industry Watches 'Medical Tourism,'" February 27, 2007, National Public Radio, podcast accessed January 15, 2009. <http://www.npr.org/templates/story/story.php?storyId=7615619>

12. H.R. 2355, 109th Congress, "Health Care Choice Act of 2005," <http://thomas.loc.gov/>

13. "Findings from a Survey of Registered Voters in the United States," December 10, 2008, *Grove Insight*, accessed January 19, 2009. <http://www.consumerwatchdog.org/resources/healthcarepollmemo. pdf> The following question was asked: "There is federal legislation that would make it mandatory for every American to show proof that they have health insurance coverage or face tax penalties. If an individual does not receive full coverage through an employer, or if a person does not qualify for government assistance, then they would be required to pay for a policy. Do you favor or oppose this legislation or are you undecided?" 40% "oppose, strongly," 13% "oppose, not strongly," 31% were "undecided," 5% "favor, not strongly," and 10% "favor, strongly."

14. Institute for Health Freedom, at http://www.forhealthfreedom.org/

15. "Public Attitudes Toward Medical Privacy," Gallop Organization poll submitted to the Institute for Health Freedom, September 2000, accessed January 15, 2009. <http://forhealthfreedom.org/Gallupsurvey/IHF-Gallup.pdf> The following question was asked: "Who do you think should be allowed to see your medical records without your permission? I am going to read you a list of some groups; for each, please tell me whether you favor or oppose allowing them to see YOUR medical records without FIRST obtaining YOUR permission." (emphasis in original) Several groups were listed. In response to "government agencies," 92% of respondents were opposed. 1,000 adults were polled by random telephone number dialing.

16. Ibid. The following question was asked: "There has been a lot of discussion lately about REQUIRING that all patient medical records be stored in a national computerized database. The database would store

medical records on patients over their lifetime. Others would be able to use the information without first obtaining a patients' permission. Would you favor or oppose keeping your medical records this way?" 88% were opposed.

17. David Hogberg, Ph.D., "Sweden's Single-Payer Health System Provides a Warning to Other Nations," May 2007, *The National Center for Public Policy Research*, accessed January 15, 2009. <http://www.nationalcenter.org/NPA555_Sweden_Health_Care.html>

www.ingramcontent.com/pod-product-compliance
Lightning Source LLC
Chambersburg PA
CBHW070628290526
45790CB00001B/41